NEXT GENERATION
SCIENCE
STANDARDS

For States, By States

Volume 2: Appendixes

NGSS Lead States

THE NATIONAL ACADEMIES PRESS
WASHINGTON, D.C.
www.nap.edu

THE NATIONAL ACADEMIES PRESS

500 Fifth Street, NW   Washington, DC 20001

www.nap.edu

International Standard Book Number-13: 978-0-309-27227-8
International Standard Book Number-10: 0-309-27227-0
Library of Congress Control Number: 2013939525

Next Generation Science Standards: For States, By States
is published as a two-volume set:
Volume 1: The Standards—Arranged by Disciplinary Core Ideas and by Topics
Volume 2: Appendixes

Additional copies of this publication are available from the
National Academies Press, 500 Fifth Street, NW, Keck 360,
Washington, DC 20001;
(800) 624-6242 or (202) 334-3313; http://www.nap.edu.

 is a registered trademark of Achieve, Inc., on behalf
of the lead states and partners.

Printed in the United States of America

Suggested citation: NGSS Lead States. 2013. *Next Generation Science Standards:
For States, By States.* Washington, DC: The National Academies Press.

Cover Photo Credits

Clockwise, from top right: Elementary school age boy with magnifying glass,
©iStock/fstop123; Tungurahua volcano eruption, ©iStock/Elena Kalistratova; High
school students, ©iStock/Christopher Futcher; Sunrise, ©iStock/alxpin; Students in
biology lab, ©iStock/fstop123; Buttercup stem, ©iStock/Oliver Sun Kim

CONTENTS

The contents of the first volume of this two-volume publication are listed below.

PREFACE

The Next Generation Science Standards (NGSS), authored by a consortium of 26 states facilitated by Achieve, Inc., are the culmination of a 3-year, multi-step process jointly undertaken by the National Research Council (NRC), the National Science Teachers Association, the American Association for the Advancement of Science, and Achieve, Inc., with support from the Carnegie Corporation of New York.

The NRC, the operating arm of the National Academy of Sciences (NAS) and the National Academy of Engineering (NAE), began the process by releasing *A Framework for K–12 Science Education: Practices, Crosscutting Concepts, and Core Ideas* in July 2011. The *Framework,* authored by a committee of 18 individuals who are nationally and internationally known in their respective fields, describes a new vision for science education rooted in scientific evidence and outlines the knowledge and skills that all students need to learn from kindergarten through the end of high school. It is the foundational document for the NGSS.

Following release of the *Framework,* the consortium of 26 lead partner states, working with a team of 41 writers with expertise in science and science education and facilitated by Achieve, Inc., began the development of rigorous and internationally benchmarked science standards that are faithful to the *Framework.* As part of the development process, the standards underwent multiple reviews, including two public drafts, allowing anyone interested in science education an opportunity to inform the content and organization of the standards. Thus the NGSS were developed through collaboration between states and other stakeholders in science, science education, higher education, business, and industry.

As partners in this endeavor, the NAS, NAE, NRC, and the National Academies Press (NAP) are deeply committed to the NGSS initiative. While this document is not the product of an NRC expert committee, the final version of the standards was reviewed by the NRC and was found to be consistent with the *Framework.* These standards, built on the *Framework,* are essential for enhancing learning for all students and should enjoy the widest possible dissemination, given the vital national importance of high-quality education. That is why we decided to publish the NGSS through the NAP, a unit otherwise solely dedicated to publishing the work of this institution.

The NGSS represent a crucial step forward in realizing the *Framework*'s vision for science education in classrooms throughout our nation. The standards alone, however, will not create high-quality learning opportunities for all students. Numerous changes are now required at all levels of the K–12 education system so that the standards can lead to improved science teaching and learning, including modifications to curriculum, instruction, assessment, and professional preparation and development for teachers. The scientific and science education communities must continue to work together to create these transformations in order to make the promise of the NGSS a reality for all students.

Washington, DC, June 2013

RALPH J. CICERONE
President
National Academy of Sciences
Chair
National Research Council

CHARLES M. VEST
President
National Academy of Engineering
Vice Chair
National Research Council

HARVEY V. FINEBERG
President
Institute of Medicine

NATIONAL RESEARCH COUNCIL REVIEW OF THE NEXT GENERATION SCIENCE STANDARDS

In accordance with the procedures approved by the Executive Office of the Division of Behavioral and Social Sciences and Education (DBASSE) at the National Research Council (NRC), the Next Generation Science Standards (NGSS) were reviewed in early 2013 by individuals chosen for their technical expertise and familiarity with the Research Council's 2011 report *A Framework for K–12 Science Education: Practices, Crosscutting Concepts, and Core Ideas* (*Framework*). The purpose of the review was to evaluate whether the NGSS, as developed during a 2-year process by 26 lead states under the guidance of Achieve, Inc., remained consistent with the *Framework*, which was intended to provide the scientific consensus upon which to base new K–12 science standards. The developers of the NGSS used the *Framework* as the basis for their work in terms of developing both the structure and content of the standards. The NRC asked reviewers to direct their comments to three points:

- Are the NGSS consistent with the vision for K–12 science education presented in the *Framework*?
- To what extent do the NGSS follow the specific recommendations for standards developers put forward by the *Framework* committee (see Chapter 12 of the *Framework*)?
- For consistency with the *Framework*, are other changes needed?

The review process determined that the NGSS, released to the public in April 2013 and published in this volume, are consistent with the content and structure of the *Framework*.

The following individuals participated in the review of the NGSS: Philip Bell, Professor of the Learning Sciences, The Geda and Phil Condit Professor of Science and Math Education, University of Washington; Rodolfo Dirzo, Bing Professor in Ecology, Department of Biology, Stanford University; Kenji Hakuta, Professor of Education, School of Education, Stanford University; Kim A. Kastens, Lamont Research Professor and Adjunct Full Professor, Lamont-Doherty Earth Observatory, Department of Earth and Environmental Sciences, Columbia University; Jonathan Osborne, Shriram Family Professor of Science Education, Graduate School of Education, Stanford University; Brian J. Reiser, Professor, Learning Sciences, School of Education and Social Policy, Northwestern University; Carl E. Wieman, Professor, Department of Physics, University of British Columbia; and Lauress (Laurie) L. Wise, Principal Scientist, Education Policy Impact Center, HumRRO, Monterey, CA.

The review of the NGSS was overseen by Patricia Morison, Associate Executive Director for Reports and Communications for DBASSE, and Suzanne Wilson, member of the NRC Board on Science Education and Professor, Michigan State University. Appointed by the NRC, they were responsible for making certain that an independent examination of the NGSS was carried out in accordance with institutional procedures.

GLOSSARY

A   Algebra (CCSS Connection)

AAAS   American Association for the Advancement of Science

AYP   annual yearly progress

BF   Building Functions (CCSS Connection)

CC   Counting and Cardinality (CCSS Connection)

CC   crosscutting concept

CCR   college and career ready

CCSS   Common Core State Standards

CCSSM   Common Core State Standards for Mathematics

CED   Creating Equations (CCSS Connection)

CR   Chemical Reactions (Topic Name)

DCI   disciplinary core idea

E   Energy (Topic Name)

ED   Engineering Design (Topic Name)

EE   Expressions and Equations (CCSS Connection)

ELA   English Language Arts

ELL   English language learner

ES   Earth's Systems (Topic Name)

ESEA   Elementary and Secondary Education Act

ESS   earth and space sciences

ETS   engineering, technology, and applications of science

F   Functions (CCSS Connection)

FB   foundation box

FI   Forces and Interactions (Topic Name)

G   Geometry (CCSS Connection)

GBE   grade-band endpoint

GDRO   Growth, Development, and Reproduction of Organisms (Topic Name)

HI   Human Impacts (Topic Name)

HS   high school

IC   Making Inferences and Justifying Conclusions (CCSS Connection)

ID   Interpret Data (CCSS Connection)

IDEA   Individuals with Disabilities Education Act

IEP   individualized education program

IF   Interpreting Functions (CCSS Connection)

IRE   Interdependent Relationships in Ecosystems (Topic Name)

IVT   Inheritance and Variation of Traits (Topic Name)

K   kindergarten

LEP   limited English proficiency

LS   life sciences

MD   Measurement and Data (CCSS Connection)

MEOE   Matter and Energy in Organisms and Ecosystems (Topic Name)

MP   Mathematical Practice (Topic Name)

MS   middle school

N   Number and Quantity (CCSS Connection)

NAE   National Academy of Engineering

NAEP   National Assessment of Educational Progress

NAGC   National Association for Gifted Children

NBT   Number and Operations in Base Ten (CCSS Connection)

NCES   National Center for Educational Statistics

NCLB   No Child Left Behind Act

NF   Number and Operations—Fractions (CCSS Connection)

NGSS	Next Generation Science Standards		TELA	Technology and Engineering Literacy Assessment
NOS	Nature of Science		TIMSS	Trends in International Mathematics and Science Study
NRC	National Research Council			
NS	The Number System (CCSS Connection)		W	Waves (Topic Name)
NSA	Natural Selection and Adaptations (Topic Name)		W	Writing (CCSS Connection)
NSE	Natural Selection and Evolution (Topic Name)		WC	Weather and Climate (Topic Name)
NSF	National Science Foundation		WER	Waves and Electromagnetic Radiation (Topic Name)
NSTA	National Science Teachers Association		WHST	Writing in History/Social Studies, Science, and Technical Subjects (CCSS Connection)

OA Operations and Algebraic Thinking (CCSS Connection)

PE performance expectation

PISA Program for International Student Assessment

PS physical sciences

Q Quantities (CCSS Connection)

R&D research and development

RI Reading Informational Text (CCSS Connection)

RL Reading Literature (CCSS Connection)

RP Ratios and Proportional Relationships (CCSS Connection)

RST Reading in Science and Technical Subjects (CCSS Connection)

SEP science and engineering practice

SF Structure and Function (Topic Name)

SFIP Structure, Function, and Information Processing (Topic Name)

SL Speaking and Listening (CCSS Connection)

SP Statistics and Probability (CCSS Connection)

SPM Structures and Properties of Matter (Topic Name)

SS Space Systems (Topic Name)

SSE Seeing Structure in Expressions (CCSS Connection)

STEM science, technology, engineering, and mathematics

STS science, technology, and society

NEXT GENERATION
SCIENCE
STANDARDS

For States, By States

Volume 2: Appendixes

CONCEPTUAL SHIFTS IN THE NEXT GENERATION SCIENCE STANDARDS

The Next Generation Science Standards (NGSS) provide an important opportunity to improve not only science education but also student achievement. Based on *A Framework for K–12 Science Education: Practices, Crosscutting Concepts, and Core Ideas* (*Framework*), the NGSS are intended to reflect a new vision for American science education. The following conceptual shifts in the NGSS demonstrate what is new and different about the NGSS:

1. K–12 science education should reflect the interconnected nature of science as it is practiced and experienced in the real world.

> The framework is designed to help realize a vision for education in the sciences and engineering in which students, over multiple years of school, actively engage in scientific and engineering practices and apply crosscutting concepts to deepen their understanding of the core ideas in these fields. (NRC, 2012, p. 12)

The vision represented in the *Framework* is new in that students must be engaged at the nexus of the three dimensions:

- **Science and Engineering Practices,**
- **Crosscutting Concepts, and**
- **Disciplinary Core Ideas.**

Currently, most state and district standards express these dimensions as separate entities, leading to their separation in both instruction and assessment. Given the importance of science and engineering in the 21st century, students require a sense of contextual understanding with regard to scientific knowledge, how it is acquired and applied, and how science is connected through a series of concepts that help further our understanding of the world around us. Student performance expectations have to include a student's ability to apply a practice to content knowledge. Performance expectations thereby focus on understanding and application as opposed to memorization of facts devoid of context. The *Framework* goes on to emphasize that

> learning about science and engineering involves integration of the knowledge of scientific explanations (i.e., content knowledge) and the practices needed to engage in scientific inquiry and engineering design. Thus the framework seeks to illustrate how knowledge and practice must be intertwined in designing learning experiences in K–12 science education. (NRC, 2012, p. 11)

2. The Next Generation Science Standards are student performance expectations—NOT curriculum.

Even though within each performance expectation Science and Engineering Practices (SEPs) are partnered with a particular Disciplinary Core Idea (DCI) and Crosscutting Concept (CC) in the NGSS, these intersections do not predetermine how the three are linked in curriculum, units, or lessons. Performance expectations simply clarify the expectations of what students will know and be able to do by the end of the grade or grade band. Additional work will be needed to create coherent instructional programs that help students achieve these standards.

As stated previously, past science standards at both the state and district levels have treated the three dimensions of science as separate and distinct entities, leading to preferential treatment in assessment or instruction. It is essential to understand that the emphasis placed on a particular Science and Engineering Practice or Crosscutting Concept in a performance expectation is not intended to limit instruction, but to make clear the intent of the assessments.

An example of this is illustrated in two performance expectations in high school physical sciences that use the practice of modeling. Models are basically used for three reasons: (1) to represent or describe, (2) to collect data, or (3) to predict. The first use is typical in schools because models and representations are usually synonymous. However, the use of models to collect data or to predict phenomena is new. For example:

> Construct models to explain changes in nuclear energies during the processes of fission, fusion, and radioactive decay and the nuclear interactions that determine nuclear stability.

and

Use system models (computer or drawings) to construct molecular-level explanations to predict the behavior of systems where a dynamic and condition-dependent balance between a reaction and the reverse reaction determines the numbers of all types of molecules present.

In the first performance expectation, models are used with nuclear processes to explain changes. A scientific explanation requires evidence to support the explanation, so students will be called on to construct a model for the purpose of gathering evidence to explain these changes. Additionally, they will be required to use models to both explain and predict the behavior of systems in equilibrium. Again, the models will have to be used to collect data, but they will be further validated in their ability to predict the state of a system. In both cases, students will need a deep understanding of the content, as well as proficiency in the ability to construct and use models for various applications. The practice of modeling will need to be taught throughout the year—and indeed throughout the entire K–12 experience—as opposed to during one two-week unit of instruction.

The goal of the NGSS is to be clear about which practice students are responsible for in terms of assessment, but these practices and crosscutting concepts should occur throughout each school year.

3. The science concepts in the Next Generation Science Standards build coherently from K–12.

The focus on a few Disciplinary Core Ideas is a key aspect of a coherent science education. The *Framework* identified a basic set of core ideas that are meant to be understood by the time a student completes high school:

> To develop a thorough understanding of scientific explanations of the world, students need sustained opportunities to work with and develop the underlying ideas and to appreciate those ideas' interconnections over a period of years rather than weeks or months. . . . This sense of development has been conceptualized in the idea of learning progressions. . . . If mastery of a core idea in a science discipline is the ultimate educational destination, then well-designed learning progressions provide a map of the routes that can be taken to reach that destination.

Such progressions describe both how students' understanding of the idea matures over time and the instructional supports and experiences that are needed for them to make progress. (NRC, 2012, p. 26)

There are two key points that are important to understand:

- First, focus and coherence must be a priority. What this means to teachers and curriculum developers is that the same ideas or details are not covered each year. Rather, a progression of knowledge occurs from grade band to grade band that gives students the opportunity to learn more complex material, leading to an overall understanding of science by the end of high school. Historically, science education was taught as a set of disjointed and isolated facts. The *Framework* and the NGSS provide a more coherent progression aimed at overall scientific literacy with instruction focused on a smaller set of ideas and an eye on what students should have already learned and what they will learn at the next level.

- Second, the progressions in the NGSS automatically assume that previous material has been learned by students. Choosing to omit content at any grade level or band will impact the success of students in understanding the core ideas and will put additional responsibilities on teachers later in the process.

4. The Next Generation Science Standards focus on deeper understanding of content as well as application of content.

The *Framework* identified a smaller set of Disciplinary Core Ideas that students should know by the time they graduate from high school, and the NGSS are written to focus on the same. It is important that teachers and curriculum/assessment developers understand that the focus is on the core ideas—not necessarily the facts that are associated with them. The facts and details are important evidence, but not the sole focus of instruction. The *Framework* states:

> The core ideas also can provide an organizational structure for the acquisition of new knowledge. Understanding the core ideas and engaging in the scientific and engineering practices helps to prepare students for broader understanding, and deeper levels of scientific and engineering investigation, later on—in high school, college, and beyond. One rationale for organizing content around core ideas comes from studies comparing experts and novices in any field. Experts understand the core principles and

theoretical constructs of their field, and they use them to make sense of new information or tackle novel problems. Novices, in contrast, tend to hold disconnected and even contradictory bits of knowledge as isolated facts and struggle to find a way to organize and integrate them. . . . The assumption, then, is that helping students learn the core ideas through engaging in scientific and engineering practices will enable them to become less like novices and more like experts. (NRC, 2012, p. 25)

5. Science and engineering are integrated in the Next Generation Science Standards from kindergarten through twelfth grade.

The idea of integrating technology and engineering into science standards is not new. Chapters on the nature of technology and the human-built world were included in *Science for All Americans* (AAAS, 1989) and *Benchmarks for Science Literacy* (AAAS, 1993, 2008). Standards for science and technology were included for all grade spans in the *National Science Education Standards* (NRC, 1996).

Despite these early efforts, however, engineering and technology have not received the same level of attention in science curricula, assessments, or the education of new science teachers as the traditional science disciplines have. A significant difference in the NGSS is the integration of engineering and technology into the structure of science education. This integration is achieved by raising engineering design to the same level as scientific inquiry in classroom instruction when teaching science disciplines at all levels and by giving core ideas of engineering and technology the same status as those in other major science disciplines.

The rationale for this increased emphasis on engineering and technology rests on two positions taken in the *Framework*. One position is aspirational, the other practical.

From an aspirational standpoint, the *Framework* points out that science and engineering are needed to address major world challenges such as generating sufficient clean energy, preventing and treating diseases, maintaining supplies of food and clean water, and solving the problems of global environmental change that confront society today. These important challenges will motivate many students to continue or initiate their study of science and engineering.

From a practical standpoint, the *Framework* notes that engineering and technology provide opportunities for students to deepen their understanding of science by applying their developing scientific knowledge to the solution of practical problems. Both positions converge on the powerful idea that by integrating technology and engineering into the science curriculum, teachers can empower their students to use what they learn in their everyday lives.

6. The Next Generation Science Standards are designed to prepare students for college, careers, and citizenship.

There is no doubt that science and science education are central to the lives of all Americans. Never before has our world been so complex and science knowledge so critical to making sense of it all. When comprehending current events, choosing and using technology, or making informed decisions about one's health care, understanding science is key. Science is also at the heart of the the ability of the United States to continue to innovate, lead, and create the jobs of the future. All students no matter what their future education and career path must have a solid K–12 science education in order to be prepared for college, careers, and citizenship.

7. The Next Generation Science Standards and Common Core State Standards (English Language Arts and Mathematics) are aligned.

The timing of the release of NGSS comes as most states are implementing the Common Core State Standards (CCSS) in English Language Arts and Mathematics. This is important to science for a variety of reasons. First, there is an opportunity for science to be part of a child's comprehensive education. The NGSS are aligned with the CCSS to ensure a symbiotic pace of learning in all content areas. The three sets of standards overlap in meaningful and substantive ways and offer an opportunity to give all students equitable access to learning standards.

Some important work is already in progress regarding the implications and advantages to the CCSS and NGSS. Stanford University recently released 13 papers on a variety of issues related to language and literacy in the content areas of the CCSS and NGSS (Stanford University, 2012).

REFERENCES

AAAS (American Association for the Advancement of Science) (1989). *Science for all Americans.* New York: Oxford University Press.

AAAS. (1993, 2008). *Benchmarks for science literacy.* New York: Oxford University Press.

NRC (National Research Council). (1996). *National science education standards.* Washington, DC: National Academy Press.

NRC. (2012). *A framework for K–12 science education: Practices, cross-cutting concepts, and core ideas.* Washington, DC: The National Academies Press.

Stanford University. (2012). Understanding language. Available at: http://ell.stanford.edu/papers.

RESPONSES TO THE PUBLIC DRAFTS

EXECUTIVE SUMMARY

Several rounds of review were built into the development process of the Next Generation Science Standards (NGSS) to make sure that all educators and stakeholders would have opportunities to provide feedback. The first public draft of the NGSS was posted online from May 11 to June 1, 2012, and the second public draft was posted online from January 8 to January 29, 2013. The draft received comments from more than 10,000 individuals during each of the two public review periods, including those in lead state review teams, school and school district discussion groups, and scientific societies. The writers then used this feedback to make substantial revisions to the draft standards.

Overall, the feedback received on both public drafts of the NGSS was very positive. Almost all reviewers indicated that they liked the pedagogical vision, the integration of the three dimensions in the NGSS, and the structure of the NGSS itself. Most reviewers scored the performance expectations (PEs) highly, but some also critiqued specific issues and suggested improvements. The following themes emerged from the comments on how to improve the first public draft:

- Concern that there was too much material
- Suggestions for additional topics
- Lack of language clarity
- Concern about how engineering and technology were included and addressed
- Confusion about the role of the one practice specified in each PE
- Lack of guidance for incorporating crosscutting concepts
- Lack of specificity in connections to other standards and other subjects
- Concern about the organization of the standards
- Concern about the amount of support needed for implementation of the standards

Based on the feedback, the following changes were made between the first and second public drafts:

- 95% of the PEs were rewritten based on feedback, with more specific and consistent language used
- After a college- and career-readiness review, some content was removed
- Some content shifted grade levels in the elementary grades
- Engineering was integrated into the traditional science disciplines
- More math expectations were added to the PEs
- Course models were drafted for middle and high school
- "Nature of science" concepts were highlighted throughout the document
- The practices matrix was revised
- A new chapter was added to describe the intent and use of crosscutting concepts
- A new chapter on equity was drafted about implementation of the NGSS with diverse student groups
- A glossary of terms was added
- More flexibility in viewing the standards was provided by arranging the PEs according to both topic and disciplinary core idea (DCI)
- Additional flexibility was added to the website, allowing users to turn off pop up description boxes.

The feedback on the second public draft indicated that changes had completely addressed some issues, and the percentage of reviewers concerned about the remaining issues was greatly reduced. Those remaining issues included:

- Concern that there was still too much material
- Suggestions for a few additional topics
- Lack of language clarity
- Concern about including and addressing engineering and technology
- Confusion about the role of the one practice specified in each PE
- Concern about the amount of support needed for implementation of the standards
- Confusion about the coding/naming of PEs

Based on the feedback, the following changes were made between the second public draft and the final release of the NGSS:

- 75% of the PEs were edited to increase clarity, consistency, and specific feedback
- A review of the central focus of each DCI from *A Framework for K–12 Science Education* (*Framework*) resulted in the removal of about 33% of the PEs and associated DCIs while retaining the progression of DCIs across the grade bands
- Separate ETS1: Engineering Design PEs were added to each grade band to supplement PEs that had integrated engineering design into the traditional science disciplines
- "Storylines" with essential questions were added to the beginning of each grade band and section to describe the context and rationale for the PEs
- The "All Standards, All Students" appendix was expanded to include several vignettes about implementation of the NGSS with diverse student groups
- PE names were changed from lowercase letters to numbers to avoid confusion with the DCI names; for example, MS-LS1-a became MS-LS1-1

INTRODUCTION

Several rounds of review were built into the development process of the NGSS to make sure that all educators and stakeholders would have opportunities to provide feedback. The first public draft of the NGSS was posted online from May 11 to June 1, 2012, and the second public draft was posted online from January 8 to January 29, 2013. The draft received comments from more than 10,000 individuals during each of the two public review periods, including those working together in lead state review teams, school and school district discussion groups, and scientific society commenters.

Feedback on the public drafts was reviewed, coded into sortable spreadsheets, and summarized for state and writing team consideration. Where feedback was unclear or conflicting, lead state teams engaged in additional discussions. The writers then used this feedback, along with that of the college- and career-readiness reviews, to make substantial revisions to the draft standards. As a result of the first public review and subsequent state review, 95% of the PEs were rewritten. After the second public draft review period, 75% of the PEs were edited to add clarity and consistency across the document.

Overall, the feedback received on both public drafts of the NGSS was overwhelmingly positive. Almost all reviewers indicated that they liked the pedagogical vision described in the *Framework*, and the integration of the three dimensions in the NGSS: Science and Engineering Practices, Disciplinary Core Ideas, and Crosscutting Concepts. The structure of the NGSS received high praise, including the foundation boxes that show the source of the language and ideas in the PEs. The presence of clarification statements, assessment boundaries, as well as connections to other standards and the Common Core State Standards, were also almost universally approved. While these elements were applauded, some commenters suggested improvements regarding specific wording and foundation box connections.

In addition to the overall positive feedback the first draft received, there were critiques of specific issues. The following themes emerged from the comments about ways to improve the first public draft:
- Concern that there was too much material
- Suggestions for additional topics
- Lack of language clarity
- Concern about how engineering and technology were included and addressed
- Confusion about the role of the one practice specified in each PE
- Lack of guidance for incorporating crosscutting concepts
- Lack of specificity in connections to other standards and other subjects
- Concern about the organization of the standards
- Concern about the amount of support needed for implementation of the standards

Based on this feedback and on additional interim reviews of the standards by the lead states, many changes were made to the standards between the first and second public drafts. The feedback on the second public draft indicated that the changes to the draft had completely addressed some of the issues and had greatly reduced the percentage of reviewers who had concerns about the remaining issues. Those remaining issues included:

- Concerns that there was still too much material
- Suggestions for a few additional topics to include
- Lack of language clarity
- Concerns about including and addressing engineering and technology
- Confusion about the role of the one practice specified in each PE
- Concern about the amount of support that will be needed for implementation of the standards

Below is a representative sampling of how each issue identified above was addressed, after a thorough review of the feedback.

Too Much Material

The *Framework* and the NGSS set out to define a small set of core ideas that build on each other coherently through the grade levels. While most reviewers of both the first and second public drafts indicated that proficiency in the standards was sufficient for student success at the next level, they also noted that practical classroom time constraints could prevent many students from getting to the depth of skills and knowledge required by the standards.

In the first public draft, several topics, such as nuclear processes, were identified as being beyond the scope of knowledge necessary for college and career readiness. These topics, for example, were deemed important only for those students who planned to continue in science, technology, engineering, and mathematics (STEM) career paths. Similarly, some topics in the elementary levels were deemed more appropriate at either a higher or lower grade level.

To address these issues, the standards underwent extensive review to ensure that all content is both necessary and sufficient for student success after high school in the 21st century. In the K–5 standards, several PEs were shifted from one grade level to the next based on the feedback.

In June 2012, university and community college faculty met with workforce-readiness experts to examine all of the standards in depth. Their feedback, together with that from the first public draft review, led to deletion of many PEs and a greater focus in many discipline areas. In addition, reviews from cross-disciplinary

teams of higher education faculty and the Lead State Review in September led to a further reduction in the content designated in the DCIs.

Feedback on the January 2013 draft indicated that the previous reductions in content were not sufficient to allow for the instruction time necessary to build student proficiency in all of the practices, core ideas, and crosscutting concepts. Therefore, additional content was removed by deleting both the PEs and associated DCI endpoints that covered content beyond the central focus of each core idea. For example, the central focus of HS.LS2.B is the effect of cell division and differentiation on growth, so the DCI endpoints that described the details of cellular differentiation were deleted from the expectations of the standards. The teachers on the NGSS writing team then performed a validity check with the PEs to ensure that the scope of the expectations was practical within the realities of a typical school year. In many cases, the deleted endpoints could serve as the beginnings of instructional extensions when time allows.

In addition, changes were made to ensure that the practice and core idea pairings for each PE were appropriate for all students at each grade level. Writers ensured that all of the K–12 PEs would be implementable within realistic timeframes. The knowledge and skills required by particular PEs are not intended to be taught independently of others at the same grade level and should take into account student knowledge and skills learned at previous grade levels. For instance, in high school physical sciences, one would not teach chemical reactions without also addressing the law of conservation of mass, and these skills should build on associated middle school endpoints.

Suggestions on Inclusion/Exclusion of Certain Topics

While recognizing the sizable amount of content mastery expected of all students in the NGSS draft, many reviewers of both public drafts voiced concerns about the omission of particular areas of content. As writers were tasked with creating a set of standards faithful to the *Framework*, many of these concerns paralleled those raised during the *Framework* development process. Major themes from the feedback on the first public draft included requests for more ocean science context to be used in examples, for computer science concepts to be added, and for "nature of science" concepts to be made more explicit.

One of the important components to the vision of the *Framework* and the NGSS is the focus on a smaller set of core ideas that build over time. With the practical constraints of class time availability and the commitment to remain within the scope of the *Framework*, the NGSS writers were not able to add new core ideas to the standards. They were, however, able to add more context and examples demonstrating potential connections to ocean science and computer science between the first and second public drafts. In addition, where nature of science connections already existed in the standards, they were made more explicit in the second public draft and called out in the appropriate foundation boxes. This addition received very positive feedback from most reviewers.

In both the first and second public drafts, many reviewers expressed concern that specific content normally included in high school elective courses was not in the NGSS, including thermodynamics, stoichiometry, solution chemistry, and nitrogen cycles. Much of this feedback indicated a misunderstanding of the purpose of the NGSS. In contrast to many current state standards, the NGSS specify content and skills required of *all* students and are not intended to replace high school course standards. The NGSS are meant to specify the knowledge and skills that will provide a thorough foundation for student success in any chosen field and they can be supplemented with further in-depth study in particular upper-level science courses.

A key consideration with regard to missing or additional content was its relation to college and career readiness in science. As described, a large team of postsecondary faculty and hiring managers from across the country met to review the May draft specifically to determine if the content represented, as understood by high school graduates, would allow for success in postsecondary education and training. In each discipline (earth/space, biology/life, chemistry, and physics), the outcome did not support adding additional content. In some cases, like stoichiometry, the conceptual understanding for why chemists do stoichiometry was already in the standards. The teams wanted to make the mathematical practice more explicit through the clarification statements, without

having a separate PE requiring that all students do gram-to-gram calculations.

A small number of reviewers in both public draft review periods asked that evolution not be included in the standards. However, an understanding of evolution was identified in the *Framework* as the basis for understanding all of the natural sciences. As such, it was included in the NGSS.

In their feedback on the first public draft, several commenters perceived that "inquiry" was missing from the standards. A few emphasized the importance of students' joy and passion for learning, indicating that this should be made explicit in the standards documents.

The concept and practice of "inquiry" has not been omitted from the NGSS—instead, it is now specified in the eight practices throughout every PE.

In addition, many reviewers requested more guidance for implementation with diverse student groups. A thorough discussion of equity and diversity issues had been planned for inclusion in the standards. A draft version was included in the second public draft of the NGSS, and an expanded version with several vignettes is included in the final release. Each PE and associated examples have been reviewed for appropriateness with all student groups and for relevance to student interests. The writers were committed to the creation of a document that will help encourage all students to engage in and enjoy the study of science.

Some reviewers of both public drafts requested that the standards specify the intermediate knowledge necessary for scaffolding toward eventual student outcomes. However, the NGSS are a set of goals. They are PEs for the end of instruction—not a curriculum. Many different methods and examples could be used to help support student understanding of the DCIs and science and engineering practices, and the writers did not want to prescribe any curriculum or constrain any instruction. It is therefore outside the scope of the standards to specify intermediate knowledge and instructional steps. For example, MS-LS3-1 includes, as a student outcome, some general knowledge of the role of gene mutations. No part of the NGSS specifies the student outcome of defining a gene—it is instead implicit that in order to demonstrate proficiency on MS-LS3-1, students will have to be introduced to the concept of a gene through curriculum and instruction.

Clarity of Language

Many reviewers of the first public draft remarked that the language in the PEs was unclear and not user friendly enough to support consistent implementation—that multiple users would have different interpretations of the same language. More examples and guidance for instruction, assessment, and curriculum development were requested. Requests for clarification were particularly abundant in the feedback describing the practices; the feedback suggested confusion about the meaning and scope of certain practices—particularly "developing and using models."

In early drafts of the standards, the writers purposefully did not control for consistent language, in order to provide several different writing styles as models. Based on the public draft feedback and additional feedback from lead states, the different writing styles were assessed and the highest-rated writing style was then adapted for all of the standards. All PEs were carefully reviewed for clarity of language. Although some examples were added, the writers were careful to use language that was general enough to avoid prescribing curriculum and to ensure that PEs could be met in multiple ways. To help clarify the meaning of each practice, a separate chapter on the practices was added to this draft of the NGSS.

The percentage of people with concerns about language clarity was much lower when reviewing the second public draft. Because some concerns still remained, however, the PEs that received the highest scores for clarity were used as models for editing most of the other PEs. This created clearer and more consistent language, more closely aligned to that in the *Framework*.

Inclusion of Engineering and Technology

The initial inclusion of engineering practices and core ideas in the May 2012 draft NGSS generated a large number of comments. Most reviewers responded positively to the inclusion. Others indicated that engineering should not be in the science standards because of the total amount of content already present in the traditional disciplines and the scarcity of teachers with training in this subject. Still others requested that additional engineering content be added to the NGSS. Of those who liked the inclusion of engineering, many voiced concern that having separate engineering PEs, especially in middle school and high school, would either lead to instruction separated from science content or to an omission of the engineering components altogether.

Upon direction from the lead states, writers integrated the ETS1 (Engineering Design) core ideas into the other disciplines for the January 2013 draft. For example, some PEs described the outcomes from both physical sciences and core ideas and engineering design core ideas. This integration resulted in a reduction of the total number of PEs. In the January 2013 draft, there were two different ways to view these same integrated PEs: listed within the traditional disciplines and listed in separate Engineering Design standards.

Feedback on the integration of engineering in the January 2013 draft was mixed. Reviewers enthusiastically praised the idea of integration as a way to help ensure that engineering design core ideas would be incorporated into science instruction, but commented that the intended engineering design core ideas were not always explicit. The feedback indicated that the integration was not consistently successful.

The writers therefore reintroduced a small set of separate PEs addressing ETS1 core ideas at each grade band, to ensure that the engineering design core ideas from the *Framework* would be clearly represented. In addition, some of the successfully-integrated DCIs are still present throughout the other disciplinary standards.

In addition to this core idea integration, the engineering, technology, and application of science (ETS) core ideas from the *Framework* are included in the other two dimensions of the draft NGSS. Engineering practices are incorporated into PEs at every grade level. Due to their crosscutting nature, ETS2 (Links Among Engineering, Technology, Science, and Society) core ideas have been integrated throughout the standards in a manner similar to that of crosscutting concepts. A thorough discussion of the inclusion of engineering in the NGSS is provided in Appendixes I and J.

Specifying One Practice in Each Performance Expectation

While the NGSS draft was widely praised for integrating practices throughout the standards, many reviewers in both the first and second public drafts remarked that specifying a particular practice in each PE was too restrictive and that it would be interpreted as prescribing instruction.

Response

The writers, upon direction from the lead states, have revised the front matter documents to provide a more detailed explanation of the nature of PEs—that they specify student outcomes and *not* instruction. To help support student learning, *all practices* should be used in instruction throughout each discipline and each year.

It is important to note that the Science and Engineering Practices are not teaching strategies—they are indicators of achievement as well as important learning goals in their own right. As such, the *Framework* and the NGSS ensure that the practices are not treated as afterthoughts. Coupling practice with content gives the learning context, whereas practices alone are activities and content alone is memorization. It is through integration that science begins to make sense and allows student to apply the material.

State standards have traditionally represented practices and core ideas as two separate entities. However, observations from science education researchers have indicated that the result of having these two dimensions separate is that they are either taught separately or the practices are not taught at all.

Implementation Support Needed

Almost every reviewer in both public drafts noted that the vision laid out in the *Framework* and embodied by the NGSS will likely require additional professional development and possibly large-scale changes in education systems to ensure that all students can meet all of these standards. For example, it was noted that science is not currently taught at the K–3 level in many schools and that many students do not take chemistry, physics, and earth sciences classes at the high school level. To help them fully understand the vision of the NGSS, reviewers requested vignettes of classroom instruction showing integration of the three dimensions and inclusion of engi-

neering practices and concepts. Many reviewers also commented that implementation of the standards will, in practice, be impossible until aligned assessments are proposed.

Response

The NGSS writers recognize the differences between current education practice and that envisioned by the *Framework*. Many organizations, including the National Science Teachers Association, are currently planning for programs and support for teachers and states that adopt and implement the standards. The National Research Council is now researching ways to assess the kind of science education envisioned in the *Framework*. Ultimately, the decision of what assessment to use or develop will be up to each state choosing to adopt the NGSS.

COLLEGE AND CAREER READINESS

INTRODUCTION

Postsecondary education is now seen as critical to ensure the nation's long-term economic security, to respond to the transformation in both the nature and number of current and projected jobs, and to enable social mobility. Yet, alarmingly, the United States has fallen from ranking 1st among industrialized nations in both high school completion rates and the percentage of adults with a 2- or 4-year degree, to 22nd in high school graduation and 14th in the percentage of 25- to 34-year-olds with a 2- or 4-year degree (OECD, 2012a, p. 26). On the 30th anniversary of the *Nation at Risk* report, key indicators point to our nation being more at risk than ever (Kirwan, 2013):

- 60% of U.S. jobs are predicted to require some form of post-secondary education by the end of the decade (Georgetown University Center on Education and the Workforce, 2013).

- The U.S. Department of Labor notes that companies have reported more than three million job openings every month since February 2011 because of an absence of applicants with the skills to fill these positions (Woellert, 2012). The National Science Foundation also reports that there are currently between two and three million unfilled positions in the STEM areas of science, technology, engineering, and mathematics.

- The shortfall in STEM employees is likely to increase. The Department of Commerce shows that in the past 10 years, STEM jobs grew at three times the rate of non-STEM jobs, a trend likely to continue and accelerate (Langdon et al., 2011).

Postsecondary education also increases an individual student's chances for a decent, well-paying job. The unemployment rate for recent high school graduates without a college degree was more than 30%, while for recent college graduates, it was under 6% (Shierholtz et al., 2012). And in terms of earnings, a holder of a bachelor's degree is likely to realize a million dollars more over a lifetime than an individual with only a high school diploma. More troubling is a grim reality underlying these statistics: a child born into a family in the lowest quartile of income has a less than 8% chance of earning a postsecondary degree. The Organisation for Economic Co-operation and Development (OECD) observes that children of less-educated parents in the United States have a tougher time climbing the educational ladder than in almost any other developed country (OECD, 2012a, p. 102). The American dream that one's birth circumstances do not control one's destiny is fast slipping away.

The last decade has seen an emerging consensus that effective preparation for student success in postsecondary education and careers includes a strong background in science. In particular, the best science education seems to be one based on integrating rigorous content with the practices that scientists and engineers routinely use in their work—including application of mathematics. The larger context, and perhaps the primary impetus for this consensus, is the paradigm shift in our worldview of educational priorities, a direct result of the advent of the information age and global economy. To remain economically competitive, countries are pressed to substantially increase the number of students who can put knowledge to use in the service of new frontiers—discovering new knowledge, solving challenging problems, and generating innovations (NSF, 2012). Beyond the needs of the economy, an education grounded in acquiring and applying knowledge positions students to improve their options in a rapidly changing menu of jobs, where few students will stay in the same job throughout their working lives. In sum, today's new reality demands that science and engineering become accessible to the many, not the few. And because the needed proficiencies are acquired over time, students must experience how science and engineering are conducted in the workplace throughout their K–12 schooling (NRC, 2007).

Scientists and engineers have always integrated content and practices in their work, but that has not been the case with science instruction. As former president of the National Academy of Sciences, Bruce Alberts, stated, "rather than learning how to think scientifically, students are generally being told about science and asked to remember facts" (Alberts, 2009). Traditional instruction has emphasized lectures, note-taking, reading, and assessment that tested recall, offering little opportunity for in-depth study or research (NRC, 2007). Laboratory activities, when offered, generally consisted of cookbook or confirmatory experiences. Research indicates that most lab experiences do not integrate well with other classroom instruction and infrequently include teacher and student analysis and discussion, thereby making it difficult for students to connect learning about science content with learning the processes of science (NRC, 2005). This situation stands in stark contrast to the real work of science and engineering, where new knowledge and innovation are prized. The shift in what the world needs and values requires that K–12 science education undergo a huge transition, from a focus on knowledge itself to a focus on putting that knowledge to use—a transition that in and of itself necessitates a corresponding leap in rigor. Meeting this challenge head-on, the Next Generation Science Standards (NGSS) constructed each performance expectation by linking concepts and practices that build coherently over time throughout K–12, thereby helping to ensure that students who meet the NGSS will be prepared to succeed in science courses in both 2- and 4-year institutions.

The first step in developing the NGSS was the development of *A Framework for K–12 Science Education: Practices, Crosscutting Concepts, and Core Ideas (Framework)*. The National Research Council (NRC) led the undertaking in partnership with the American Association for the Advancement of Science (AAAS), the National Science Teachers Association (NSTA), and Achieve, Inc. The intent of the *Framework* was to describe a coherent vision of science education by (1) viewing learning as a developmental progression; (2) focusing on a limited number of core ideas to allow for in-depth learning (both cross-disciplinary concepts with applicability across science and engineering and concepts central to each of the disciplines); and (3) emphasizing that learning about science and engineering involves integration of content knowledge and the practices needed to engage in scientific inquiry and engineering design (NRC, 2012a, pp. 10–11). The NGSS kept the vision of the *Framework* intact by focusing on a rigorous set of core concepts that are articulated for each grade

band (K–2, 3–5, 6–8, 9–12) and anchored to real-world science and engineering practices. This appendix reviews the evidence for basing K–12 standards on rigorous content, science and engineering practices, mathematics, and the benefits of integrating content with practices.

IMPORTANCE OF RIGOROUS CONTENT FOR COLLEGE AND CAREER READINESS IN SCIENCE

The first challenge facing the developers of the *Framework* was to identify the core conceptual knowledge that all students need to know and that also provides a foundation for those who will become the scientists, engineers, technologists, and technicians of the future (NRC, 2012a). Not all content is equally worth learning. Some science concepts deserve the lion's share of instruction because they have explanatory or predictive power or provide a framework that facilitates learning and applying new knowledge. To that end, the NRC convened members of the scientific community and engaged them in a rigorous, 2-year iterative process of formulating and refining the document based on multiple, critical reviews involving key organizations, distinguished scientists, mathematicians, engineers, and science educators, as well as the public. The resulting *Framework* sets forth not only the core ideas in the major science disciplines (life, physical, and earth and space sciences), but also the crosscutting concepts that have applicability to most fields in science and engineering. In keeping with the idea that learning is a developmental progression, the natural and cognitive scientists who developed the *Framework* further articulated what students should know by the end of each grade band. Significantly, the *Framework* also embraces the core concepts and essential practices of engineering, and in doing so, opens a window of interest and career opportunities not previously available to most K–12 students.

Once the *Framework* was completed, the NGSS writing team used the content to construct the NGSS performance expectations. Throughout the 2-year development process, the disciplinary core ideas (DCIs), and the related learning progressions from the *Framework,* along with their incorporation into the student performance expectations, were reviewed multiple times by a large group of expert reviewers (including major science, engineering, and mathematics associations), by the state teams in each of the 26 lead states as well as some additional states, and by the general public. In addition, Achieve convened postsecondary faculty and business representatives on two separate occasions to evaluate the content of the standards as being both necessary and sufficient for college and career readiness for all students. The comprehensive nature and thoroughness of the review process should ensure that the NGSS express the content expectations that will allow all students to be successful in advanced science courses and postsecondary careers.

Both the *Framework* and the NGSS reflect current thinking about the need for greater depth and rigor in K–12 science schooling. College Board, for example, has had a rich history in defining college and career readiness. "In order for a student to be college-ready in science, he or she must . . . have knowledge of the overarching ideas in the science disciplines (i.e., earth and space science, life science, physical science, and engineering) and how the practices of science are situated within this content" (College Board, 2010, p. 3). The content represented in the *Framework* is also in line with the content identified in the College Board *Standards for College Success* (2009), which defines the rigorous knowledge and skills students need to develop and master in order to be ready for college and 21st-century careers. These were developed to . . . help students successfully transition into Advanced Placement (AP) and college-level courses. College Board standards, like the *Framework*, are based on (1) overarching unifying concepts that are important across the science disciplines but also often apply to other fields such as mathematics and technology, and (2) like the *Framework,* are based on the core ideas of each science discipline (College Board, 2009). For students pursuing postsecondary coursework in science, core content clearly plays a key role. By virtue of being based on the content from the *Framework,* the NGSS provide a strong foundation for students to be successful in advanced science coursework.

ACT takes a similar, though not identical, stance as College Board with respect to core content. The ACT assessment assumes "that students are in the process of taking the core science course of study (three years or more of science in high school) that will prepare them for college-level work, and have completed a course in Biology and a course in Physical Science and/or Earth Science by the time they take the ACT" (ACT, 2011, p. 20). Based on their available data, ACT builds the case that students are better prepared for postsecondary work when the practices are used over 3 years of science in high school. ACT concludes [*sic*]: "Postsecondary expectations clearly state the process and inquiry skill in science are critical as well as rigorous understanding of fundamental (not advanced) science topics" (ACT, 2011, p. 9). However, while both ACT and College Board argue for winnowing content, ACT goes further, making the case that studying advanced content is not a quality predictor of postsecondary success. ACT goes on to state, "Therefore, for example, including a great deal of advanced science topics among the Next Generation standards would conflict with available empirical evidence" (ACT, 2011, p. 9). Postsecondary faculty report that a firm grasp of core concepts is more important than a weak grasp of advanced topics. Thus, a few components originally included in the *Framework* and early drafts of the NGSS were eliminated over time, based on the reviews of faculty in 2- and 4-year institutions in NGSS lead states, as well as on the ACT research.

ACT is not alone in arguing for a more limited coverage of content. Recent research examining the relationship between the performance of college students in introductory science courses and the amount of content covered in their high school courses concluded that "students who reported covering at least one major topic in depth, for a month or longer, in high school were found to earn higher grades in college science than did students who reported no coverage in depth. Students reporting breadth in their high school course, covering all major topics, did not appear to have any advantage in Chemistry or Physics and a significant disadvantage in Biology" (Schwartz et al., 2009, p. 1). Additional research supports limiting coverage, but offers little in the way of advising standards or policy developers *what* content should be eliminated. In fact, little empirical evidence exists on the content alignment between high school science and postsecondary expectations beyond ACT's data. Given the lack of empirical evidence in the field, the most fruitful path to support college and career readiness in science is to involve postsecondary faculty working with high school faculty to align content expectations.

From an international perspective, science content plays a prominent role in preparing K–12 students. In its international science benchmarking study of 10 countries (Canada [Ontario], Chinese Taipei, England, Finland, Hong Kong, Hungary, Ireland, Japan, Singapore, and South Korea) Achieve found evidence of strong science content, including far more attention to physical science concepts in primary and lower secondary grades than is typical of most states in the United States (Achieve, 2010, p. 59). However, the presentation of content is different than in the United States. Standards in 7 of the 10 countries present integrated science content (content drawn from the major disciplines) each year from primary through grade 10, allowing students to specialize later in high school (Achieve, 2010, p. 42). These countries clearly see that a minimum amount of science knowledge is necessary for all students to become scientifically literate. Requiring that all students study integrated science content through grade 10 before enrolling in discipline-specific courses is a significant departure from the current structures in most U.S. states. Importantly, an integrated program through grade 10 also speaks to the possibility of capitalizing on student interest. Students could choose to pursue a course of study later in high school that fully prepares them for postsecondary careers, such as entry-level positions in health-related fields. Singapore has pursued this approach to great advantage. In making recommendations to the Carnegie's Commission on Mathematics and Science Education, mathematics expert Phillip Daro observed that Singapore's educational system "illustrates how it is possible to design multiple pathways to college entrance while still serving more specialized interests in the student population" (Carnegie Corporation of New York, 2009, p. 25).

Students need to be able to make sense of the world and approach problems not previously encountered—new situations, new phenomena, and new information. To achieve this level of proficiency students need a solid grasp of key science concepts and the ability to relate that knowledge across disciplines.

Finally, as seen in the next section, students will need to be able to apply and communicate that knowledge flexibly across various disciplines, proficiencies they can acquire through the continual exploration of DCIs, science and engineering practices, and crosscutting concepts.

IMPORTANCE OF SCIENCE AND ENGINEERING PRACTICES IN COLLEGE AND CAREER READINESS IN SCIENCE

Empirical data and related research show direct support for students engaging in, and being held accountable for, proficiency in the science and engineering practices. The NRC has published a great deal of research in the recent past that supports the need for students to engage in science and engineering practices as they learn content. While no one document prior to the *Framework* includes all eight of the science and engineering practices described in the *Framework*, they are clear in the literature as a whole. Documents supporting the practices in the *Framework* include *Taking Science to School*; *Ready, Set, SCIENCE!*; and *America's Lab Report*. Findings from *Taking Science to School* (NRC, 2007, p. 342) show that students learn science more effectively when they actively engage in the practices of science. Linn and Hsi (2000) (as cited in the NRC's *America's Lab Report* [2005]) found that a quality integrated experience with practice and content led not only to greater mastery, but importantly, also more interest in science.

Streamlining the overwhelming amount of science content to target essential key ideas was the first but not the only challenge in building the *Framework*. In identifying and characterizing science and engineering practices, developers had to confront common classroom instructional practices where students are told that there is "a scientific method," typically presented as a fixed linear sequence of steps that students apply in a superficial or scripted way.

> This approach often obscures or distorts the processes of inquiry as they are practiced by scientists. Practices, such as reasoning carefully about the implications of models and theories; framing questions and hypotheses so that

they can be productively investigated; systematically analyzing and integrating data to serve as evidence to evaluate claims; and communicating and critiquing ideas in a scientific community are vital parts of inquiry. However, they tend to be missed when students are taught a scripted procedure designed to obtain a particular result in a decontextualized investigation. Furthermore, these higher-level reasoning and problem-solving practices require a reasonable depth of familiarity with the content of a given scientific topic if students are to engage in them in a meaningful way. Debates over content versus process are not in step with the current views of the nature of science. . . . Science is seen as a fundamentally social enterprise that is aimed at advancing knowledge through the development of theories and models that have explanatory and predictive power and that are grounded in evidence. In practice this means that content and process are deeply intertwined. (NRC, 2012b, p. 127)

Historically, College Board emphasized content in its advanced placement science examinations, but is now giving increased attention to the practices that scientists routinely use. To wit: "Central to science is the goal of establishing lines of evidence and using that evidence to develop and refine testable explanations and make predictions about natural phenomena. Standards documents must reflect this goal of science by focusing on developing, in all students, the competencies necessary for constructing testable, evidence-based explanations and predictions" (College Board, 2010, p. 4). The new Advanced Placement (AP) Biology Exam and the relatively new *Standards for College Success* (SCS) reflect the new perspective in that both utilize scientific practices extensively. Both the AP redesign and the SCS identify performance expectations requiring practice and content to be in context of one another. Given the research that led College Board to make these decisions, the NRC utilized these two projects as a basis for the development of the *Framework*. College Board work and now the NGSS focus on understanding rather than memorization because greater understanding has been found to positively influence college performance (Tai et al., 2005, 2006). College Board states: "In order for a student to

be college-ready in science, he or she must: (1) have knowledge of the overarching ideas in the science disciplines (i.e., earth and space science, life science, physical science, and engineering) and how the practices of science are situated within this content; (2) have a rich understanding of the nature and epistemology of science, scientific discourse, and the integration of science, technology, and society; (3) have metacognitive skills and self-efficacy related to the practices of science" (College Board, 2010, p. 3). This definition and the underlying research leave no doubt as to science practices being a critical component of readiness.

ACT's evidence for incorporating science practices derives from extensive years of collecting and analyzing data with regard to judging the preparedness of high school graduates for postsecondary science courses. ACT conducts a national curriculum survey every 3 years that compares expectations of introductory level postsecondary instructors with what is actually taught by middle and high school teachers and uses the results to update teacher information and the ACT assessments. The past two surveys have shown that postsecondary instructors greatly value the use of process or inquiry skills (science and engineering practices in the language of NGSS), and, in fact, value these skills equally to content. ACT notes [*sic*]: "Postsecondary expectations clearly state the process and inquiry skill in science are critical as well as rigorous understanding of fundamental (not advanced) science topics" (ACT, 2011, p. 9). In their college placement services ACT also uses empirical data derived from the performance of college students to set the ACT College Readiness Benchmarks. Students who meet a benchmark on the ACT test or ACT Compass have approximately a 50% chance of receiving a B or better in their introductory level Biology course (ACT, 2013).

While ACT's position on college and career readiness in science acknowledges the need for students to pursue a rigorous program of science courses in high school, ACT also calls for integrating practices, based on their survey results. Notably, the ACT assessment focuses more on skill application than content. ACT (2011) states, "The Science Test, on the EXPLORE, PLAN, and ACT tests, measures the student's interpretation, analysis, evaluation, reasoning, and problem-solving skills required in the natural sciences. The test assumes that students are in the process of taking the core science course of study (three years or more of science in high school) that will prepare them for college-level work, and have completed a course in Biology and a course in Physical Science and/or Earth Science by the time they take the ACT" (p. 20). The ACT's WorkKeys Applied Technology Assessment also values these skills and empirically affirms that knowledge and usage of these skills better prepares students for career options than content knowledge alone.

College Board's and ACT's position with regard to the critical role of practices in preparing students for success in college-level science is echoed by David Conley in his book *College Knowledge* (2005). He identified students' ability to conduct meaningful research and use practices that lead toward quality research as a college- and career-ready indicator, stating that successful students:

- Formulate research questions and develop a plan for research.
- Use research to support and develop their own opinions.
- Identify claims in their work that require outside support or validation.

Science and engineering practices are also receiving increased attention in higher education. For example, recent "studies are converging on a view of engineering education that not only requires students to develop a grasp of traditional engineering fundamentals, such as mechanics, dynamics, mathematics, and technology, but also to develop the skills associated with learning to imbed this knowledge in real-world situations. This not only demands skills of creativity, teamwork, and design, but in global collaboration, communication, management, economics, and ethics. Furthermore, the rapid pace of change of technology seems fated to continue for many decades to come. This will require the engineers we are training today to learn to be lifelong learners and to learn to develop adaptive expertise" (Hatano and Inagaki, 1986; Pellegrino, 2006; Redish and Smith, 2008, p. 2).

The AP science curricula, the AAAS publication *Vision and Change*, and the *Scientific Foundations for Future Physicians* identify overlapping science practices that are in line with the *Framework*. For example, the importance of modeling emerges in the life science documents and is used as an exemplar in Redish and Smith's (2008) work on skill development in engineering, noted above. Modeling is also built into both the Common Core State Standards (CCSS) for Mathematics and the *Framework*.

As noted earlier, making science accessible to a far greater number of students than is now the case is a critical issue. A growing body of evidence suggests that student engagement in practices helps reduce achievement gaps (Barton et al., 2008; Brotman and Moore, 2008; Enfield et al., 2008; Lee et al., 2005; Page, 2007). Specifically, one study found no significant difference in performance between subgroups (gender, ethnicity, or economically disadvantaged) when inquiry was used in instruction, as opposed to traditional classroom instruction where a significant achievement gap between subgroups of students was found (Wilson et al., 2010). In addition, Lee and colleagues (2006) found that while student achievement increased overall with inquiry-focused instruction, students from non-mainstreamed or less privileged backgrounds showed much higher gains than their mainstreamed, more privileged counterparts (Lee et al., 2006).

From an international perspective, science and engineering practices are seen as necessary for literacy as well as proficiency. The OECD's *Programme for International Student Assessment 2015 Scientific Literacy Assessment Framework* (2012) states that a scientifically literate person is able to engage in discourse by explaining phenomena scientifically, evaluate and design scientific enquiry, and interpret data and evidence scientifically. It is worth noting that in Japan, a nation whose students outscore U.S. students on both PISA and TIMSS, classroom activity patterns are quite different than those characteristic of U.S. classrooms. Japanese students contribute their ideas in solving problems collectively and critically discuss alternative solutions to problems. Students in classroom environments like these come to expect that these public, social acts of reasoning and dialogue are a regular part of classroom life and learning across the disciplines (Linn, 2000; Stigler and Hiebert, 1999).

At the other end of the educational spectrum, Coles conducted research on the science content knowledge and skills necessary for both higher education and the workforce in the United Kingdom by interviewing groups from each sector. He found that employers and higher education professionals have more in common than not in their views of what science skills makes one qualified for their specific sector, noting: "[t]he number of components common to employers and higher education tutors is about twice the number of components specific to employers and about twice the number of components specific to tutors in higher education." Young and Glanfield (1998) add support to this finding, stating, "under the impact of information technology, the skills needed in different occupational sectors are converging as more and more jobs demand generic and abstract rather than sector-specific skills" (p. 7).

Graduates of 2- and 4-year colleges have as their goal securing employment and being successful on the job. Listening to what employers seek in candidates is critical because the skills employers seek need to be learned over the course of a K–postsecondary education. A number of recent reports point to gaps in preparation for work. One study earmarked five assets that are important to employers but hardest to find in candidates: These, in rank order, are Communication Skills, Positive Attitude, Adaptable to Change, Teamwork Skills, and Strategic Thinking and Analytics (Millennial Branding and Experience Inc., 2012). Another study asked employers to rate the importance of candidate skills/qualities. The results resonate with the previous study as employers cited, in rank order, the following top five abilities: work in a team structure, verbally communicate with persons inside and outside the organization, make decisions and solve problems, obtain and process information, plan, and organize and prioritize work (National Association of Colleges and Employers, 2012). Still another study found that 95% of all employers surveyed say they give hiring preference to graduates with skills that will enable them to contribute to innovation in the workplace, reflecting concern for the nation's continuing ability to compete (The Association of American Colleges and Universities, 2013). These skills are likely to be acquired when students engage in projects based on the science and engineering practices and core content described in the *Framework* and prescribed in the performance expectations of the NGSS.

IMPORTANCE OF MATHEMATICS FOR COLLEGE AND CAREER READINESS IN SCIENCE

The *Framework* calls out mathematical thinking as a specific practice for good reason. "Mathematics is the bedrock of science, engineering and technology—it is the ability to quantitatively describe and measure objects, events, and processes that makes science so powerful in extending human knowledge. Moreover, because of the rapid and almost unimaginable increase in the power of computers, advances in science now depend routinely on techniques of mathematical models, remote imaging, data mining, and probabilistic calculations that were unthinkable a decade ago" (Achieve, 2010, p. 53).

Complementing the research supporting the integration of practices and disciplinary content in science education, research on math education suggests that instruction should not only emphasize core ideas, but also emphasize inquiry, relevance, and a multilayered vision of proficiency (Carnegie Corporation of New York, 2009).

From the international perspective, the lack of inclusion of mathematics explicitly in science standards was found to be a shortcoming in the countries studied (Achieve, 2010). In a review of the top performing countries based on PISA, reviewers found that mathematics integration was left to mathematics standards and curriculum documents. It is important to be aware that the math-science connection is not obvious to students. How science standards address and incorporate mathematics can make a difference in how easily students develop quantitative habits of mind. As a result, in developing the NGSS, explicit steps were taken to include mathematics in the development of the standards to help ensure students would receive a coherent education in two mutually supportive content areas. In fact the NGSS identify related Common Core State Standards for Mathematics for each science standard.

In addition to the inclusion of mathematics in the practices, there is evidence that mathematics is a key predictor of success in college science. While there is limited empirical data about the exact boundaries of college and career readiness in science, there has been data that supports a direct correlation between mathematics and success in college course work, or even the likelihood of successfully graduating with a 4-year degree. Proficiency in mathematics is a critical component of high school preparation leading to college success: "the highest level of mathematics reached in high school continues to be a key marker in precollegiate momentum, with the tipping point of momentum toward a bachelor's degree now firmly above Algebra 2" (Adelman, 2006, p. xix).

Sadler and Tai (2007) found that the number of years of mathematics was a significant predictor of college success across all college science subjects. Further, they found that more advanced mathematics in high school was a "pillar" that supports success in college science coursework. In like vein, Conley found college- and career-ready graduates had a firm grasp on mathematics and the ability to apply it across other disciplines. In addition, he found in surveys with college faculty that mathematics was considered an even better predictor of college science than high school science courses. Beyond success in postsecondary science, "there is a strong correlation between preparedness for college mathematics and the actual completion of a college degree. Students who need remediation in mathematics are considered at risk for academic failure and for retention and perseverance in their post-secondary education" (Ali and Jenkins, 2002, p. 11). The combination of the CCSS and the NGSS provide all students the opportunity for advanced studies in mathematics and science. The NGSS were developed specifically taking into account the new mathematics expectations described in the CCSS.

Experts at home and abroad understand that mathematics is key to understanding and communicating scientific ideas. In the words of mathematician and educator Sol Garfunkel on the future of American students, "We know that their future will involve many different jobs and the need to master current and future technologies. We know that they will need creativity, independence, imagination, and problem-solving abilities in addition to skills proficiency. In other words, students will increasingly need mathematical understanding and awareness of the tools mathematics provides in order to achieve their career goals" (Garfunkel, 2009).

It is easy to see why mathematics is, and will continue to be, a quality indicator of success. If there are any prerequisites to postsecondary science courses, it is usually a mathematics requirement. Students who are prepared for postsecondary education will be able to exhibit evidence of the effective transfer of mathematics and disciplinary literacy skills to science. As the NGSS move into adoption and implementation, work to develop specific examples of the further integration of mathematics and science will be critical.

INTEGRATION OF PRACTICE AND CORE IDEAS

Neither rigorous content nor science and engineering practices alone are sufficient for success in postsecondary institutions and careers. Rather it is the linking of the practices to core content that increases student learning, as the *Framework* underscores: "Learning is defined as the combination of both knowledge and practice, not separate content and process learning goals" (p. 254). Additional research backs up the NRC's assertion. While practices are found in literature to be important predictors of achievement in science (Conley, 2005; Redish and Smith, 2008; von Secker, 2002; Wilson et al., 2010), it is also clear that students should use them in the context of quality and rigorous content.

One often overlooked aspect of combining demanding practices with strong content in standards is the effect on rigor. Even the most demanding of content is diluted if the expected student performance is basically dependent on rote memorization, i.e., calls for students to "describe," "identify," "recall," "define," "state," or "recognize." It is also well to keep in mind that calling for application of mathematics in a performance generally raises the level of rigor.

An instructive illustration is a learning outcome from Kansas's previous Science Education Standards (Kansas adopted the NGSS as its new state science education standards in June 2013) as compared with a related NGSS performance expectation.

Kansas 2007 Science Education Standards, Grades 8–11, Chemistry, HS.2A.2.2	NGSS Physical Sciences Grades 9–12, HS-PS1-1
"The student understands the periodic table lists elements according to increasing atomic number. This table organizes physical and chemical trends by groups, periods, and sub-categories."	"Use the periodic table as a model to predict the relative properties of elements based on the patterns of electrons in the outermost energy level of atoms."

While the organization of the periodic table is addressed by both sets of standards, it is clear that the NGSS raise the level of rigor by calling for a more demanding performance than does this example from the 2007 Kansas standards.

Another illustration can be found in Kansas's previous Biology standards:

Kansas 2007 Science Education Standards, Grades 8–11, Biology, HS.3.3.4	NGSS Life Sciences Grades 9–12, HS-LS3-3
"The student understands organisms vary widely within and between populations. Variation allows for natural selection to occur."	"Apply concepts of statistics and probability to explain the variation and distribution of expressed traits in a population."

Calling for students to apply math concepts in explaining trait variation, as the NGSS do, bumps up the rigor of the expected student performance. Incorporating practices with content seems to have a positive effect on ensuring all students learn content at a deep level. Researchers found that students in project-based science classrooms performed better than comparison students on designing fair tests, justifying claims with evidence, and generating explanations. They also exhibited more negotiation and collaboration in their group work and a greater tendency to monitor and evaluate their work (Kolodner et al., 2003). In addition, von Secker (2002) found a greater content mastery and retention when teachers use inquiry-oriented practices. Results from the 2011 National Assessment of Educational Progress (NAEP) in science corroborate the positive effect on learning content when

science practices are used in conjunction with content. On the eighth-grade teacher questionnaire, teachers reported how often their students engaged in hands-on activities or investigations in science by selecting one of four responses: "never or hardly ever," "once or twice a month," "once or twice a week," or "every day or almost every day." Students who did hands-on projects every day or almost every day scored higher on average than those who did hands-on projects less frequently (NCES, 2011, p. 10). Furthermore, among higher-achieving grade 8 students who scored above the 75th percentile, 77% had teachers who reported that their students engage in hands-on activities once a week or more (NCES, 2011, p. 11).

The research regarding the value of integrating practices with content is compelling: preparedness for postsecondary work should be rooted in a student's ability to use science and engineering practices in the context of rigorous content. Using the practices in absence of content is akin to asking students to learn the steps in the so-called scientific method. That will not result in preparedness but rather is likely to result in students continuing to have a disjointed view of science and a lack of ability to pursue their own interests or research today's problems. Students proficient in applying the practices in context will be able to apply a blend of science and engineering practices, crosscutting concepts, and DCIs to make sense of the world and approach problems not previously encountered, engage in self-directed planning, monitoring, and evaluation, and employ valid and reliable research strategies.

Prior to the release of the NGSS, most U.S. states had standards that did not clearly integrate inquiry and content. This integration of science process skills and domain-specific knowledge is still often missing from the classroom. Many standards, curriculum documents, and textbooks have separate sections on inquiry and science practices, and research indicates that many teachers follow the lead of these resources by teaching practices separately from conceptual content (NRC, 2007). Often, when students engage in science and engineering practices through laboratory experiments, these experiences have been isolated from the flow of classroom instruction and lacking in clear learning goals tied to content knowledge (NRC, 2005). Standards that balance and integrate inquiry and content can enhance student learning and better prepare them for success in postsecondary institutions and careers. As research has repeatedly shown that standards can have a large influence on curriculum, instruction, and assessment (Berland and McNeill, 2010; Krajcik et al., 2008; NRC, 2007), it is important for standards to specify the learning outcomes we expect from students, including that they can use practices to demonstrate knowledge of core ideas.

CONCLUSION

Economic and education statistics make it clear that the United States is not educating enough students who can succeed in a global information economy fueled by advances and innovation in science, engineering, and technology. Research findings indicate that our current system of science education, which places more value on science as a knowledge base than as a way of thinking, is ineffective. Too few students are experiencing success in postsecondary institutions and therefore lack the wherewithal to qualify for gainful employment, including STEM fields, where the nation is seeing the most growth in jobs. They are, in effect, being closed out of middle class opportunities. However, as the research studies referenced in this appendix indicate there is a more productive path to follow in science education that entails linking important core content to the practices that scientists and engineers use as they go about their work. This shift in emphasis requires that we control the amount and kind of content, giving priority to powerful concepts that have currency because of their utility in explaining phenomena, predicting outcomes or displaying broad applicability in many fields, and that we use the practices in conjunction with core content throughout the grades.

The *Framework* identifies the content students are expected to know in order to be scientifically literate and to have an adequate foundation for further study and that content was deemed appropriate for success in college and career by science education experts and postsecondary instructors and employers. The *Framework* also describes the practices that characterize science and engineering work and explains what they look like

in primary, upper elementary, and in middle and high school classrooms.

To reiterate, during the development of the NGSS, states remained focused on the vision of the *Framework* from the NRC, staying true to the cornerstones of rigorous core content, science and engineering practices, and links to mathematics. To ensure fidelity to that vision, teams of postsecondary faculty and business professionals from across the 26 lead states were convened to review the standards in terms of practice and content. Like the NRC, these groups confirmed that the design and development of the NGSS were guided by the best available evidence to ensure that students who meet the standards have the knowledge and skills to succeed in entry level science courses in technical training programs and in 2- and 4-year colleges. The evidence indicates this can best be accomplished through an approach that promotes in-depth understanding of a focused set of core concepts and interdisciplinary ideas, integrated with the regular application of those understandings through the practices of scientific inquiry.

Benchmarking has become a central concept in improving systems. And many countries are looking to Singapore as a model. Singapore's Educational System is recognized today as "world class," but that is a relatively recent turn of events. In just a slightly longer time period than it took the United States to relinquish its leadership role in terms of percent of students earning high school diplomas and postsecondary degrees, Singapore went from an impoverished nation with a largely illiterate population to being a model in education, a major telecommunications hub, and a leader in consumer electronics, pharmaceuticals, financial services, and information technology. Singapore's metamorphosis is attributed to its exemplary program of ensuring that most students are educated to take advantage of growing opportunities for employment in STEM fields. Because of the differences in size, scope, and complexity, it is difficult to imagine the United States fully implementing Singapore's system. However, much of education in the United States is controlled by states, and they could individually use Singapore's model to good advantage.

It is worth noting that as part of the education policy shift, "the government developed in 2004 the 'Teach Less, Learn More Initiative,' which moved instruction further away from rote memorization and repetitive tasks on which it had originally focused to deeper conceptual understanding and problem-based learning" (CIEB, 2012). Instruction has shifted toward one that includes active engagement with science practices (CIEB, 2012). This stance certainly resonates with that taken by the *Framework* and the NGSS.

In closing, when it comes to developing standards, rigorous content is an important indicator of student readiness for success in postsecondary education and careers, but it is not enough. Proficiency with science and engineering practices is also an indicator of readiness, but it is not sufficient in the absence of rigorous content. In the end, as the research shows, it is the science and engineering practices learned in conjunction with rigorous content that best prepares students for success in postsecondary education and careers. More research is needed around the alignment of high school and postsecondary expectations, course pathways, and flexible options that engage students' interests and best prepare students for postsecondary and career opportunities.

REFERENCES

ABET. (2009). *ABET criteria for evaluating engineering programs.* Baltimore, MD.

Achieve. (2010). *International science benchmarking report: Taking the lead in science education: Forging next-generation science standards.* Washington, DC.

ACT. (2011). Science for college and careers: A resource for developers of the next generation science standards. Unpublished manuscript, commissioned by Achieve.

ACT. (2013). What are ACT's college readiness benchmarks? Available at: http://www.act.org/research/policymakers/pdf/benchmarks.pdf.

Adams, C. (2012, December 12). K–12, higher ed. unite to align learning in Minnesota. *Education Week.* Available at: http://www.edweek.org/ew/articles/2012/12/12/14minn.h32.html?r=1637415706.

Alberts, B. (2009). Redefining science education. *Science* 23. Available at: http://www.sci-ips.com/pdf/reflections/Reflections_29.pdfhttp://www.sciencemag.org/content/323/5913/437.full.

American Association for the Advancement of Science. (2011). *Vision and change in undergraduate biology education.* Washington, DC.

American Association of Universities. (2011). *AAU undergraduate STEM initiative.* Available at: http://www.aau.edu/policy/article.aspx?id=12588.

American Society of Plant Biologists. (2012). *Core concepts and learning objectives in undergraduate plant biology.* Available at: http://my.aspb.org/blogpost/722549/152613/Core-Concepts-and-Learning-Objectives-in-Undergraduate-Plant-Biology?hhSearchTerms=core+and+concepts&terms=.

Association of American Colleges and Universities. (2013). *It takes more than a major: Employer priorities for college learning and student success.* Washington, DC: Hart Research Associates.

Association of American Medical Colleges and Howard Hughes Medical Institute. (2009). *Scientific Foundations for Future Physicians.* Washington, DC.

Association of Public and Land Grant Universities. (2013). *Science and Mathematics Teacher Imperative.* Available at: http://www.aplu.org/page.aspx?pid=584.

Barton, A. C., Tan, E., and Rivet, A. (2008). Creating hybrid spaces for engaging school science among urban middle school girls. *American Educational Research Journal* 45(1):68–103.

Berland, L. K., and McNeill, K. L. (2010). A learning progression for scientific argumentation: Understanding student work and designing supportive instructional contexts. *Science Education* 94(1):765–793.

Brotman, J. S., and Moore, F. M. (2008). Girls and science: A review of four themes in the science education literature. *Journal of Research in Science Teaching* 45(9):971–1,002.

Carnegie Corporation of New York. (2009). *The opportunity equation: Transforming mathematics and science education for citizenship and the global economy.*

Carnevale, A. P., Smith, N., and Melton, M. (2011). STEM. Washington, DC: Georgetown University Center on Education and the Workforce. Available at: http://cew.georgetown.edu/stem.

Carnevale, A. P., Rose, S. J., and Hanson, A. R. (2012). *Certificates: Gateway to gainful employment and college degrees.* Georgetown University Center on Education and the Workforce. Available at: http://www9.georgetown.edu/grad/gppi/hpi/cew/pdfs/Certificates. FullReport.061812.pdf.

CIEB (Center on International Education Benchmarking). (2012). *Singapore Overview.* Available at: http://www.ncee.org/programs-affiliates/center-on-international-education-benchmarking/top-performing-countries/singapore-overview.

Coles, M. (1998). Science for employment and higher education. *International Journal of Science Education* 20:5,609–5,621.

College Board. (2009). *Science: College Board standards for college success.*

College Board. (2010). *College readiness in science.* Unpublished manuscript, commissioned by Achieve.

Common Core State Standards for English Language Arts & Literacy in History/Social Studies, Science, and Technical Subjects, Appendix A: Research Supporting Key Elements of the Standards, Glossary of Key Terms. Available at: http://www.corestandards.org/assets/Appendix_A.pdf.

Conley, D. T. (2005). *College knowledge: What it really takes for students to succeed and what we can do to get them ready.* San Francisco, CA: Jossey-Bass Education Series.

Conley, D. T. (2010). *College and career ready: Helping all students succeed beyond high school.* San Francisco, CA: Jossey-Bass Education Series.

Enfield, M., Smith, E. L., and Grueber, D. J. (2008). "A sketch is like a sentence": Curriculum structures that support teaching epistemic practices of science. *Science Education* 92(4):608–630.

Garfunkel, S. (2009). *Math to work.* Prepared for the Carnegie-IAS Commission on Mathematics and Science Education. Available at: OpportunityEquation.org/go/garfunkel.

Georgetown University Center on Education and the Workforce. (2013). Recovery: Job growth and education requirements through 2020. Georgetown University Center on Education and the Workforce. PowerPoint. June 26, 2013. Available at: http://www.slideshare.net/CEWGeorgetown/projections2020-powerpoint-final.

Kansas State Department of Education. (2007). Kansas Science Education Standards.

Kirwan, W. E. (2013, April). *Upgrade America 2013.* Speech presented at the Business Coalition for Student Achievement, Washington, DC.

Kolodner, J. L., Camp, P. J., Crismond, D., Fasse, B., Gray, J., and Holbrook, J. (2003). Problem-based learning meets case-based reasoning in the middle-school science classroom: Putting learning by design into practice. *Journal of the Learning Sciences* 12(4):495–547.

Krajcik, J., McNeill, K. L., and Reiser, B. J. (2008). Learning-goals-driven design model: Curriculum materials that align with national standards and incorporate project-based pedagogy. *Science Education* 92(1):1–32.

Langdon, D., McKittrick, G., Beede D., Khan, B., and Doms, M. (2011, July). STEM: Good jobs now and for the future. Department of Commerce, Economics and Statistics Administration. Available at: http://www.esa.doc.gov/Reports/stem-good-jobs-now-and-future.

Lee, O., Deaktor, R. A., Hart, J. E., Cuevars, P., and Enders, C. (2005). An instructional intervention's impact on the science and literacy achievement of culturally and linguistically diverse elementary students. *Journal of Research in Science Teaching* 42(8):857–887.

Lee, O., Buxton, C., Lewis, S., and LeRoy, K. (2006). Science inquiry and student diversity: Enhanced abilities and continuing difficulties after an instructional intervention. *Journal of Research in Science Teaching* 607–636.

Linn, M. C. (2000). Designing the knowledge integration environment. *International Journal of Science Education* 22(8):781–796.

Linn, M. C., and Hsi, S. (2000). *Computers, teachers, peers.* Mahwah, NJ: Lawrence Erlbaum.

Millennial Branding and Experience Inc. (2012). Student Employment Gap Study. Available at: http://millennialbranding.com/2012/05/millennial-branding-student-employment-gap-study.

National Association of Colleges and Employers. (2012). *Job outlook 2012.*

National Association of State Directors of Career Technical Education Consortium. Plans of study. Available at: http://www.careertech.org/career-clusters/resources/plans.html.

NCES (National Center for Education Statistics). (2011). *The nation's report card: Science 2011* (NCES 2012-465). Washington, DC: National Center for Education Statistics, Institute of Education Sciences, U.S. Department of Education.

NRC (National Research Council). (2002). *Learning and understanding: Improving advanced study of mathematics and science in U.S. high schools.* Washington, DC: The National Academies Press.

NRC. (2004). *The engineer of 2020: Visions of engineering in the new century.* Washington, DC: The National Academies Press.

NRC. (2005). *America's lab report: Investigations in high school science.* Washington, DC: The National Academies Press.

NRC. (2007). *Taking science to school: Learning and teaching science in grades K–8.* Washington, DC: The National Academies Press.

NRC. (2009). *A new biology for the 21st century.* Washington, DC: The National Academies Press.

NRC. (2012a). *A framework for K–12 science education: Practices, crosscutting concepts, and core ideas*. Washington, DC: The National Academies Press.

NRC. (2012b). *Education for life and work: Developing transferable knowledge and skills in the 21st century.* Washington, DC: The National Academies Press.

NSF (National Science Foundation). (2012). *Overview.* Science and engineering indicators. Available at: http://www.nsf.gov/statistics/seind12/c0/c0i.htm.

OECD (Organisation for Economic Co-operation and Development). (2012a). Education at a glance 2012: OECD indicators, OECD Publishing. Available at: http://dx.doi.org/10.1787/eag-2012-en.

OECD. (2012b). Programme for International Student Assessment 2015 Scientific Literacy Assessment Framework.

Page, S. (2007). The difference: How the power of diversity creates better groups, firms, schools, and societies. Woodstock, England: Princeton University Press.

President's Council of Advisors on Science and Technology. (2012). *Engage to excel: Producing one million additional college graduates with degrees in science, technology, engineering, and mathematics.* Washington, DC: Office of Science, Technology, and Policy.

Redish, E. F., and Smith, K. A. (2008). Looking beyond content: Skill development for engineers. *Journal of Engineering Education* 97:295–307.

Sadler, P. M., and Tai, R. H. (2007). The two high-school pillars supporting college science. *Science* 317:457–458.

Schwartz, M. S., Sadler, P. M., Sonnert, G., and Tai, R. H. (2009). Depth vs breadth: How content coverage in high school science courses relates to later success in college science coursework. *Science Education* 93:798–826. doi: 10.1002/sce.20328.

Sharp, P. A., Cooney, C. L., Kastner, M. A., Lees, J., Sasisekharan, R., Yaffe, M. B., Bhatia, S., Jacks, T. E., Lauffenburger, D. A., Langer, R., Hammond, P. T., and Sur, M. (2011, January). *The third revolution: The convergence of the life sciences, physical sciences, and engineering.* White paper from MIT's Washington Office.

Sharp, P. A., and Langer, R. (2011). Promoting convergence in biomedical science. *Science* 333:527.

Shierholz, H., Sabadish, N., and Wething, H. (2012, May 3). The class of 2012: Labor market for young graduates remains grim. *Economic Policy Institute.* Available at: http://www.epi.org/publication/bp340-labor-market-young-graduates.

Stigler, J. W., and Hiebert, J. (1999). *The teaching gap: Best ideas from the world's teachers for improving education in the classroom.* New York: The Free Press.

Tai, R. H., Sadler, P. M., and Loehr, J. F. (2005). Factors influencing success in introductory college chemistry. *Journal of Research in Science Teaching* 42(9):987–1012.

Tai, R. H., Liu, C. Q., Maltese, A. V., and Fan, X. (2006). Planning early for careers in science. *Science* 312(5777):1143–1144.

von Secker, C. (2002). Effects of inquiry-based teacher practices on science excellence and equity. *Journal of Educational Research* 95(3):151–160.

The William and Flora Hewlett Foundation. (2010). *Education program strategic plan.* Available at: http://www.hewlett.org/uploads/documents/Education_Strategic_Plan_2010.pdf.

Wilson, C., Taylor, J., Kowalski, S., and Carlson, J. (2010). The Relative effects and equity of inquiry-based and commonplace science teaching on students' knowledge, reasoning, and argumentation. *Journal of Research in Science Teaching* 47(3):276–301.

Woellert, L. (2012, July 25). Companies say 3 million unfilled positions in skill crisis: Jobs. Bloomberg. Available at: http://www.bloomberg.com/news/2012-07-25/companies-say-3-million-unfilled-positions-in-skill-crisis-jobs.html.

Wood, W. B. (2009). Revising the AP biology curriculum. *Science* 325:1627–1628.

Young, M., and Glanfield, K. (1998). Science in post-compulsory education: towards a framework for a curriculum of the future. *Studies in Science Education* 32:1–20.

"ALL STANDARDS, ALL STUDENTS": MAKING THE NEXT GENERATION SCIENCE STANDARDS ACCESSIBLE TO ALL STUDENTS

The Next Generation Science Standards (NGSS) are being developed at a historic time when major changes in education are occurring at the national level. On one hand, student demographics across the nation are changing rapidly, as teachers have seen the steady increase of student diversity in the classrooms. Yet, achievement gaps in science and other key academic indicators among demographic subgroups have persisted. On the other hand, national initiatives are emerging for a new wave of standards through the NGSS as well as the Common Core State Standards (CCSS) for English language arts and literacy and for mathematics. As these new standards are cognitively demanding, teachers must make instructional shifts to enable all students to be college and career ready.

The NGSS are building on the National Research Council's consensus reports in recent years, including *Taking Science to School* (2007) and its companion report for practitioners, *Ready, Set, SCIENCE!* (2008), *Learning Science in Informal Environments* (2009), and most notably *A Framework for K–12 Science Education* (2012). These reports consistently highlight that when provided with equitable learning opportunities, students from diverse backgrounds are capable of engaging in scientific practices and constructing meaning in both science classrooms and informal settings.

This Appendix, accompanied by seven case studies of diverse student groups, addresses what classroom teachers can do to ensure that the NGSS are accessible to all students; hence the title: *All Standards, All Students*. Successful application of science and engineering practices (e.g., constructing explanations, engaging in argument from evidence) and understanding of how crosscutting concepts (e.g., patterns, structure and function) play out across a range of disciplinary core ideas (e.g., structure and properties of matter, earth materials and systems) will demand increased cognitive expectations of all students. Making such connections has typically been expected only of "advanced," "gifted," or "honors" students. The NGSS are intended to provide a foundation for all students, including those who can and should surpass the NGSS performance expectations. At the same time, the NGSS make it clear that these increased expectations apply to those students who have traditionally struggled to demonstrate mastery even in the previous generation of less cognitively demanding standards. The goal of the chapter and the case studies is to demonstrate that NGSS are extended to all students.

Throughout this chapter and the case studies, the terms "dominant" and "non-dominant" groups are used with reference to student diversity (Gutiérrez and Rogoff, 2003). The dominant group(s) does not refer to numerical majority, but rather to social prestige and institutionalized privilege. This is particularly the case now as student diversity is increasing in the nation's classrooms. Even where the dominant group(s) is the numerical minority, the privileging of its academic backgrounds persists. In contrast, non-dominant groups have traditionally been underserved by the education system. Thus, the term "non-dominant" highlights a call to action that the education system meets the learning needs of the nation's increasingly diverse student population.

The chapter highlights the practicality and utility of implementation strategies that are grounded in theoretical or conceptual frameworks. It consists of three parts. First, it discusses both *learning opportunities and challenges* that the NGSS present to student groups that have traditionally been underserved in science classrooms. Second, it describes effective strategies for *implementation* of the NGSS in classrooms, schools, homes, and communities. Finally, it provides the *context* of student diversity by addressing changing demographics, persistent science achievement gaps, and education policies affecting non-dominant student groups.

The seven case studies (available at: www.nextgenscience.org) illustrate science teaching and learning of non-dominant student groups as they engage in the NGSS. Several caveats are offered to understand the purpose of the case studies. First, the case studies are not intended to prescribe science instruction, but to illustrate an example or prototype for implementation of effective classroom strategies with diverse student groups. Given the vast range of student diversity across varied educational settings, teachers and schools will implement the NGSS to meet the learning needs of specific student groups in local contexts. Second, each case study highlights one identified group (e.g., economically disadvantaged students, English language learners [ELLs]). In reality, however, students could belong to multiple categories of diversity (e.g., ELLs who are racial and ethnic minorities from economically disadvantaged backgrounds). Third, as there is wide variability among students within each group, "essentializing" on the basis of a group label must be avoided. For example, ELLs form a heterogeneous group with differences in ethnic backgrounds, proficiency level in home language and English, socioeconomic status, immigration history, quality of prior schooling, parents' education level, etc.

In identifying student diversity, the case studies address the four accountability groups defined in No Child Left Behind (NCLB) Act of 2001 and the reauthorized Elementary and Secondary Education Act (ESEA), Section 1111(b)(2)(C)(v):

- economically disadvantaged students,
- students from major racial and ethnic groups,
- students with disabilities, and
- students with limited English proficiency.

Further, student diversity is extended by adding three groups:

- girls,
- students in alternative education programs, and
- gifted and talented students.

Each of the seven case studies consists of three parts that parallel the chapter. Each case study starts with a vignette of science instruction to illustrate learning opportunities as well as use of effective classroom strategies connections to the NGSS and the CCSS for English language arts and mathematics. The vignette emphasizes what teachers can do to successfully engage students in learning the NGSS. Then each case study provides a brief summary of the research literature on effective classroom strategies for the student group highlighted. Each case study ends with the context for the student group—demographics, science achievement, and education policy. The contextual information relies heavily on government reports addressing student diversity broadly, including the ESEA, U.S. Census, National Center for Education Statistics (including the National Assessment of Educational Progress), and Common Core of Data. The contextual information also comes from government reports addressing specific student groups such as students in alternative education programs or gifted and talented students.

The case studies were written by members of the NGSS Diversity and Equity Team with expertise on specific student groups. In working on their case studies, many members piloted the NGSS in their own science instruction. The case studies represent science disciplines across grade levels:

- economically disadvantaged students—ninth grade chemistry
- students from major racial and ethnic groups—eighth grade life sciences
- students with disabilities—sixth grade space sciences
- students with limited English proficiency—second grade earth sciences
- girls—third grade engineering
- students in alternative education programs—tenth and eleventh grade chemistry
- gifted and talented students—fourth grade life sciences

Collectively, this chapter and the seven case studies make contributions in several ways. First, they focus on *issues of student diversity and equity in relation to the NGSS specifically* as the NGSS present both learning opportunities and challenges to all students, particularly non-dominant student groups. Second, they are intended for *education policies* as they highlight emerging national initiatives through the NGSS as well as the CCSS for English language arts and mathematics. Third, they are intended for *classroom practice* as the case studies were written by members of the NGSS Diversity and Equity Team who are themselves teachers working with diverse student groups. Fourth, they highlight key findings in *research literature on student diversity and equity* for seven demographic groups of students in science education. This is noteworthy because research for each student group tends to exist independently from the others. Finally, for each student group, the case studies provide context in terms of *demographics, science achievement, and education policy.*

NGSS: LEARNING OPPORTUNITIES AND DEMANDS FOR NON-DOMINANT STUDENT GROUPS

The NGSS offer a clear vision of rigorous science standards by blending science and engineering practices with disciplinary core ideas and crosscutting concepts across K–12. In addition, the NGSS make connections to the CCSS for English language arts and literacy and for mathematics. For the student groups that have traditionally been underserved in science education, the NGSS offer both learning opportunities and challenges. Instead of making a long list of opportunities and challenges, major considerations are discussed below. Then, learning opportunities and challenges are illustrated in the seven case studies for economically disadvantaged students, racial or ethnic minority students, students with disabilities, English language learners, girls, students in alternative education programs, and gifted and talented students.

NGSS Connections to CCSS for English Language Arts and Mathematics

The NGSS make connections across school curricula. For example, students understand the crosscutting concept of patterns not only across science disciplines but also across other subject areas of language arts, mathematics, social studies, etc. Likewise, the crosscutting concept of cause and effect can be used to explain phenomena in the earth sciences as well as to examine character or plot development in literature. Thus, students develop mastery of crosscutting concepts through repeated and contrastive experiences across school curricula.

The requirements and norms for classroom discourse are shared across all the science disciplines and indeed across all the subject areas. The convergence of disciplinary practices across the CCSS for English language arts and literacy, the CCSS for mathematics, and the NGSS is highlighted in Figure D-1. For example, students are expected to engage in argumentation from evidence; construct explanations; obtain, synthesize, evaluate, and communicate information; and build a knowledge base through content-rich texts across the three subject areas. Such convergence is particularly beneficial for students from non-dominant groups who are pressed for instructional time to develop literacy and numeracy at the cost of other subjects, including science.

The integration of subject areas strengthens science learning for all students, particularly students who have traditionally been underserved. In the current climate of accountability policies which are dominated by reading and mathematics, science tends to be de-emphasized. This is due to the perceived urgency of developing basic literacy and numeracy for students in low-performing schools, including, but not limited to, ELLs and students with limited literacy development. Thus, allocation and utilization of instructional time across subject areas will benefit these students. Furthermore, the convergence of core ideas, practices, and crosscutting concepts across subject areas offers multiple entry points to build and deepen understanding for these students.

Initiatives are emerging to identify language demands and opportunities as ELLs engage in the NGSS as well as the CCSS for English language arts and literacy and for mathematics. For example, the Understanding Language Initiative (ell.stanford.edu) is aimed at heightening educator awareness of the critical role that language plays in the CCSS and the NGSS. Its long-term goal is to help educators understand that the new standards cannot be achieved without providing specific attention to the language demands inherent to each subject area. This initiative seeks to improve academic outcomes for ELLs by drawing attention to critical aspects of instructional practices and by advocating for necessary policy supports at the state and local levels.

Inclusion of Engineering

The inclusion of engineering along with science in the NGSS has major implications for non-dominant student groups. First, from an epistemological perspective, the NGSS reinterpret a traditional view of epistemology and the history of science. For example, *Science for All Americans* stated:

> The recommendations in this chapter focus on the development of science, mathematics, and technology in Western culture, but not on how that development drew from earlier Egyptian, Chinese, Greek, and Arabic cultures. The sciences accounted for in this book are largely part of a tradition of thought that happened to develop in Europe during the last 500 years—a tradition to which most people from all cultures contribute today. (AAAS, 1989, p. 136)

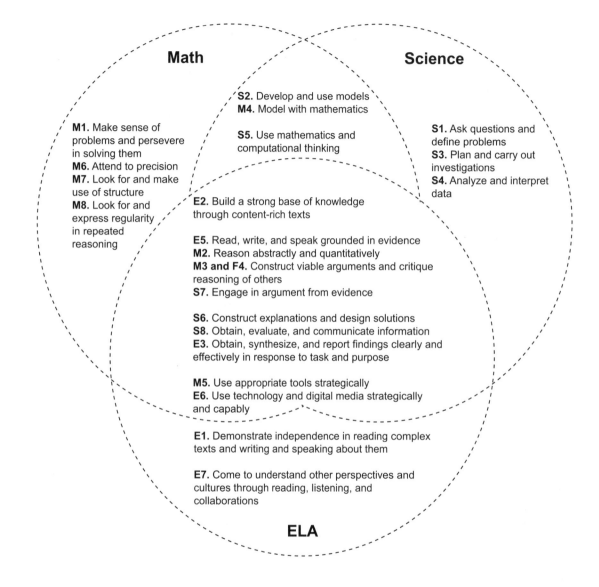

Math

Science

S2. Develop and use models
M4. Model with mathematics

S5. Use mathematics and computational thinking

M1. Make sense of problems and persevere in solving them
M6. Attend to precision
M7. Look for and make use of structure
M8. Look for and express regularity in repeated reasoning

S1. Ask questions and define problems
S3. Plan and carry out investigations
S4. Analyze and interpret data

E2. Build a strong base of knowledge through content-rich texts

E5. Read, write, and speak grounded in evidence
M2. Reason abstractly and quantitatively
M3 and F4. Construct viable arguments and critique reasoning of others
S7. Engage in argument from evidence

S6. Construct explanations and design solutions
S8. Obtain, evaluate, and communicate information
E3. Obtain, synthesize, and report findings clearly and effectively in response to task and purpose

M5. Use appropriate tools strategically
E6. Use technology and digital media strategically and capably

E1. Demonstrate independence in reading complex texts and writing and speaking about them

E7. Come to understand other perspectives and cultures through reading, listening, and collaborations

ELA

FIGURE D-1 Relationships and convergences found in the CCSS for Mathematics (practices), CCSS for English Language Arts and Literacy (student portraits), and the *Framework* (science and engineering practices).
NOTE: The letter and number set preceding each phrase denotes the discipline and number designated by the content standards. The *Framework* was used to guide the development of the NGSS.
SOURCE: We acknowledge Tina Cheuk for developing Figure D-1 as part of the Understanding Language initiative at Stanford University (ell.stanford.edu).

At that time, although the goal of *Science for All Americans* was visionary, the definition of science in terms of Western science while ignoring historical contributions from other cultures presented a limited or distorted view of science. The NGSS, by emphasizing engineering, recognize the contributions of other cultures historically. This (re)defines the epistemology of science or what counts as science, which, in turn, defines or determines school science curriculum.

Second, from a pedagogical perspective, engineering has the potential to be inclusive of students who have traditionally been marginalized in the science classroom and do not see science as being relevant to their lives or future. By solving problems through engineering in local contexts (e.g., gardening, improving air quality, cleaning water pollution in the community), students gain knowledge of science content, view science as relevant to their lives and future, and engage in science in socially relevant and transformative ways (Rodriguez and Berryman, 2002).

Finally, from a global perspective, engineering offers opportunities for "innovation" and "creativity" at the K–12 level. Engineering is a field that is critical to innovation, and exposure to engineering activities (e.g., robotics and invention competitions) can spark interest in the study of science, technology, engineering, and mathematics or future careers (NSF, 2010). Although exposure to engineering at the pre-collegiate level is currently rare (NAE and NRC, 2009), the NGSS make exposure to engineering at the pre-collegiate level no longer a rarity, but a necessity. This opportunity is particularly important for students who traditionally have not recognized science as relevant to their lives or future and for students who come from multiple languages and cultures in this global community.

Focus on Practices

The ways we describe student engagement in science have evolved over time. Terms such as "hands-on" and "minds-on" have traditionally been used to describe when students engage in science. Then, *National Science Education Standards* (NRC, 1996, 2000) highlighted "scientific inquiry" as the core of science teaching and learning through which students "develop knowledge and understanding of scientific ideas, as well as an understanding

of how scientists study the natural world" (p. 23). In the NGSS, "inquiry-based science" is refined and deepened by the explicit definition of the set of eight science and engineering practices, which have major implications for non-dominant student groups (for details, see Lee et al., 2013, Quinn et al., 2012).

Engagement in any of the science and engineering practices involves both scientific sense-making and language use (see Figure D-1). Students engage in these practices for the scientific sense-making process, as they transition from their naïve conceptions of the world to more scientifically based conceptions. Engagement in these practices is also language intensive and requires students to participate in classroom science discourse. Students must read, write, and visually represent as they develop models and construct explanations. They speak and listen as they present their ideas or engage in reasoned argumentation with others to refine their ideas and reach shared conclusions.

These science and engineering practices offer rich opportunities and demands for language learning while they support science learning for all students, especially English language learners, students with language processing difficulties, students with limited literacy development, and students who are speakers of social or regional varieties of English that are generally referred to as "non-standard English." When supported appropriately, these students are capable of learning science through their emerging language and by comprehending and carrying out sophisticated language functions (e.g., arguing from evidence, constructing explanations, developing models) using less-than-perfect English. By engaging in such practices, moreover, they simultaneously build on their understanding of science and their language proficiency (i.e., capacity to do more with language).

Crosscutting Concepts

Crosscutting concepts are overarching scientific themes that emerge across all scientific disciplines. These themes provide the context for new disciplinary core ideas and enable students to "develop a cumulative, coherent, and useable understanding of science and engineering" (NRC, 2012, p. 83). Thus, crosscutting concepts bridge the engineering, physical, life, and earth/space sciences and offer increased rigor across science disciplines over

K–12. Although *Science for All Americans* (AAAS, 1989) identified "common themes" and *National Science Education Standards* (NRC, 1996) identified "unifying concepts and processes," the NGSS bring crosscutting concepts to the forefront as one of three dimensions of science learning.

Crosscutting concepts offers frameworks to conceptualize disciplinary core ideas. In this way, students think of science learning not as memorization of isolated or disconnected facts, but as integrated and interrelated concepts. This is a fundamental understanding of science that is often implied as background knowledge for students in "gifted," "honors," or "advanced" programs. Through the NGSS, explicit teaching of crosscutting concepts enables less privileged students, most from non-dominant groups, to make connections among big ideas that cut across science disciplines. This could result in leveling the playing field for students who otherwise might not have exposure to such opportunities.

IMPLEMENTATION OF EFFECTIVE STRATEGIES

To make the NGSS accessible to all students, implementation of effective strategies capitalizes on learning opportunities while being aware of the demands that the NGSS present to non-dominant student groups, as described in the previous section. Unfortunately, existing research literature does not address students' performance expectations as envisioned in the NGSS based on the mastery of science and engineering practices, crosscutting concepts, and disciplinary core ideas. Furthermore, the existing research literature addresses non-dominant student groups separately. For example, research on race or ethnicity, research on English language learners, research on students with disabilities, and research on gender comprise distinct research traditions (for effective strategies for non-dominant groups in science classrooms, see Special Issue in *Theory Into Practice*, 2013; for a discussion of classroom strategies and policy issues, see Lee and Buxton, 2010).

There seem to be common themes that unite these distinct research areas. In describing "equitable learning opportunities" for non-dominant student groups, Lee and Buxton (2010) highlight the following themes: (1) value and respect the experiences that all students bring from their backgrounds (e.g., homes or communities), (2) articulate students' background knowledge (e.g., cultural or linguistic knowledge) with disciplinary knowledge, and (3) offer sufficient school resources to support student learning.

First, to value and respect the experiences that all students bring from their backgrounds, it is important to make diversity visible. In the process of making diversity visible, there are both connections and disconnections between home/community and classroom/school. Effective teachers understand how disconnections may vary among different student groups, as well as how to capitalize on connections. These teachers bridge diverse students' background knowledge and experiences to scientific knowledge and practices.

Second, to articulate students' background knowledge with disciplinary knowledge of science, it is important to capitalize on "funds of knowledge" (González et al., 2005). Funds of knowledge are culturally based understandings and abilities that develop over time in family and neighborhood contexts, and the social and intellectual resources contained in families and communities can serve as resources for academic learning. Effective teachers ask questions that elicit students' funds of knowledge related to science topics. They also use cultural artifacts and community resources in ways that are academically meaningful and culturally relevant.

Finally, school resources constitute essential elements of a school's organizational context for teaching and learning. School resources to support student learning involve material resources, human resources (or capital), and social resources (or capital). School resources are likely to have a greater impact on the learning opportunities of non-dominant students who have traditionally been underserved in science education. In schools and classrooms where non-dominant students reside, resources are often scarce, forcing allocations of the limited resources for some areas (e.g., reading and mathematics) and not others (e.g., science and other non-tested subject areas).

Below, each of these themes is described as it relates to classroom strategies, home and community connections, and school resources—all of which can enable non-dominant student groups to engage in the NGSS.

Effective Classroom Strategies

Key features of effective classroom strategies from the research literature on each of the non-dominant groups are summarized below. In recognition of the fact that each area of research literature has been developing as an independent body of knowledge, the description of strategies is provided for each group. Yet, it is noted that while some strategies are unique to a particular group (e.g., home language use with ELLs, accommodations or modifications for students with disabilities), other strategies apply to all students broadly (e.g., multiple modes of representation). More detailed descriptions are provided in each of the seven case studies, including the four accountability groups defined in ESEA and three additional groups. While effective science instruction of the NGSS will be based on the existing research literature, the NGSS will also stimulate new directions for research to actualize the standards' vision for all students.

Economically disadvantaged students. Strategies to support economically disadvantaged students include (1) connecting science education to students' sense of "place" as physical, historical, and sociocultural dimensions; (2) applying students' funds of knowledge and cultural practices; (3) using project-based science learning as a form of connected science; and (4) providing school resources and funding for science instruction.

Students from major racial and ethnic groups. Effective strategies for students from major racial and ethnic groups fall into the following categories: (1) culturally relevant pedagogy, (2) community involvement and social activism, (3) multiple representation and multimodal experiences, and (4) school support systems, including role models and mentors of similar racial or ethnic backgrounds.

Students with disabilities. Students with disabilities have their Individualized Education Programs (IEPs), specific to each individual that mandate the accommodations and modifications that teachers must provide to support student learning in the regular education classroom. By definition, accommodations allow students to overcome or work around their disabilities with the same performance expectations of their peers, whereas modifications generally change the curriculum or performance expectations for a specific student. Two approaches for providing accommodations and modifications are widely used by general education teachers

in their classrooms: (1) differentiated instruction and (2) Universal Design for Learning.

Students with limited English proficiency. The research literature indicates five areas where teachers can support both science and language learning for English language learners: (1) literacy strategies for all students, (2) language support strategies with ELLs, (3) discourse strategies with ELLs, (4) home language support, and (5) home culture connections.

Girls. The research literature points to three main areas where schools can positively impact girls' achievement, confidence, and affinity with science and engineering: (1) instructional strategies to increase girls' science achievement and their intentions to continue studies in science, (2) curricula to improve girls' achievement and confidence in science by promoting images of successful females in science, and (3) classrooms' and schools' organizational structure in ways that benefit girls in science (e.g., after-school clubs, summer camps, and mentoring programs).

Students in alternative education programs. The research literature focuses on school-wide approaches to promote increased attendance and high school graduation. Specific factors, taken collectively, correspond with alienation from school prior to dropping out. Public alternative schools employ strategies to counteract these factors and increase student engagement: (1) structured after-school opportunities, (2) family outreach, (3) life skills training, (4) safe learning environment, and (5) individualized academic support.

Gifted and talented students. Gifted and talented students may have such characteristics as intense interests, rapid learning, motivation and commitment, curiosity, and questioning skills. Teachers can employ effective differentiation strategies to promote the science learning of gifted and talented students in four domains: (1) fast pacing, (2) level of challenge (including differentiation of content), (3) opportunities for self-direction, and (4) strategic grouping.

Home and Community Connections to School Science

While it has long been recognized that building home-school connections is important for the academic success of non-dominant student groups, in practice this is rarely done in an effective manner. There are tensions as parents and families want their children to maintain the cultural and linguistic practices of their heritage while also wanting their children to participate fully in the dominant school culture. A challenge facing schools is the perceived disconnect between school science practices and home and community practices of non-dominant student groups. Traditionally, research on home-school connections looked at how the family and home environments of non-dominant student groups measured up to the expectations and practices of the dominant group. The results were interpreted in terms of deficits in students' family and home environments, as compared to their dominant counterparts. In contrast, more recent research has identified resources and strengths in the family and home environments of non-dominant student groups (Calabrese Barton et al., 2004). Students bring to the science classroom funds of knowledge from their homes and communities that can serve as resources for academic learning and teachers should understand and find ways to activate this prior knowledge (González et al., 2005). Science learning builds on tasks and activities that occur in the social contexts of day-to-day living, whether or not the school chooses to recognize this.

Through the NGSS, students can engage in science and engineering practices, crosscutting concepts, and disciplinary core ideas by connecting school science to their out-of-school experiences in home and community contexts. Several approaches build connections between home/community and school science: (1) increase parent involvement in their children's science classroom by encouraging parents' roles as partners in science learning, (2) engage students in defining problems and designing solutions of community projects in their neighborhoods (typically engineering), and (3) focus on science learning in informal environments.

Parent involvement in school science. Concerted efforts should be made to support and encourage parent involvement in promoting positive engagement and achievement of non-dominant student groups in science classrooms. Siblings and peers can serve as role models on academic achievement. Parents without academic background in science can still be partners in their children's science education by setting high expectations for academic success and higher education. Teachers can form partnerships with parents, facilitating dialogue to solicit their help with homework and their attendance at science-related events in the school.

To promote parents' involvement in school science, schools can play a part to address parents' needs from the school and remove roadblocks to participation. Schools may need to individually invite underserved families on science-related field trips, making certain that particular concerns are met (e.g., child care, translation, transportation) so that the parents are able to attend. Teachers can create homework assignments that invite joint participation of the child and parent to complete a task together (e.g., observe the phases of the moon, record water use in the house). A non-evaluative survey related to science content can generate classroom discussions that bridge home and school. Homework assignments can encourage dialogue, increase interest among both parents and students, and solicit home language support for science learning.

Parents from non-dominant backgrounds feel comfortable with the school when they perceive the school as reflecting their values, and such parents, in turn, are most likely to partner with the school. For example, a science camp focused on African American achievement had high parental participation because its goals highlighted issues related to African American identity and culture (Simpson and Parsons, 2008). Teachers can also increase parent involvement by relating after-school and summer school themes around values that are important to the families and communities.

Student engagement with school science in community contexts. Strategies that involve the community underscore the importance of connecting the school science curriculum to the students' lives and the community in which they live. It is through these connections that students who have traditionally been alienated from science recognize science as relevant to their lives and future, deepen their understanding of science concepts, develop agency in science, and consider careers in science.

Science learning in community contexts may take different approaches. First, both disciplinary and informal education experts underscore the connection between science and the neighborhood that the students reside in. Effective approaches can include engaging in outdoor exploration (e.g., bird surveys, weather journal) and analyzing local natural resources (e.g., landforms in the neighborhood, soil composition).

Second, the community context for science education capitalizes on the community resources and funds of knowledge to make science more culturally, linguistically, and socially relevant for diverse student groups (González et al., 2005). For example, a teacher could tap into the community as a resource by recruiting a community member(s) to assist an upper elementary class, as students investigate the pollution along a river near the school. By bringing the neighborhood and community into the science classroom, students learn that science is not only applicable to events in the classroom, but it also extends to what they experience in their homes and what they observe in their communities.

Finally, "place-based" science education is consistent with culturally relevant pedagogy (Ladson-Billings, 1995). Through social activism, students develop critical consciousness of social inequities, especially as such inequities exist in their communities. When youth find science education to be empowering and transformative, they are likely to embrace and further investigate what they are learning, instead of being resistant to learning science. Thus, school science should be reconceptualized to give a more central role to students' lived experiences and identities.

Science learning in informal environments. Informal environments for science learning (e.g., museums, nature centers, zoos, etc.) have the potential to broaden participation in science and engineering for youth from non-dominant communities. Informal environments may also include non-institutional opportunities that are not traditionally recognized by school systems (e.g., community gardens, woodlots, campgrounds). However, informal institutions face challenges in reaching and serving non-dominant groups, as reflected in low attendance patterns. Although research on how to structure science learning opportunities to better serve non-dominant groups in informal environments is sparse, it highlights two promising insights and practices (NRC, 2009).

First, informal environments for science learning should be developed and implemented with the interests and concerns of particular cultural groups and communities in mind. Project goals should be mutually determined by educators and the communities and cultural groups being served. It is also important to develop strategies that help learners identify with science in personally meaningful ways. Having community-based contacts that are familiar and safe can be critical in engaging families in science explorations and conversations and even, at a more basic level, in helping

non-dominant groups see museums as worthwhile destinations for their families.

Second, environments should be developed in ways that expressly draw upon participants' cultural practices, including everyday language, linguistic practices, and cultural experiences. In designed environments, such as museums, bilingual or multilingual labels provide access to the specific content and facilitate conversations and sense-making among participants. Developing peer networks may be particularly important to foster sustained participation of non-dominant groups. Designed spaces that serve families should consider visits by extended families. Members of diverse cultural groups can play a critical role in the development and implementation of programs, serving as designers, advisers, front-line educators, and evaluators of such efforts.

School Resources for Science Instruction

School resources to support student learning generally fall into three categories (Gamoran et al., 2003; Penuel et al., 2009). First, material resources include time available for teaching, professional development, and collaboration among teachers. Material resources also include curricular materials, equipment, supplies, and expenditures for school personnel and other purposes related to teaching and learning. Second, human capital includes individual knowledge, skills, and expertise that might become a part of the stock of resources available in an organization. In schools, human capital involves teachers' knowledge, including content knowledge, pedagogical knowledge, and pedagogical content knowledge, as well as principal leadership. Finally, social capital concerns the relationships among individuals in a group or organization, including such norms as trust, collaboration, common values, shared responsibility, a sense of obligation, and collective decision making.

School resources are likely to have a greater impact on the learning opportunities of non-dominant student groups. This is because the dominant student group is more likely to have the benefits of other supports for their learning, such as better-equipped schools, more material resources at home, and highly educated parents. In contrast, the academic success of non-dominant students depends more heavily on the quality of their school environment; yet, it is these students who are less likely to have access to high-quality learning environments. Thus, inequitable resources are a central concern. The NGSS present both opportunities and challenges to reconceptualize the allocation and utilization of school resources.

Material resources. Science receives less instructional time (a form of material resources) than language arts and mathematics, which are both considered to be basic skills. Particularly, science instruction in low-performing schools is often limited and tightly regulated due to the urgency of developing basic literacy and numeracy. In addition, under the demands of accountability policies, schools devote extended time and attention to the heavily tested subjects of language arts and mathematics, leaving limited time for science.

The NGSS capitalize on the synergy with the CCSS for English language arts and literacy and for mathematics. The standards across the three subject areas share common shifts to focus on core concepts and practices that build coherently across K–12. Science and engineering practices in the NGSS (e.g., argumentation from evidence) share commonalities with those of the CCSS for English language arts and for mathematics (see Figure D-1). Furthermore, the CCSS for literacy require strong content knowledge, informational texts, and text complexity across subject areas, including science. In a similar manner, the NGSS make connections to the CCSS. Such synergy will help effective use of instructional time among English language arts, mathematics, and science.

Human capital. While all students deserve access to highly qualified teachers, schools serving non-dominant student groups require the most effective teachers to enable students to overcome achievement gaps (Marx and Harris, 2006). The NGSS require science teachers who possess knowledge of disciplinary core ideas, science and engineering practices, and crosscutting concepts. For non-dominant student groups, teachers should also be able to connect science to students' home and community experiences as the students engage in the NGSS. Such expectations present both opportunities and challenges to teacher preparation and professional development for urban or low-performing schools where non-dominant student groups tend to be concentrated.

The NGSS are built on continuity of learning progressions across grade levels. This presents both opportunities and challenges to students who are highly mobile or transient. On one hand, the

nationwide purview of the NGSS may help these students by providing them with consistent standards among states, districts, and schools. On the other hand, this assumption may impede the ability of new immigrant students to catch up as they are unable to draw from a base of years of shared experiences. Likewise, students who miss school because of homelessness or other reasons for mobility may struggle to fill gaps in understanding.

Social capital. The conditions of urban or low-performing schools are not conducive to building social resources in the form of trust, collaboration, and high expectations collectively. Urban settings present challenges, including overcrowding, management issues, and emotional concerns related to conditions of poverty in students' homes.

The NGSS reinforce the need for collaboration among teachers of different specializations and subject areas beyond the traditional forms of collaboration. Science teachers need to work with special education teachers and teachers of ELLs in order to foster a deeper understanding of science. In addition, science, math, and English language arts teachers need to work together in order to address both the opportunities and demands for meaningful connections among these subject areas. Furthermore, collaboration needs to involve the entire school personnel, including teachers, administrators, counselors, etc. Utilization and development of social capital among school personnel is key to effective implementation of the NGSS with all students, particularly students from non-dominant groups.

CONTEXT

To engage all students in learning the NGSS, it is important to understand the context that influences science learning by diverse student groups. This section briefly describes student demographics, science achievement, and education policies affecting non-dominant student groups. More details are presented in each of the seven case studies in terms of economically disadvantaged students, racial or ethnic minority students, students with disabilities, English language learners, girls, students in alternative education programs, and gifted and talented students.

Student Demographics

The student population in the United States is increasingly more diverse:

- **Economically disadvantaged students.** The American Community Survey report from the U.S. Census Bureau summarized the poverty data (U.S. Census Bureau, 2012). Overall, 21.6% of children in the United States live in poverty, the highest poverty rate since the poverty survey began in 2001. The poverty rate was the highest for blacks at 38.2% and Hispanics at 32.3%, compared to whites at 17.0% and Asians at 13.0%. According to the *Common Core of Data* report, 48% of students were eligible for free or reduced-price lunches in 2010–2011. A greater number of students live in poverty in the cities compared to suburban areas, towns, and rural areas.

- **Students from major racial or ethnic minority groups.** The student population in the United States is increasingly more diverse racially and ethnically. According to the 2010 U.S. Census, 36% of the U.S. population is composed of racial minorities, including 16% Hispanics, 13% blacks, 5% Asians, and 1% American Indian or Native Alaskans (U.S. Census Bureau, 2012). Among the school-age population under 19 years old in 2010, 45% were minorities. It is projected that the year 2022 will be the turning point when minorities will become the majority in terms of percentage of the school-age population.

- **Students with disabilities.** The number of children and youth ages 3–21 receiving special education services under the Individuals with Disabilities Education Act (IDEA) rose from 4.1 million to 6.7 million between 1980 and 2005, or from 10% to 14% of the student enrollment (National Center for Education Statistics [NCES], 2011). That number decreased to 6.5 million or 13% of student enrollment by 2009.

- **Students with limited English proficiency.** More than 1 in 5 students (21%) speak a language other than English at home, and Limited English Proficient (LEP) students (the federal term) have more than doubled from 5% in 1993 to 11% in 2007. The 11% of LEP students does not count those who were classified as LEP when younger but who are now considered proficient in English or during a monitoring period.

- **Students in alternative education programs.** Reporting the demographics of students in alternative education is difficult due to wide inconsistencies in definitions across the nation. A significant proportion of students who attend public alternative schools specifically targeting dropout prevention are economically disadvantaged students, racial and ethnic minorities, and English language learners (NCES, 2012).

- **Gifted and talented students.** Reporting the demographics of gifted and talented students is difficult due to wide inconsistencies in definitions, assessments to identify these students, and funding for programs across the nation. The National Association for Gifted Children (NAGC, 2012) defines giftedness as "those who demonstrate outstanding levels of aptitude or competence in one or more domains" and estimates that this definition describes approximately three million or roughly 6% of all students in K–12.

Several caveats are made with regard to student diversity. First, each demographic subgroup is not a homogenous or monolithic group, and there is a great deal of variability among members of a group. For example, categories of disabilities include specific learning disabilities, speech and language impairments, other health impairments, intellectual disability, emotional disturbance, developmental delay, autism, multiple disabilities, hearing impairment, visual impairment, orthopedic impairment, deaf-blindness, and traumatic brain injury. These categories could be classified as cognitive, emotional, and physical disabilities. Such variability among members of a group cautions that essentializing should be avoided.

Second, there is a significant overlap among non-dominant student groups. For example, most ELLs are racial or ethnic minorities. In addition, 60% of economically disadvantaged students, including large proportions of racial or ethnic minorities and ELLs, live in cities (NCES, 2012). As a result, these students face multiple challenges in achieving academic success.

Finally, specific student groups are either overrepresented or underrepresented in education programs. For example, females are underrepresented in engineering and physics (NSF, 2012). Racial or ethnic minority students, economically disadvantaged students, and ELLs are underrepresented in gifted and talented programs, whereas they are overrepresented in special education programs (Harry and Klingner, 2006).

Science Achievement

While the student population in the United States is becoming more diverse, science achievement gaps persist by demographic subgroups. The results of international and national science assessments indicate the need for a two-pronged approach to enhancing student science outcomes. Achievement gaps must be closed among demographic subgroups of students, while improved science outcomes should be promoted for all students. In the report *Preparing the Next Generation of STEM Innovators*, the National Science Board states, "In America, it should be possible, even essential, to elevate the achievement of low-performing at-risk groups while simultaneously lifting the ceiling of achievement for our future innovators" (NSF, 2010, p. 16).

U.S. students have not ranked favorably on international comparisons of science achievement as measured by the Trends in International Mathematics and Science Study (TIMSS) and the Program for International Student Assessment (PISA). Although TIMSS science results for U.S. fourth and eighth graders showed positive trends since its first administration in 1995 through the latest administration in 2007, PISA results for 15-year-olds did not corroborate trends indicated by TIMSS. When it comes to applying science in meaningful ways (e.g., using scientific evidence, identifying scientific issues, and explaining phenomena scientifically) as measured by PISA, U.S. students performed in the bottom half of the international comparison and did not show significant improvements since its first administration in 2000 through its latest administration in 2009.

At the national level, the National Assessment of Educational Progress (NAEP) provides data for U.S. students' science performance over time. Focusing only on more recent NAEP science assessments in 1996, 2000, 2005, 2009, and 2011, achievement gaps persist among demographic subgroups of students across grades 4, 8, and 12. Results are reported by family income level (based on eligibility for the National School Lunch Program), race or ethnicity, students with disabilities, English language learners, gender, and type of school (public or private). It is noted that these subgroups represent the accountability groups defined in ESEA.

The framework for NAEP science involves science content in three areas (physical sciences, life sciences, and earth and space sciences) and four science practices (identifying science principles, using science principles, using scientific inquiry, and using technological design). Two developments are noteworthy in relation to the NGSS. First, the 2009 NAEP science assessment included interactive computer and hands-on tasks to measure how well students were able to reason through complex problems and apply science to real-life situations. This approach could pave a way for assessment of science and engineering practices in NGSS. Second, the first-ever NAEP Technology and Engineering Literacy Assessment (TELA) is currently under development. The initial assessment, planned for 2014, will be a probe—a smaller-scale, focused assessment on a timely topic that explores a particular question or issue. This approach could be used for assessment of engineering in the NGSS.

A clear understanding of science achievement gaps should take into account certain methodological limitations in how these gaps are measured and reported. Science achievement is typically measured by standardized tests administered to national and international student samples. A strength of these measures is that they provide access to large data sets that allow for the use of powerful statistical analyses. However, these measures also present limitations.

First, standardized tests provide only a general picture of how demographic variables relate to science achievement. For example, "Hispanic" is likely to be treated as a single category of race or ethnicity, masking potentially important differences in performance among Mexican Americans, Puerto Ricans, and Cuban Americans. Similarly, the group of students with disabilities (SDs) is generic, referring to students who usually have IEPs and could include both learning disabled (LD) or emotionally disturbed (ED). Thus, achievement data are generally lumped together for very different disabilities. Such overgeneralization hinders more nuanced understanding of achievement gaps, thereby limiting the potential effectiveness of educational interventions aimed at reducing these gaps.

Second, standardized tests have the potential to reinforce stereotypes, both positive and negative, of certain demographic groups

(Rodriguez, 1998). For example, the "model minority" stereotype of Asian American students as strong performers in mathematics and science may well be supported by generalized test data for the racial category of Asian American. However, such a result masks great disparities within this group, such as Southeast Asian refugees with limited literacy development in their homes or communities. These students are less likely to have their needs met in equitable ways if teachers presume that they "naturally" learn science and mathematics with little trouble. In contrast, high-achieving Hispanic or African American students may be disadvantaged by teachers or counselors who underestimate them and set low expectations of their academic success.

Finally, standardized tests do not analyze or report interactions between demographic variables. For example, as racial/ethnic minority students are disproportionately represented in free or reduced-price lunch programs, science achievement gaps between race/ethnicity and socioeconomic status are confounded. In a similar manner, science achievement gaps between race/ethnicity and gender are confounded.

Educational Policies

Passage of the NCLB Act of 2001 (the reauthorized ESEA) ushered in a new era of high-stakes testing and accountability policies. Districts and schools are accountable for making an adequate level of achievement gain each year, referred to as annual yearly progress (AYP). The theory behind ESEA (NCLB) assumes that states, districts, and schools will allocate resources to best facilitate the attainment of AYP. Decisions concerning resources and practices are determined largely by test scores on state assessments.

Although ESEA is most often associated with accountability systems, there is a second property of ESEA that has also been a focus of attention. ESEA mandates that each state report AYP disaggregated for demographic subgroups of students. Mandating this disaggregated reporting of AYP results in potentially desirable outcomes: (a) each of the groups is publicly monitored to examine achievement and progress; (b) resources are allocated differentially to these groups to enhance the likelihood that they meet AYP; and (c) if AYP is not met for these groups in schools receiving Title I funding, students are provided with additional

academic assistance through Supplemental Educational Services (e.g., tutoring) and the right to transfer to another public school. Schools, districts, and states cannot hide historically underperforming demographic groups, because ESEA forces the states to publicly monitor these groups and to be accountable for their performance. On the undesirable side, however, all of the added attention to high-stakes testing does not necessarily result in improved teaching. In fact, the increased emphasis on testing could detract from academically rigorous learning opportunities that are often lacking with students from certain demographic subgroups. Similarly, calling more public attention to the failures of schools to adequately meet the needs of these students does little to ensure that they will receive instruction that is more engaging, more intellectually challenging, or more culturally or socially relevant.

Although ESEA mandates reporting of AYP for reading and mathematics, the same is not true for science. With respect to science, ESEA only requires that by the 2007–2008 school year each state would have science assessments to be administered and reported for formative purposes at least once during grades 3–5, grades 6–9, and grades 10–12. However, it is up to each state to decide whether to include high-stakes science testing in state accountability systems or AYP reporting. Although science accountability policies affect all students, the impact is far greater for student groups that have traditionally been underserved in the education system.

Separate from federal and state policies that apply to all students, specific policies apply to specific student groups. According to the ESEA:

- Title I is the largest federally funded educational program intended for "improving the academic achievement of the disadvantaged" in order to meet "the educational needs of low-achieving children in our Nation's highest-poverty schools, limited English proficient children, migratory children, children with disabilities, Indian children, neglected or delinquent children, and young children in need of reading assistance."
- Title I, Part H, states that the Dropout Prevention Act aims "to provide for school dropout prevention and reentry and to raise academic achievement levels by providing grants that (1) challenge all children to attain their highest academic potential; and (2) ensure that all students have substantial and ongoing

opportunities to attain their highest academic potential through school-wide programs proven effective in school drop-out prevention and reentry."

- Title III addresses "language instruction for limited English proficient and immigrant students."
- Title VII is designed for "Indian, Native Hawaiian, and Alaska Native education."
- Title IX prevents gender-based discrimination within federally funded educational programs. Title IX states, "No person in the United States shall, on the basis of sex, be excluded from participation in, be denied the benefits of, or be subjected to discrimination under any education program or activity receiving federal financial assistance" (Public Law No. 92318, 86 Stat. 235).
- Title IX, Part A, SEC. 9101 (22), provides a federal definition and federal research funding for gifted and talented students: "The term gifted and talented, when used with respect to students, children, or youth, means students, children, or youth who give evidence of high achievement capability in areas such as intellectual, creative, artistic, or leadership capacity, or in specific academic fields, and who need services or activities not ordinarily provided by the school in order to fully develop those capabilities."
- The Individuals with Disabilities Education Act (IDEA) is a law ensuring services to children with disabilities.

CONCLUSIONS AND IMPLICATIONS

The NGSS offer a vision of science teaching and learning that presents both learning opportunities and demands for all students, particularly student groups that have traditionally been underrepresented in the science classroom. Furthermore, the NGSS are connected to the CCSS for English language arts and mathematics. Changes in the new standards occur as student demographics in the nation become increasingly diverse while science achievement gaps persist among demographic subgroups.

The academic rigor and expectations of the NGSS are less familiar to many science teachers than conventional or traditional teaching practices and require shifts for science teaching, which are consistent with shifts for teaching CCSS for English language arts and mathematics (see Figure D-1). Science teachers need

to acquire effective strategies to include all students regardless of racial, ethnic, cultural, linguistic, socioeconomic, and gender backgrounds. While effective classroom strategies that enable students to engage in the NGSS will draw from the existing research literature, the NGSS will also stimulate new research agenda. For example, future research may identify ways to make connections between school science and home/community for non-dominant student groups as they engage in the NGSS. Future research may explore how to utilize and allocate school resources to support student learning in terms of material resources, human capital, and social capital in relation to the NGSS.

Effective implementation of the NGSS for all students, including non-dominant student groups, will require shifts in the education support system. Key components of the support system include teacher preparation and professional development, principal support and leadership, public-private-community partnerships, formal and informal classroom experiences that require considerable coordination among community stakeholders, technological capabilities, network infrastructure, cyber-learning opportunities, access to digital resources, online learning communities, and virtual laboratories. As the NGSS implementation takes root over time, these components of the education system will also evolve and change accordingly.

REFERENCES

AAAS (American Association for the Advancement of Science). (1989). *Science for all Americans.* New York: Oxford University Press.

Calabrese Barton, A., Drake, C., Perez, J. G., St. Louis, K., and George, M. (2004). Ecologies of parental engagement in urban education. *Educational Researcher* 33:3–12.

Gamoran, A., Anderson, C. W., Quiroz, P. A., Secada, W. G., Williams, T., and Ashmann, S. (2003). *Transforming teaching in math and science: How schools and districts can support change.* New York: Teachers College Press.

González, N., Moll, L. C., and Amanti, C. (2005). *Funds of knowledge: Theorizing practices in households, communities, and classrooms.* Mahwah, NJ: Lawrence Erlbaum Associates.

Gutiérrez, K., and Rogoff, B. (2003). Cultural ways of learning: Individual traits or repertoires of practice. *Educational Researcher* 32:19–25.

Harry, B., and Klingner, J. K. (2006). *Why are so many minority students in special education?: Understanding race and disability in schools.* New York: Teachers College Press.

Ladson-Billings, G. (1995). Toward a theory of culturally relevant pedagogy. *American Educational Research Journal* 32:465–491.

Lee, O., and Buxton, C. A. (2010). *Diversity and equity in science education: Theory, research, and practice.* New York: Teachers College Press.

Lee, O., Quinn, H., and Valdés, G. (2013). Science and language for English language learners: Language demands and opportunities in relation to Next Generation Science Standards. *Educational Researcher* 42:223–233.

Marx, R. W., and Harris, C. J. (2006). No Child Left Behind and science education: Opportunities, challenges, and risks. *The Elementary School Journal* 106:467–477.

NAE and NRC (National Academy of Engineering and National Research Council). (2009). *Engineering in K–12 education: Understanding the status and improving the prospects.* L. Katehi, G. Pearson, and M. Feder (Eds.). Washington, DC: The National Academies Press.

NAGC (National Association for Gifted Children). (2010). Redefining giftedness for a new century: Shifting the paradigm. Available at: http://www.nagc.org/uploadedFiles/About_NAGC/Redefining%20 Giftedness%20for%20a%20New%20Century.pdf.

NCES (National Center for Education Statistics). (2011). *The condition of education 2011* (NCES 2011-033). Washington, DC: U.S. Department of Education, Institute of Education Sciences.

NCES. (2012). *The condition of education 2012* (NCES 2012-045). Washington, DC: U.S. Department of Education, Institute of Education Sciences.

NRC (National Research Council). (1996). *National science education standards.* Washington, DC: National Academy Press.

NRC. (2000). *Inquiry and the National Science Education Standards: A guide for teaching and learning.* Washington, DC: National Academy Press.

NRC. (2007). *Taking science to school: Learning and teaching science in grades K–8.* Washington, DC: The National Academies Press.

NRC. (2008). *Ready, set, SCIENCE!: Putting research to work in K–8 science classrooms.* Washington, DC: The National Academies Press.

NRC. (2009). *Learning science in informal environments: People, places, and pursuits.* Washington, DC: The National Academies Press.

NRC. (2012). *A framework for K–12 science education: Practices, cross-cutting themes, and core ideas.* Washington, DC: The National Academies Press.

NSF (National Science Foundation). (2010). *Preparing the next generation of STEM innovators: Identifying and developing our nation's human capital.* Washington, DC: NSF.

NSF. (2012). *Science and engineering indicators 2012: A broad base of quantitative information on the U.S. and international science and engineering enterprise.* Washington, DC: NSF.

Penuel, W., Riel, M., Krause, A., and Frank, K. (2009). Analyzing teachers' professional interactions in a school as social capital: A social network approach. *Teachers College Record* 111(1):124–163.

Quinn, H., Lee, O., and Valdés, G. (2012). *Language demands and opportunities in relation to Next Generation Science Standards for English language learners: What teachers need to know.* Stanford, CA: Stanford University, Understanding Language Initiative at Stanford University. Available at: ell.stanford.edu.

Rodriguez, A. (1998). Busting open the meritocracy myth: Rethinking equity and student achievement in science education. *Journal of Women and Minorities in Science and Engineering* 4:195–216.

Rodriguez, A. J., and Berryman, C. (2002). Using sociotransformative constructivism to teach for understanding in diverse classrooms: A beginning teacher's journey. *American Educational Research Journal* 39:1017–1045.

Simpson, J. S., and Parsons, E. (2008). African American perspectives and informal science educational experiences. *Science Education* 93:293–321.

Special issue on diversity and equity in science education. (2013). *Theory into Practice* 52(1).

U.S. Census Bureau. (2012). *Statistical abstract of the United States, 2012.* Washington, DC: Government Printing Office. Available at: http://www.census.gov/compendia/statab/cats/education.html.

DISCIPLINARY CORE IDEA PROGRESSIONS IN THE NEXT GENERATION SCIENCE STANDARDS

Following the vision of *A Framework for K–12 Science Education* (*Framework*), the Next Generation Science Standards (NGSS) are intended to increase coherence in K–12 science education. The following excerpt from the *Framework* explains the approach in more detail:

> First, it is built on the notion of learning as a developmental progression. It is designed to help children continually build on and revise their knowledge and abilities, starting from their curiosity about what they see around them and their initial conceptions about how the world works. The goal is to guide their knowledge toward a more scientifically based and coherent view of the natural sciences and engineering, as well as of the ways in which they are pursued and their results can be used.

> Second, the framework focuses on a limited number of core ideas in science and engineering both within and across the disciplines. The committee made this choice in order to avoid the shallow coverage of a large number of topics and to allow more time for teachers and students to explore each idea in greater depth. Reduction of the sheer sum of details to be mastered is intended to give time for students to engage in scientific investigations and argumentation and to achieve depth of understanding of the core ideas presented. Delimiting what is to be learned about each core idea within each grade band also helps clarify what is most important to spend time on, and avoid the proliferation of detail to be learned with no conceptual grounding.

> Third, the framework emphasizes that learning about science and engineering involves integration of the knowledge of scientific explanations (i.e., content knowledge) and the practices needed to engage in scientific inquiry and engineering design. Thus the framework seeks to illustrate how knowledge and practice must be intertwined in designing learning experiences in K–12 science education. (NRC, 2012)

DISCIPLINARY CORE IDEA PROGRESSION

The *Framework* describes the progression of disciplinary core ideas in the grade-band endpoints. The progressions are summarized in this section of the NGSS appendixes, which describe the content that occurs at each grade band. Some of the sub-ideas within the disciplinary core ideas overlap significantly. Readers will notice there is not always a clear division between those ideas, so several progressions are divided among more than one sub-idea. The purpose of these diagrams is to briefly describe the content at each grade band for each disciplinary core idea across K–12. This progression is for reference only. The full progressions can be seen in the *Framework*. In addition, the NGSS show the integration of the three dimensions. This document in no way endorses separating the disciplinary core ideas from the other two dimensions.

REFERENCE

NRC (National Research Council). (2012). *A framework for K–12 science education: Practices, crosscutting concepts, and core ideas.* Washington, DC: The National Academies Press.

	K–2	3–5	6–8	9–12
PS1.A Structure of matter (includes PS1.C Nuclear processes)	Matter exists as different substances that have observable different properties. Different properties are suited to different purposes. Objects can be built up from smaller parts.	Matter exists as particles that are too small to see, and so matter is always conserved even if it seems to disappear. Measurements of a variety of observable properties can be used to identify particular materials.	The fact that matter is composed of atoms and molecules can be used to explain the properties of substances, diversity of materials, states of matter, phase changes, and conservation of matter.	The sub-atomic structural model and interactions between electrical charges at the atomic scale can be used to explain the structure and interactions of matter, including chemical reactions and nuclear processes. Repeating patterns of the periodic table reflect patterns of outer electrons. A stable molecule has less energy than the same set of atoms separated; one must provide at least this energy to take the molecule apart.
PS1.B Chemical reactions	Heating and cooling of substances cause changes that are sometimes reversible and sometimes not.	Chemical reactions that occur when substances are mixed can be identified by the emergence of substances with different properties; the total mass remains the same.	Reacting substances rearrange to form different molecules, but the number of atoms is conserved. Some reactions release energy and others absorb energy.	Chemical processes are understood in terms of collisions of molecules, rearrangement of atoms, and changes in energy as determined by properties of the elements involved.
PS2.A Forces and motion	Pushes and pulls can have different strengths and directions, and can change the speed or direction of an object's motion or start or stop it.	The effect of unbalanced forces on an object results in a change of motion. Patterns of motion can be used to predict future motion. Some forces act through contact; some forces act even when the objects are not in contact. The gravitational force of Earth acting on an object near Earth's surface pulls that object toward the planet's center.	The role of the mass of an object must be qualitatively accounted for in any change of motion due to the application of a force.	Newton's Second Law of Motion ($F = ma$) and the conservation of momentum can be used to predict changes in the motion of macroscopic objects.
PS2.B Types of interactions			Forces that act at a distance involve fields that can be mapped by their relative strength and effect on an object.	Forces at a distance are explained by fields that can transfer energy and that can be described in terms of the arrangement and properties of the interacting objects and the distance between them. These forces can be used to describe the relationship between electrical and magnetic fields.
PS2.C Stability and instability in physical systems	N/A	N/A	N/A	N/A

	K–2	3–5	6–8	9–12
PS3.A Definitions of energy	N/A	Moving objects contain energy. The faster an object moves, the more energy it has. Energy can be moved from place to place by moving objects or through sound, light, or electrical currents. Energy can be converted from one form to another.	Kinetic energy can be distinguished from the various forms of potential energy. Energy changes to and from each type can be tracked through physical or chemical interactions. The relationship between the temperature and the total energy of a system depends on the types, states, and amounts of matter.	The total energy within a system is conserved. Energy transfer within and between systems can be described and predicted in terms of the energy associated with the motion or configuration of particles (objects). ------------------------------ Systems move toward stable states.
PS3.B Conservation of energy and energy transfer	[Content found in PS3.D]			
PS3.C Relationship between energy and forces	Bigger pushes and pulls cause bigger changes in an object's motion or shape.	When objects collide, contact forces transfer energy so as to change the objects' motions.	When two objects interact, each exerts a force on the other, and these forces can transfer energy between them.	A field contains energy that depends on the arrangement of the objects in the field.
PS3.D Energy in chemical processes and everyday life	Sunlight warms Earth's surface.	Energy can be "produced," "used," or "released" by converting stored energy. Plants capture energy from sunlight, which can later be used as fuel or food.	Sunlight is captured by plants and used in a reaction to produce sugar molecules, which can be reversed by burning those molecules to release energy.	Photosynthesis is the primary biological means of capturing radiation from the sun. Energy cannot be destroyed; it can be converted to less useful forms.
PS4.A Wave properties	Sound can make matter vibrate, and vibrating matter can make sound.	Waves are regular patterns of motion, which can be made in water by disturbing the surface. Waves of the same type can differ in amplitude and wavelength. Waves can make objects move.	A simple wave model has a repeating pattern with a specific wavelength, frequency, and amplitude, and mechanical waves need a medium through which they are transmitted. This model can explain many phenomena, including sound and light. Waves can transmit energy.	The wavelength and frequency of a wave are related to one another by the speed of the wave, which depends on the type of wave and the medium through which it is passing. Waves can be used to transmit information and energy.
PS4.B Electromagnetic radiation	Objects can be seen only when light is available to illuminate them.	An object can be seen when light reflected from its surface enters our eyes. ------------------------------	The construct of a wave is used to model how light interacts with objects.	Both an electromagnetic wave model and a photon model explain features of electromagnetic radiation broadly and describe common applications of electromagnetic radiation.
PS4.C Information technologies and instrumentation	People use devices to send and receive information.	Patterns can encode, send, receive, and decode information.	Waves can be used to transmit digital information. Digitized information is comprised of a pattern of ones and zeros.	Large amounts of information can be stored and shipped around as a result of being digitized.

Life Sciences Progression
INCREASING SOPHISTICATION OF STUDENT THINKING

	K–2	3–5	6–8	9–12
LS1.A Structure and function	All organisms have external parts that they use to perform daily functions.	Organisms have both internal and external macroscopic structures that allow for growth, survival, behavior, and reproduction.	All living things are made up of cells. In organisms, cells work together to form tissues and organs that are specialized for particular body functions.	Systems of specialized cells within organisms help perform essential functions of life. Any one system in an organism is made up of numerous parts. Feedback mechanisms maintain an organism's internal conditions within certain limits and mediate behaviors.
LS1.B Growth and development of organisms	Parents and offspring often engage in behaviors that help the offspring survive.	Reproduction is essential to every kind of organism. Organisms have unique and diverse life cycles.	Animals engage in behaviors that increase the odds of reproduction. An organism's growth is affected by both genetic and environmental factors.	Growth and division of cells in organisms occur by mitosis and differentiation for specific cell types.
LS1.C Organization for matter and energy flow in organisms	Animals obtain food they need from plants or other animals. Plants need water and light.	Food provides animals with the materials and energy they need for body repair, growth, warmth, and motion. Plants acquire material for growth chiefly from air, water, and process matter and obtain energy from sunlight, which is used to maintain conditions necessary for survival.	Plants use the energy from light to make sugars through photosynthesis. Within individual organisms, food is broken down through a series of chemical reactions that rearrange molecules and release energy.	The hydrocarbon backbones of sugars produced through photosynthesis are used to make amino acids and other molecules that can be assembled into proteins or DNA. Through cellular respiration, matter and energy flow through different organizational levels of an organism as elements are recombined to form different products and transfer energy.
LS1.D Information processing	Animals sense and communicate information and respond to inputs with behaviors that help them grow and survive.	Different sense receptors are specialized for particular kinds of information; animals use their perceptions and memories to guide their actions.	Each sense receptor responds to different inputs, transmitting them as signals that travel along nerve cells to the brain; the signals are then processed in the brain, resulting in immediate behavior or memories.	N/A
LS2.A Interdependent relationships in ecosystems	Plants depend on water and light to grow and on animals for pollination or to move their seeds around.	The food of almost any animal can be traced back to plants. Organisms are related in food webs in which some animals eat plants for food and other animals eat the animals that eat plants, while decomposers restore some materials to the soil.	Organisms and populations are dependent on their environmental interactions with both other living things and non-living factors, any of which can limit their growth. Competitive, predatory, and mutually beneficial interactions vary across ecosystems, but the patterns are shared.	Ecosystems have carrying capacities resulting from biotic and abiotic factors. The fundamental tension between resource availability and organism populations affects the abundance of species in any given ecosystem.

(Continued)

	K–2	3–5	6–8	9–12
LS2.B Cycles of matter and energy transfer in ecosystems	[Content found in LS1.C and ESS3.A]	Matter cycles between the air and soil and among organisms as they live and die.	The atoms that make up the organisms in an ecosystem are cycled repeatedly between the living and non-living parts of the ecosystem. Food webs model how matter and energy are transferred among producers, consumers, and decomposers as the three groups interact within an ecosystem.	Photosynthesis and cellular respiration provide most of the energy for life processes. Only a fraction of matter consumed at the lower level of a food web is transferred up, resulting in fewer organisms at higher levels. At each link in an ecosystem elements are combined in different ways and matter and energy are conserved. Photosynthesis and cellular respiration are key components of the global carbon cycle.
LS2.C Ecosystem dynamics, functioning, and resilience	N/A	When the environment changes some organisms survive and reproduce, some move to new locations, some move into the transformed environment, and some die.	Ecosystem characteristics vary over time. Disruptions to any part of an ecosystem can lead to shifts in all of its populations. The completeness or integrity of an ecosystem's biodiversity is often used as a measure of its health.	If a biological or physical disturbance to an ecosystem occurs, including one induced by human activity, the ecosystem may return to its more or less original state or become a very different ecosystem, depending on the complex set of interactions within the ecosystem.
LS2.D Social interactions and group behavior	N/A	Being part of a group helps animals obtain food, defend themselves, and cope with changes.	N/A	Group behavior has evolved because membership can increase the chances of survival for individuals and their genetic relatives.
LS3.A Inheritance of traits	Young organisms are very much, but not exactly, like their parents and also resemble other organisms of the same kind.	Different organisms vary in how they look and function because they have different inherited information; the environment also affects the traits that an organism develops.	Genes chiefly regulate specific proteins, which affect an individual's traits.	DNA carries instructions for forming species' characteristics. Each cell in an organism has the same genetic content, but genes expressed by cells can differ.
LS3.B Variation of traits			In sexual reproduction each parent contributes half the genes acquired by the offspring, resulting in variation between parent and offspring. Genetic information can be altered because of mutations, which may result in beneficial, negative, or no change to proteins in or traits of an organism.	The variation and distribution of traits in a population depend on genetic and environmental factors. Genetic variation can result from mutations caused by environmental factors or errors in DNA replication or from chromosomes swapping sections during meiosis.

	K–2	3–5	6–8	9–12
LS4.A Evidence of common ancestry and diversity	N/A	Some living organisms resemble organisms that once lived on Earth. Fossils provide evidence about the types of organisms and environments that existed long ago.	The fossil record documents the existence, diversity, extinction, and change of many life forms and their environments through Earth's history. The fossil record and comparisons of anatomical similarities between organisms enable the inference of lines of evolutionary descent.	The ongoing branching that produces multiple lines of descent can be inferred by comparing DNA sequences, amino acid sequences, and anatomical and embryological evidence of different organisms.
LS4.B Natural selection	N/A	Differences in characteristics between individuals of the same species provide advantages in survival and reproduction.	Both natural and artificial selection result from certain traits giving some individuals an advantage in survival and reproduction, leading to predominance of certain traits in a population.	Natural selection occurs only if there is variation in the genes and traits of organisms in a population. Traits that positively affect survival can become more common in a population.
LS4.C Adaptation	N/A	Particular organisms can survive only in particular environments. ---	Species can change over time in response to changes in environmental conditions through adaptation by natural selection acting over generations. Traits that support successful survival and reproduction in the new environment become more common.	Evolution results primarily from genetic variation of individuals in a species, competition for resources, and proliferation of organisms better able to survive and reproduce. Adaptation means that the distribution of traits in a population, as well as species' expansion, emergence, or extinction, can change when conditions change.
LS4.D Biodiversity and humans	A range of different organisms lives in different places.	Populations of organisms live in a variety of habitats. Change in those habitats affects the organisms living there.	Changes in biodiversity can influence humans' resources and the ecosystem services they rely on.	Biodiversity is increased by the formation of new species and reduced by extinction. Humans depend on biodiversity but also have adverse impacts on it. Sustaining biodiversity is essential to supporting life on Earth.

	K–2	3–5	6–8	9–12
ESS1.A The universe and its stars	Patterns of movement of the sun, moon, and stars as seen from Earth can be observed, described, and predicted.	Stars range greatly in size and distance from Earth, and this can explain their relative brightness. --------------------------------------	-------------------------------------- The solar system is part of the Milky Way, which is one of many billions of galaxies.	Light spectra from stars are used to determine their characteristics, processes, and life cycles. Solar activity creates the elements through nuclear fusion. The development of technologies has provided astronomical data that provide empirical evidence for the Big Bang theory.
ESS1.B Earth and the solar system		Earth's orbit and rotation and the orbit of the moon around Earth cause observable patterns.	The solar system contains many varied objects held together by gravity. Solar system models explain and predict eclipses, lunar phases, and seasons.	Kepler's Laws describe common features of the motions of orbiting objects. Observations from astronomy and space probes provide evidence for explanations of solar system formation. Changes in Earth's tilt and orbit cause climate changes such as ice ages.
ESS1.C The history of planet Earth	Some events on Earth occur very quickly; others can occur very slowly.	Certain features on Earth can be used to order events that have occurred in a landscape.	Rock strata and the fossil record can be used as evidence to organize the relative occurrence of major historical events in Earth's history.	The rock record resulting from tectonic and other geoscience processes as well as objects from the solar system can provide evidence of Earth's early history and the relative ages of major geologic formations.
ESS2.A Earth's materials and systems	Wind and water change the shape of the land.	Four major Earth systems interact. Rainfall helps to shape the land and affects the types of living things found in a region. Water, ice, wind, organisms, and gravity break rocks, soils, and sediments into smaller pieces and move them around.	Energy flows and matter cycles within and among Earth's systems, including the sun and Earth's interior as primary energy sources. Plate tectonics is one result of these processes.	Feedback effects exist within and among Earth's systems.
ESS2.B Plate tectonics and large-scale system interactions	Maps show where things are located. The shapes and kinds of land and water in any area can be mapped.	Earth's physical features occur in patterns, as do earthquakes and volcanoes. Maps can be used to locate features and determine patterns in those events.	Plate tectonics is the unifying theory that explains the movements of rocks at Earth's surface and geologic history. Maps are used to display evidence of plate movement.	Radioactive decay within Earth's interior contributes to thermal convection in the mantle.

	K–2	3–5	6–8	9–12
ESS2.C The roles of water in Earth's surface processes	Water is found in many types of places and in different forms on Earth.	Most of Earth's water is in the ocean and much of Earth's fresh water is in glaciers or underground.	Water cycles among land, ocean, and atmosphere and is propelled by sunlight and gravity. Density variations of sea water drive interconnected ocean currents. Water movement causes weathering and erosion, changing landscape features. --------------------------------- Complex interactions determine local weather patterns and influence climate, including the role of the ocean.	The planet's dynamics are greatly influenced by water's unique chemical and physical properties.
ESS2.D Weather and climate	Weather is the combination of sunlight, wind, snow or rain, and temperature in a particular region and time. People record weather patterns over time.	Climate describes patterns of typical weather conditions over different scales and variations. Historical weather patterns can be analyzed.		The role of radiation from the sun and its interactions with the atmosphere, ocean, and land are the foundation for the global climate system. Global climate models are used to predict future changes, including changes influenced by human behavior and natural factors.
ESS2.E Biogeology	Plants and animals can change their local environment. --------------------------------- Living things need water, air, and resources from the land, and they live in places that have the things they need. Humans use natural resources for everything they do.	Living things can affect the physical characteristics of their environment.	[Content found in LS4.A and LS4.D]	The biosphere and Earth's other systems have many interconnections that cause a continual co-evolution of Earth's surface and life on it
ESS3.A Natural resources		Energy and fuels that humans use are derived from natural sources and their use affects the environment. Some resources are renewable over time, others are not.	Humans depend on Earth's land, ocean, atmosphere, and biosphere for different resources, many of which are limited or not renewable. Resources are distributed unevenly around the planet as a result of past geologic processes.	Resource availability has guided the development of human society and the use of natural resources has associated costs, risks, and benefits.
ESS3.B Natural hazards	In a region some kinds of severe weather are more likely than others. Forecasts allow communities to prepare for severe weather.	A variety of hazards result from natural processes; humans cannot eliminate hazards but can reduce their impacts.	Some natural hazards can be predicted by mapping the history of those natural hazards in a region and understanding related geologic forces.	Natural hazards and other geologic events have shaped the course of human history at local, regional, and global scales.
ESS3.C Human impacts on Earth systems	Things people do can affect the environment, but they can make choices to reduce their impacts.	Societal activities have had major effects on land, ocean, atmosphere, and even outer space. Societal activities can also help protect Earth's resources and environments.	Human activities have altered the biosphere, sometimes damaging it, although changes to environments can have different impacts for different living things. Activities and technologies can be engineered to reduce people's impacts on Earth.	Sustainability of human societies and of the biodiversity that supports them requires responsible management of natural resources, including the development of technologies.
ESS3.D Global climate change	N/A	N/A	Human activities affect global warming. Decisions to reduce the impact of global warming depend on understanding climate science, engineering capabilities, and social dynamics.	Global climate models used to predict changes continue to be improved, although discoveries about the global climate system are ongoing and continually needed.

SCIENCE AND ENGINEERING PRACTICES IN THE NEXT GENERATION SCIENCE STANDARDS

A Framework for K–12 Science Education (*Framework*) provides the blueprint for developing the Next Generation Science Standards (NGSS). The *Framework* expresses a vision in science education that requires students to operate at the nexus of three dimensions of learning: Science and Engineering Practices, Disciplinary Core Ideas, and Crosscutting Concepts. The *Framework* identified a small number of disciplinary core ideas that all students should learn with increasing depth and sophistication, from kindergarten through twelfth grade. Key to the vision expressed in the *Framework* is for students to learn these disciplinary core ideas in the context of science and engineering practices. The importance of combining science and engineering practices and disciplinary core ideas is stated in the *Framework* as follows:

> Standards and performance expectations that are aligned to the framework must take into account that students cannot fully understand scientific and engineering ideas without engaging in the practices of inquiry and the discourses by which such ideas are developed and refined. At the same time, they cannot learn or show competence in practices except in the context of specific content. (NRC, 2012, p. 218)

The *Framework* specifies that each performance expectation must combine a relevant practice of science or engineering, with a core disciplinary idea and crosscutting concept, appropriate for students of the designated grade level. That guideline is perhaps the most significant way in which the NGSS differs from prior standards documents. In the future, science assessments will not assess students' understanding of core ideas separately from their abilities to use the practices of science and engineering. These two dimensions of learning will be assessed together, showing students not only "know" science concepts, but also that students

can use their understanding to investigate the natural world through the practices of science inquiry, and can solve meaningful problems through the practices of engineering design. The *Framework* uses the term "practices," rather than "science processes" or "inquiry" skills, for a specific reason:

> We use the term "practices" instead of a term such as "skills" to emphasize that engaging in scientific investigation requires not only skill but also knowledge that is specific to each practice. (NRC, 2012, p. 30)

The eight practices of science and engineering that the *Framework* identifies as essential for all students to learn, and describes in detail, are listed below:

1. Asking questions (for science) and defining problems (for engineering)
2. Developing and using models
3. Planning and carrying out investigations
4. Analyzing and interpreting data
5. Using mathematics and computational thinking
6. Constructing explanations (for science) and designing solutions (for engineering)
7. Engaging in argument from evidence
8. Obtaining, evaluating, and communicating information

RATIONALE

Chapter 3 of the *Framework* describes each of the eight practices of science and engineering and presents the following rationale for why they are essential:

> Engaging in the practices of science helps students understand how scientific knowledge develops; such direct involvement gives them an appreciation of the wide range of approaches that are used to investigate, model, and explain the world. Engaging in the practices of engineering likewise helps students understand the work of engineers, as well as the links between engineering and science. Participation in these practices also helps students form an understanding of the crosscutting concepts and disciplinary ideas of science and engineering; moreover,

it makes students' knowledge more meaningful and embeds it more deeply into their worldview.

The actual doing of science or engineering can also pique students' curiosity, capture their interest, and motivate their continued study; the insights thus gained help them recognize that the work of scientists and engineers is a creative endeavor—one that has deeply affected the world they live in. Students may then recognize that science and engineering can contribute to meeting many of the major challenges that confront society today, such as generating sufficient energy, preventing and treating disease, maintaining supplies of fresh water and food, and addressing climate change.

Any education that focuses predominantly on the detailed products of scientific labor—the facts of science—without developing an understanding of how those facts were established or that ignores the many important applications of science in the world misrepresents science and marginalizes the importance of engineering. (NRC, 2012, pp. 42–43)

As suggested in the rationale above, Chapter 3 derives the eight practices based on an analysis of what professional scientists and engineers do. It is recommended that users of the NGSS read that chapter carefully, as it provides valuable insights into the nature of science and engineering, as well as the connections between these two closely allied fields. The intent of this section of the NGSS appendixes is more limited—to describe what each of these eight practices implies about what students can do. Its purpose is to enable readers to better understand the performance expectations. A "practices matrix" is included, which lists the specific capabilities included in each practice for each grade band (K–2, 3–5, 6–8, 9–12).

GUIDING PRINCIPLES

The development process of the standards provided insights into science and engineering practices. These insights are shared in the following guiding principles:

Students in grades K–12 should engage in all eight practices over each grade band. All eight practices are accessible at some level to young children; students' abilities to use the practices grow over time. However, the NGSS only identify the capabilities that students are expected to acquire by the end of each grade band (K–2, 3–5, 6–8, and 9–12). Curriculum developers and teachers determine strategies that advance students' abilities to use the practices.

Practices grow in complexity and sophistication across the grades. The *Framework* suggests how students' capabilities to use each of the practices should progress as they mature and engage in science learning. For example, the practice of "planning and carrying out investigations" begins at the kindergarten level with guided situations in which students have assistance in identifying phenomena to be investigated and how to observe, measure, and record outcomes. By upper elementary school, students should be able to plan their own investigations. The nature of investigations that students should be able to plan and carry out is also expected to increase as students mature, including the complexity of questions to be studied; the ability to determine what kind of investigation is needed to answer different kinds of questions; whether or not variables need to be controlled and if so, which are most important; and at the high school level, how to take measurement error into account. As listed in the tables in this chapter, each of the eight practices has its own progression, from kindergarten to grade 12. While these progressions are derived from Chapter 3 of the *Framework*, they are refined based on experiences in crafting the NGSS and feedback received from reviewers.

Each practice may reflect science or engineering. Each of the eight practices can be used in the service of scientific inquiry or engineering design. The best way to ensure a practice is being used for science or engineering is to ask about the goal of the activity. Is the goal to answer a question? If so, students are doing science. Is the purpose to define and solve a problem? If so, students are doing engineering. Box 3-2 in *Framework* provides a side-by-side comparison of how scientists and engineers use these practices. This chapter briefly summarizes what it "looks like" for a student to use each practice for science or engineering.

Practices represent what students are expected to do and are not teaching methods or curriculum. The *Framework* occasionally offers suggestions for instruction, such as how a science unit might begin with a scientific investigation, which then leads to the solution of an engineering problem. The NGSS avoid such suggestions because the goal is to describe what students should be able to do, rather than how they should be taught. For example, it was suggested that the NGSS to recommend certain teaching strategies such as using biomimicry—the application of biological features to solve engineering design problems. Although instructional units that make use of biomimicry seem well aligned with the spirit of the *Framework* to encourage integration of core ideas and practices, biomimicry and similar teaching approaches are more closely related to curriculum and instruction than to assessment. Hence, the decision was made not to include biomimicry in the NGSS.

The eight practices are not separate; they intentionally overlap and interconnect. As explained by Bell et al. (2012), the eight practices do not operate in isolation. Rather, they tend to unfold sequentially, and even overlap. For example, the practice of "asking questions" may lead to the practice of "modeling" or "planning and carrying out an investigation," which in turn may lead to "analyzing and interpreting data." The practice of "mathematical and computational thinking" may include some aspects of "analyzing and interpreting data." Just as it is important for students to carry out each of the individual practices, it is important for them to see the connections among the eight practices.

Performance expectations focus on some but not all capabilities associated with a practice. The *Framework* identifies a number of features or components of each practice. The practices matrix described in this section lists the components of each practice as a bulleted list within each grade band. As the performance expectations were developed, it became clear that it is too much to expect each performance to reflect all components of a given practice. The most appropriate aspect of the practice is identified for each performance expectation.

Engagement in practices is language intensive and requires students to participate in classroom science discourse. The practices offer rich opportunities and demands for language learning while advancing science learning for all students (Lee et al., in press). English language learners, students with disabilities that involve language processing, students with limited literacy development, and students who are speakers of social or regional varieties of English that are generally referred to as "non-standard English" stand to gain from science learning that involves language-intensive scientific and engineering practices. When supported appropriately, these students are capable of learning science through their emerging language and of comprehending and carrying out sophisticated language functions (e.g., arguing from evidence, providing explanations, developing models) using less-than-perfect English. By engaging in such practices, moreover, they simultaneously build on their understanding of science and their language proficiency (i.e., capacity to do more with language).

On the following pages, each of the eight practices is briefly described. Each description ends with a table illustrating the components of the practice that students are expected to master at the end of each grade band. All eight tables comprise the practices matrix. During development of the NGSS, the practices matrix was revised several times to reflect improved understanding of how the practices connect with the disciplinary core ideas.

PRACTICE 1: ASKING QUESTIONS AND DEFINING PROBLEMS

Students at any grade level should be able to ask questions of each other about the texts they read, the features of the phenomena they observe, and the conclusions they draw from their models or scientific investigations. For engineering, they should ask questions to define the problem to be solved and to elicit ideas that lead to the constraints and specifications for its solution. (NRC, 2012, p. 56)

Practice 1: Asking Questions and Defining Problems

Grades K–2	Grades 3–5	Grades 6–8	Grades 9–12

Asking questions and defining problems in K–2 builds on prior experiences and progresses to simple descriptive questions that can be tested.
• Ask questions based on observations to find more information about the natural and/or designed world(s).
• Ask and/or identify questions that can be answered by an investigation.
• Define a simple problem that can be solved through the development of a new or improved object or tool.
	Asking questions and defining problems in 3–5 builds on K–2 experiences and progresses to specifying qualitative relationships.
	• Ask questions about what would happen if a variable is changed.
	• Identify scientific (testable) and non-scientific (non-testable) questions.
	• Ask questions that can be investigated and predict reasonable outcomes based on patterns such as cause and effect relationships.
	• Use prior knowledge to describe problems that can be solved.
	• Define a simple design problem that can be solved through the development of an object, tool, process, or system and includes several criteria for success and constraints on materials, time, or cost.
		Asking questions and defining problems in 6–8 builds on K–5 experiences and progresses to specifying relationships between variables and clarifying arguments and models.
		• Ask questions
		  ○ that arise from careful observation of phenomena, models, or unexpected results, to clarify and/or seek additional information.
		  ○ to identify and/or clarify evidence and/or the premise(s) of an argument.
		  ○ to determine relationships between independent and dependent variables and relationships in models.
		  ○ to clarify and/or refine a model, an explanation, or an engineering problem.
		  ○ that require sufficient and appropriate empirical evidence to answer.
		  ○ that can be investigated within the scope of the classroom, outdoor environment, and museums and other public facilities with available resources and, when appropriate, frame a hypothesis based on observations and scientific principles.
		  ○ that challenge the premise(s) of an argument or the interpretation of a data set.
		• Define a design problem that can be solved through the development of an object, tool, process, or system and includes multiple criteria and constraints, including scientific knowledge that may limit possible solutions.
			Asking questions and defining problems in 9–12 builds on K–8 experiences and progresses to formulating, refining, and evaluating empirically testable questions and design problems using models and simulations.
			• Ask questions
			  ○ that arise from careful observation of phenomena, or unexpected results, to clarify and/or seek additional information.
			  ○ that arise from examining models or a theory, to clarify and/or seek additional information and relationships.
			  ○ to determine relationships, including quantitative relationships, between independent and dependent variables.
			  ○ to clarify and refine a model, an explanation, or an engineering problem.
			• Evaluate a question to determine if it is testable and relevant.
			• Ask questions that can be investigated within the scope of the school laboratory, research facilities, or field (e.g., outdoor environment) with available resources and, when appropriate, frame a hypothesis based on a model or theory.
			• Ask and/or evaluate questions that challenge the premise(s) of an argument, the interpretation of a data set, or the suitability of a design.
			• Define a design problem that involves the development of a process or system with interacting components and criteria and constraints that may include social, technical, and/or environmental considerations.
			• Analyze complex real-world problems by specifying criteria and constraints for successful solutions.

Scientific questions arise in a variety of ways. They can be driven by curiosity about the world, inspired by the predictions of a model, theory, or findings from previous investigations, or they can be stimulated by the need to solve a problem. Scientific questions are distinguished from other types of questions in that the answers lie in explanations supported by empirical evidence, including evidence gathered by others or through investigation.

While science begins with questions, engineering begins with defining a problem to solve. However, engineering may also involve asking questions to define a problem, such as: What is the need or desire that underlies the problem? What are the criteria for a successful solution? Other questions arise when generating ideas, or testing possible solutions, such as: What are the possible tradeoffs? What evidence is necessary to determine which solution is best?

Asking questions and defining problems also involves asking questions about data, claims that are made, and proposed designs. It is important to realize that asking a question also leads to involvement in another practice. A student can ask a question about data that will lead to further analysis and interpretation. Or a student might ask a question that leads to planning and design, an investigation, or the refinement of a design.

Whether engaged in science or engineering, the ability to ask good questions and clearly define problems is essential for everyone. The following progression of Practice 1 summarizes what students should be able to do by the end of each grade band. Each of the examples of asking questions below leads to students engaging in other scientific practices.

PRACTICE 2: DEVELOPING AND USING MODELS

Modeling can begin in the earliest grades, with students' models progressing from concrete "pictures" and/or physical scale models (e.g., a toy car) to more abstract representations of relevant relationships in later grades, such as a diagram representing forces on a particular object in a system. (NRC, 2012, p. 58)

Models include diagrams, physical replicas, mathematical representations, analogies, and computer simulations. Although models do not correspond exactly to the real world, they bring certain features into focus while obscuring others. All models contain approximations and assumptions that limit the range of validity and predictive power, so it is important for students to recognize their limitations.

In science, models are used to represent a system (or parts of a system) under study, to aid in the development of questions and explanations, to generate data that can be used to make predictions, and to communicate ideas to others. Students can be expected to evaluate and refine models through an iterative cycle of comparing their predictions with the real world and then adjusting them to gain insights into the phenomenon being modeled. As such, models are based on evidence. When new evidence is uncovered that the models cannot explain, models are modified.

In engineering, models may be used to analyze a system to see where or under what conditions flaws might develop or to test possible solutions to a problem. Models can also be used to visualize and refine a design, to communicate a design's features to others, and as prototypes for testing design performance.

Practice 2: Developing and Using Models

Grades K–2	Grades 3–5	Grades 6–8	Grades 9–12
Modeling in K–2 builds on prior experiences and progresses to include using and developing models (i.e., diagram, drawing, physical replica, diorama, dramatization, or storyboard) that represent concrete events or design solutions. • Distinguish between a model and the actual object, process, and/or events the model represents. • Compare models to identify common features and differences. • Develop and/or use a model to represent amounts, relationships, relative scales (bigger, smaller), and/or patterns in the natural and designed world(s). • Develop a simple model based on evidence to represent a proposed object or tool.	Modeling in 3–5 builds on K–2 experiences and progresses to building and revising simple models and using models to represent events and design solutions. • Identify limitations of models. • Collaboratively develop and/or revise a model based on evidence that shows the relationships among variables for frequent and regular occurring events. • Develop a model using an analogy, example, or abstract representation to describe a scientific principle or design solution. • Develop and/or use models to describe and/or predict phenomena. • Develop a diagram or simple physical prototype to convey a proposed object, tool, or process. • Use a model to test cause and effect relationships or interactions concerning the functioning of a natural or designed system.	Modeling in 6–8 builds on K–5 experiences and progresses to developing, using, and revising models to describe, test, and predict more abstract phenomena and design systems. • Evaluate limitations of a model for a proposed object or tool. • Develop or modify a model—based on evidence—to match what happens if a variable or component of a system is changed. • Use and/or develop a model of simple systems with uncertain and less predictable factors. • Develop and/or revise a model to show the relationships among variables, including those that are not observable but predict observable phenomena. • Develop and/or use a model to predict and/or describe phenomena. • Develop a model to describe unobservable mechanisms. • Develop and/or use a model to generate data to test ideas about phenomena in natural or designed systems, including those representing inputs and outputs and those at unobservable scales.	Modeling in 9–12 builds on K–8 experiences and progresses to using, synthesizing, and developing models to predict and show relationships among variables between systems and their components in the natural and designed world(s). • Evaluate merits and limitations of two different models of the same proposed tool, process, mechanism, or system in order to select or revise a model that best fits the evidence or design criteria. • Design a test of a model to ascertain its reliability. • Develop, revise, and/or use a model based on evidence to illustrate and/or predict the relationships between systems or between components of a system. • Develop and/or use multiple types of models to provide mechanistic accounts and/or predict phenomena, and move flexibly between model types based on merits and limitations. • Develop a complex model that allows for manipulation and testing of a proposed process or system. • Develop and/or use a model (including mathematical and computational) to generate data to support explanations, predict phenomena, analyze systems, and/or solve problems.

PRACTICE 3: PLANNING AND CARRYING OUT INVESTIGATIONS

Students should have opportunities to plan and carry out several different kinds of investigations during their K–12 years. At all levels, they should engage in investigations that range from those structured by the teacher—in order to expose an issue or question that they would be unlikely to explore on their own (e.g., measuring specific properties of materials)—to those that emerge from students' own questions. (NRC, 2012, p. 61)

Scientific investigations may be undertaken to describe a phenomenon or to test a theory or model for how the world works. The purpose of engineering investigations might be to find out how to fix or improve the functioning of a technological system or to compare different solutions to see which best solves a problem. Whether students are doing science or engineering, it is always important for them to state the goal of an investigation, predict outcomes, and plan a course of action that will provide the best evidence to support their conclusions. Students should design investigations that generate data to provide evidence to support claims they make about phenomena. Data are not evidence until used in the process of supporting a claim. Students should use reasoning and scientific ideas, principles, and theories to show why data can be considered evidence.

Over time, students are expected to become more systematic and careful in their methods. In laboratory experiments, students are expected to decide which variables should be treated as results or outputs, which should be treated as inputs and intentionally varied from trial to trial, and which should be controlled, or kept the same across trials. In the case of field observations, planning involves deciding how to collect different samples of data under different conditions, even though not all conditions are under the direct control of the investigator. Planning and carrying out investigations may include elements of all of the other practices.

Practice 3: Planning and Carrying Out Investigations

Grades K–2	Grades 3–5	Grades 6–8	Grades 9–12
Planning and carrying out investigations to answer questions or test solutions to problems in K–2 builds on prior experiences and progresses to simple investigations, based on fair tests, which provide data to support explanations or design solutions. • With guidance, plan and conduct an investigation in collaboration with peers (for K). • Plan and conduct an investigation collaboratively to produce data to serve as the basis for evidence to answer a question. • Evaluate different ways of observing and/or measuring a phenomenon to determine which way can answer a question. • Make observations (firsthand or from media) and/or measurements to collect data that can be used to make comparisons. • Make observations (firsthand or from media) and/or measurements of a proposed object, tool, or solution to determine if it solves a problem or meets a goal. • Make predictions based on prior experiences.	Planning and carrying out investigations to answer questions or test solutions to problems in 3–5 builds on K–2 experiences and progresses to include investigations that control variables and provide evidence to support explanations or design solutions. • Plan and conduct an investigation collaboratively to produce data to serve as the basis for evidence, using fair tests in which variables are controlled and the number of trials is considered. • Evaluate appropriate methods and/or tools for collecting data. • Make observations and/or measurements to produce data to serve as the basis for evidence for an explanation of a phenomenon or to test a design solution. • Make predictions about what would happen if a variable changes. • Test two different models of the same proposed object, tool, or process to determine which better meets criteria for success.	Planning and carrying out investigations in 6–8 builds on K–5 experiences and progresses to include investigations that use multiple variables and provide evidence to support explanations or solutions. • Plan an investigation individually and collaboratively, and in the design identify independent and dependent variables and controls, what tools are needed to do the gathering, how measurements will be recorded, and how many data are needed to support a claim. • Conduct an investigation and/or evaluate and/or revise the experimental design to produce data to serve as the basis for evidence that meet the goals of the investigation. • Evaluate the accuracy of various methods for collecting data. • Collect data to produce data to serve as the basis for evidence to answer scientific questions or to test design solutions under a range of conditions. • Collect data about the performance of a proposed object, tool, process, or system under a range of conditions.	Planning and carrying out investigations in 9–12 builds on K–8 experiences and progresses to include investigations that provide evidence for and test conceptual, mathematical, physical, and empirical models. • Plan an investigation or test a design individually and collaboratively to produce data to serve as the basis for evidence as part of building and revising models, supporting explanations for phenomena, or testing solutions to problems. Consider possible confounding variables or effects and evaluate the investigation's design to ensure variables are controlled. • Plan and conduct an investigation individually and collaboratively to produce data to serve as the basis for evidence, and in the design decide on types, how much, and accuracy of data needed to produce reliable measurements and consider limitations on the precision of the data (e.g., number of trials, cost, risk, time), and refine the design accordingly. • Plan and conduct an investigation or test a design solution in a safe and ethical manner, including considerations of environmental, social, and personal impacts. • Select appropriate tools to collect, record, analyze, and evaluate data. • Make directional hypotheses that specify what happens to a dependent variable when an independent variable is manipulated. • Manipulate variables and collect data about a complex model of a proposed process or system to identify failure points or improve performance relative to criteria for success or other variables.

PRACTICE 4: ANALYZING AND INTERPRETING DATA

Once collected, data must be presented in a form that can reveal any patterns and relationships and that allows results to be communicated to others. Because raw data as such have little meaning, a major practice of scientists is to organize and interpret data through tabulating, graphing, or statistical analysis. Such analysis can bring out the meaning of data—and their relevance—so that they may be used as evidence.

Engineers, too, make decisions based on evidence that a given design will work; they rarely rely on trial and error. Engineers often analyze a design by creating a model or prototype and collecting extensive data on how it performs, including under extreme conditions. Analysis of this kind of data not only informs design decisions and enables the prediction or assessment of performance but also helps define or clarify problems, determine economic feasibility, evaluate alternatives, and investigate failures. (NRC, 2012, pp. 61–62)

As students mature, they are expected to expand their capabilities to use a range of tools for tabulation, graphical representation, visualization, and statistical analysis. Students are also expected to improve their abilities to interpret data by identifying significant features and patterns, use mathematics to represent relationships between variables, and take into account sources of error. When possible and feasible, students should use digital tools to analyze and interpret data. Whether analyzing data for the purpose of science or engineering, it is important that students present data as evidence to support their conclusions.

Practice 4: Analyzing and Interpreting Data

Grades K–2	Grades 3–5	Grades 6–8	Grades 9–12
Analyzing data in K–2 builds on prior experiences and progresses to collecting, recording, and sharing observations. • Record information (observations, thoughts, and ideas). • Use and share pictures, drawings, and/or writings of observations. • Use observations (firsthand or from media) to describe patterns and/or relationships in the natural and designed world(s) in order to answer scientific questions and solve problems. • Compare predictions (based on prior experiences) to what occurred (observable events). • Analyze data from tests of an object or tool to determine if it works as intended.	Analyzing data in 3–5 builds on K–2 experiences and progresses to introducing quantitative approaches to collecting data and conducting multiple trials of qualitative observations. When possible and feasible, digital tools should be used. • Represent data in tables and/or various graphical displays (bar graphs, pictographs, and/or pie charts) to reveal patterns that indicate relationships. • Analyze and interpret data to make sense of phenomena, using logical reasoning, mathematics, and/or computation. • Compare and contrast data collected by different groups in order to discuss similarities and differences in their findings. • Analyze data to refine a problem statement or the design of a proposed object, tool, or process. • Use data to evaluate and refine design solutions.	Analyzing data in 6–8 builds on K–5 experiences and progresses to extending quantitative analysis to investigations, distinguishing between correlation and causation, and basic statistical techniques of data and error analysis. • Construct, analyze, and/or interpret graphical displays of data and/or large data sets to identify linear and non-linear relationships. • Use graphical displays (e.g., maps, charts, graphs, and/or tables) of large data sets to identify temporal and spatial relationships. • Distinguish between causal and correlational relationships in data. • Analyze and interpret data to provide evidence for phenomena. • Apply concepts of statistics and probability (including mean, median, mode, and variability) to analyze and characterize data, using digital tools when feasible. • Consider limitations of data analysis (e.g., measurement error) and/or seek to improve precision and accuracy of data with better technological tools and methods (e.g., multiple trials). • Analyze and interpret data to determine similarities and differences in findings. • Analyze data to define an optimal operational range for a proposed object, tool, process, or system that best meets criteria for success.	Analyzing data in 9–12 builds on K–8 experiences and progresses to introducing more detailed statistical analysis, the comparison of data sets for consistency, and the use of models to generate and analyze data. • Analyze data using tools, technologies, and/or models (e.g., computational, mathematical) in order to make valid and reliable scientific claims or determine an optimal design solution. • Apply concepts of statistics and probability (including determining function fits to data, slope, intercept, and correlation coefficient for linear fits) to scientific and engineering questions and problems, using digital tools when feasible. • Consider limitations of data analysis (e.g., measurement error, sample selection) when analyzing and interpreting data. • Compare and contrast various types of data sets (e.g., self-generated, archival) to examine consistency of measurements and observations. • Evaluate the impact of new data on a working explanation and/or model of a proposed process or system. • Analyze data to identify design features or characteristics of the components of a proposed process or system to optimize it relative to criteria for success.

PRACTICE 5: USING MATHEMATICS AND COMPUTATIONAL THINKING

Although there are differences in how mathematics and computational thinking are applied in science and in engineering, mathematics often brings these two fields together by enabling engineers to apply the mathematical form of scientific theories and by enabling scientists to use powerful information technologies designed by engineers. Both kinds of professionals can thereby accomplish investigations and analyses and build complex models, which might otherwise be out of the question. (NRC, 2012, p. 65)

Students are expected to use mathematics to represent physical variables and their relationships and to make quantitative predictions. Other applications of mathematics in science and engineering include logic, geometry, and at the highest levels, calculus. Computers and digital tools can enhance the power of mathematics by automating calculations, approximating solutions to problems that cannot be calculated precisely, and analyzing large data sets available to identify meaningful patterns. Students are expected to use laboratory tools connected to computers for observing, measuring, recording, and processing data. Students are also expected to engage in computational thinking, which involves strategies for organizing and searching data, creating sequences of steps called algorithms, and using and developing new simulations of natural and designed systems. Mathematics is a tool that is key to understanding science. As such, classroom instruction must include critical skills of mathematics. The NGSS display many of those skills through the performance expectations, but classroom instruction should enhance all of science through the use of quality mathematical and computational thinking.

Practice 5: Using Mathematics and Computational Thinking

Grades K–2	Grades 3–5	Grades 6–8	Grades 9–12
Mathematical and computational thinking in K–2 builds on prior experience and progresses to recognizing that mathematics can be used to describe the natural and designed world(s). • Decide when to use qualitative vs. quantitative data. • Use counting and numbers to identify and describe patterns in the natural and designed world(s). • Describe, measure, and/or compare quantitative attributes of different objects and display the data using simple graphs. • Use quantitative data to compare two alternative solutions to a problem.	Mathematical and computational thinking in 3–5 builds on K–2 experiences and progresses to extending quantitative measurements to a variety of physical properties and using computation and mathematics to analyze data and compare alternative design solutions. • Decide if qualitative or quantitative data are best to determine whether a proposed object or tool meets criteria for success. • Organize simple data sets to reveal patterns that suggest relationships. • Describe, measure, estimate, and/or graph quantities (e.g., area, volume, weight, time) to address scientific and engineering questions and problems. • Create and/or use graphs and/or charts generated from simple algorithms to compare alternative solutions to an engineering problem.	Mathematical and computational thinking in 6–8 builds on K–5 experiences and progresses to identifying patterns in large data sets and using mathematical concepts to support explanations and arguments. • Use digital tools (e.g., computers) to analyze very large data sets for patterns and trends. • Use mathematical representations to describe and/or support scientific conclusions and design solutions. • Create algorithms (a series of ordered steps) to solve a problem. • Apply mathematical concepts and/or processes (e.g., ratio, rate, percent, basic operations, simple algebra) to scientific and engineering questions and problems. • Use digital tools and/or mathematical concepts and arguments to test and compare proposed solutions to an engineering design problem.	Mathematical and computational thinking in 9–12 builds on K–8 experiences and progresses to using algebraic thinking and analysis, a range of linear and non-linear functions, including trigonometric functions, exponentials and logarithms, and computational tools for statistical analysis to analyze, represent, and model data. Simple computational simulations are created and used based on mathematical models of basic assumptions. • Create and/or revise a computational model or simulation of a phenomenon, designed device, process, or system. • Use mathematical, computational, and/or algorithmic representations of phenomena or design solutions to describe and/or support claims and/or explanations. • Apply techniques of algebra and functions to represent and solve scientific and engineering problems. • Use simple limit cases to test mathematical expressions, computer programs, algorithms, or simulations of a process or system to see if a model "makes sense" by comparing the outcomes with what is known about the real world. • Apply ratios, rates, percentages, and unit conversions in the context of complicated measurement problems involving quantities with derived or compound units (such as mg/mL, kg/m^3, acre-feet, etc.).

PRACTICE 6: CONSTRUCTING EXPLANATIONS AND DESIGNING SOLUTIONS

The goal of science is to construct explanations for the causes of phenomena. Students are expected to construct their own explanations, as well as apply standard explanations they learn about from their teachers or reading. The *Framework* states the following about explanations:

> The goal of science is the construction of theories that provide explanatory accounts of the world. A theory becomes accepted when it has multiple lines of empirical evidence and greater explanatory power of phenomena than previous theories. (NRC, 2012, p. 52)

An explanation includes a claim that relates how a variable or variables relate to another variable or a set of variables. A claim is often made in response to a question and in the process of answering the question, scientists often design investigations to generate data.

The goal of engineering is to solve problems. Designing solutions to problems is a systematic process that involves defining the problem, then generating, testing, and improving solutions. This practice is described in the *Framework* as follows:

> Asking students to demonstrate their own understanding of the implications of a scientific idea by developing their own explanations of phenomena, whether based on observations they have made or models they have developed, engages them in an essential part of the process by which conceptual change can occur.

> In engineering, the goal is a design rather than an explanation. The process of developing a design is iterative and systematic, as is the process of developing an explanation or a theory in science. Engineers' activities, however, have elements that are distinct from those of scientists. These elements include specifying constraints and criteria for desired qualities of the solution, developing a design plan, producing and testing models or prototypes, selecting among alternative design features to optimize the achievement of design criteria, and refining design ideas based on the performance of a prototype or simulation. (NRC, 2012, pp. 68–69)

Practice 6: Constructing Explanations and Designing Solutions

Grades K–2	Grades 3–5	Grades 6–8	Grades 9–12
Constructing explanations and designing solutions in K–2 builds on prior experiences and progresses to the use of evidence and ideas in constructing evidence-based accounts of natural phenomena and designing solutions. • Make observations (firsthand or from media) to construct an evidence-based account for natural phenomena. • Use tools and/or materials to design and/or build a device that solves a specific problem or a solution to a specific problem. • Generate and/or compare multiple solutions to a problem.	Constructing explanations and designing solutions in 3–5 builds on K–2 experiences and progresses to the use of evidence in constructing explanations that specify variables that describe and predict phenomena and in designing multiple solutions to design problems. • Construct an explanation of observed relationships (e.g., the distribution of plants in the backyard). • Use evidence (e.g., measurements, observations, patterns) to construct or support an explanation or design a solution to a problem. • Identify the evidence that supports particular points in an explanation. • Apply scientific ideas to solve design problems. • Generate and compare multiple solutions to a problem based on how well they meet the criteria and constraints of the design solution.	Constructing explanations and designing solutions in 6–8 builds on K–5 experiences and progresses to include constructing explanations and designing solutions supported by multiple sources of evidence consistent with scientific ideas, principles, and theories. • Construct an explanation that includes qualitative or quantitative relationships between variables that predicts and/or describes phenomena. • Construct an explanation using models or representations. • Construct a scientific explanation based on valid and reliable evidence obtained from sources (including students' own experiments) and the assumption that theories and laws that describe the natural world operate today as they did in the past and will continue to do so in the future. • Apply scientific ideas, principles, and/or evidence to construct, revise, and/or use an explanation for real-world phenomena, examples, or events. • Apply scientific reasoning to show why the data or evidence is adequate for the explanation or conclusion. • Apply scientific ideas or principles to design, construct, and/or test a design of an object, tool, process, or system. • Undertake a design project, engaging in the design cycle, to construct and/or implement a solution that meets specific design criteria and constraints. • Optimize performance of a design by prioritizing criteria, making tradeoffs, testing, revising, and re-testing.	Constructing explanations and designing solutions in 9–12 builds on K–8 experiences and progresses to explanations and designs that are supported by multiple and independent student-generated sources of evidence consistent with scientific ideas, principles, and theories. • Make a quantitative and/or qualitative claim regarding the relationship between dependent and independent variables. • Construct and revise an explanation based on valid and reliable evidence obtained from a variety of sources (including students' own investigations, models, theories, simulations, peer review) and the assumption that theories and laws that describe the natural world operate today as they did in the past and will continue to do so in the future. • Apply scientific ideas, principles, and/or evidence to provide an explanation of phenomena and solve design problems, taking into account possible unanticipated effects. • Apply scientific reasoning, theory, and/or models to link evidence to the claims to assess the extent to which the reasoning and data support the explanation or conclusion. • Design, evaluate, and/or refine a solution to a complex real-world problem, based on scientific knowledge, student-generated sources of evidence, prioritized criteria, and tradeoff considerations.

PRACTICE 7: ENGAGING IN ARGUMENT FROM EVIDENCE

The study of science and engineering should produce a sense of the process of argument necessary for advancing and defending a new idea or an explanation of a phenomenon and the norms for conducting such arguments. In that spirit, students should argue for the explanations they construct, defend their interpretations of the associated data, and advocate for the designs they propose. (NRC, 2012, p. 73)

Argumentation is a process for reaching agreements about explanations and design solutions. In science, reasoning and argument based on evidence are essential in identifying the best explanation for a natural phenomenon. In engineering, reasoning and argument are needed to identify the best solution to a design problem. Student engagement in scientific argumentation is critical if students are to understand the culture in which scientists live and how to apply science and engineering for the benefit of society. As such, argument is a process based on evidence and reasoning that leads to explanations acceptable by the scientific community and design solutions acceptable by the engineering community.

Argument in science goes beyond reaching agreements in explanations and design solutions. Whether investigating a phenomenon, testing a design, or constructing a model to provide a mechanism for an explanation, students are expected to use argumentation to listen to, compare, and evaluate competing ideas and methods based on their merits. Scientists and engineers engage in argumentation when investigating a phenomenon, testing a design solution, resolving questions about measurements, building data models, and using evidence to evaluate claims.

Practice 7: Engaging in Argument from Evidence

Grades K–2	Grades 3–5	Grades 6–8	Grades 9–12
Engaging in argument from evidence in K–2 builds on prior experiences and progresses to comparing ideas and representations about the natural and designed world(s). • Identify arguments that are supported by evidence. • Distinguish between explanations that account for all gathered evidence and those that do not. • Analyze why some evidence is relevant to a scientific question and some is not. • Distinguish between opinions and evidence in one's own explanations. • Listen actively to arguments to indicate agreement or disagreement based on evidence, and/or to retell the main points of the argument. • Construct an argument with evidence to support a claim. • Make a claim about the effectiveness of an object, tool, or solution that is supported by relevant evidence.	Engaging in argument from evidence in 3–5 builds on K–2 experiences and progresses to critiquing the scientific explanations or solutions proposed by peers by citing relevant evidence about the natural and designed world(s). • Compare and refine arguments based on an evaluation of the evidence presented. • Distinguish among facts, reasoned judgment based on research findings, and speculation in an explanation. • Respectfully provide and receive critiques from peers about a proposed procedure, explanation, or model by citing relevant evidence and posing specific questions. • Construct and/or support an argument with evidence, data, and/or a model. • Use data to evaluate claims about cause and effect. • Make a claim about the merit of a solution to a problem by citing relevant evidence about how it meets the criteria and constraints of the problem.	Engaging in argument from evidence in 6–8 builds on K–5 experiences and progresses to constructing a convincing argument that supports or refutes claims for either explanations or solutions about the natural and designed world(s). • Compare and critique two arguments on the same topic and analyze whether they emphasize similar or different evidence and/or interpretations of facts. • Respectfully provide and receive critiques about one's explanations, procedures, models, and questions by citing relevant evidence and posing and responding to questions that elicit pertinent elaboration and detail. • Construct, use, and/or present an oral and written argument supported by empirical evidence and scientific reasoning to support or refute an explanation or a model for a phenomenon or a solution to a problem. • Make an oral or written argument that supports or refutes the advertised performance of a device, process, or system based on empirical evidence concerning whether or not the technology meets relevant criteria and constraints. • Evaluate competing design solutions based on jointly developed and agreed-upon design criteria.	Engaging in argument from evidence in 9–12 builds on K–8 experiences and progresses to using appropriate and sufficient evidence and scientific reasoning to defend and critique claims and explanations about the natural and designed world(s). Arguments may also come from current scientific or historical episodes in science. • Compare and evaluate competing arguments or design solutions in light of currently accepted explanations, new evidence, limitations (e.g., tradeoffs), constraints, and ethical issues. • Evaluate the claims, evidence, and/or reasoning behind currently accepted explanations or solutions to determine the merits of arguments. • Respectfully provide and/or receive critiques on scientific arguments by probing reasoning and evidence, challenging ideas and conclusions, responding thoughtfully to diverse perspectives, and determining additional information required to resolve contradictions. • Construct, use, and/or present an oral and written argument or counter-arguments based on data and evidence. • Make and defend a claim based on evidence about the natural world or the effectiveness of a design solution that reflects scientific knowledge and student-generated evidence. • Evaluate competing design solutions to a real-world problem based on scientific ideas and principles, empirical evidence, and/or logical arguments regarding relevant factors (e.g., economic, societal, environmental, ethical considerations).

PRACTICE 8: OBTAINING, EVALUATING, AND COMMUNICATING INFORMATION

Any education in science and engineering needs to develop students' ability to read and produce domain-specific text. As such, every science or engineering lesson is in part a language lesson, particularly reading and producing the genres of texts that are intrinsic to science and engineering. (NRC, 2012, p. 76)

Being able to read, interpret, and produce scientific and technical text is a fundamental practice of science and engineering, as is the ability to communicate clearly and persuasively. Being a critical consumer of information about science and engineering requires the ability to read or view reports of scientific or technological advances or applications (whether found in the press, on the Internet, or in a town meeting) and to recognize the salient ideas, identify sources of errors and methodological flaws, and distinguish observations from inferences, arguments from explanations, and claims from evidence. Scientists and engineers employ multiple sources to obtain information used to evaluate the merit and validity of claims, methods, and designs. Communicating information, evidence, and ideas can be done in multiple ways: using tables, diagrams, graphs, models, interactive displays, and equations as well as orally, in writing, and through extended discussions.

Practice 8: Obtaining, Evaluating, and Communicating Information

Grades K–2	Grades 3–5	Grades 6–8	Grades 9–12
Obtaining, evaluating, and communicating information in K–2 builds on prior experiences and uses observations and texts to communicate new information. • Read grade-appropriate texts and/or use media to obtain scientific and/or technical information to determine patterns in and/or evidence about the natural and designed world(s). • Describe how specific images (e.g., a diagram showing how a machine works) support a scientific or engineering idea. • Obtain information using various texts, text features (e.g., headings, tables of contents, glossaries, electronic menus, icons), and other media that will be useful in answering a scientific question and/or supporting a scientific claim. • Communicate information or design ideas and/or solutions with others in oral and/or written forms using models, drawings, writing, or numbers that provide detail about scientific ideas, practices, and/or design ideas.	Obtaining, evaluating, and communicating information in 3–5 builds on K–2 experiences and progresses to evaluating the merit and accuracy of ideas and methods. • Read and comprehend grade-appropriate complex texts and/or other reliable media to summarize and obtain scientific and technical ideas and describe how they are supported by evidence. • Compare and/or combine across complex texts and/or other reliable media to support the engagement in other scientific and/or engineering practices. • Combine information in written text with that contained in corresponding tables, diagrams, and/or charts to support the engagement in other scientific and/or engineering practices. • Obtain and combine information from books and/or other reliable media to explain phenomena or solutions to a design problem. • Communicate scientific and/or technical information orally and/or in written formats, including various forms of media as well as tables, diagrams, and charts.	Obtaining, evaluating, and communicating information in 6–8 builds on K–5 experiences and progresses to evaluating the merit and validity of ideas and methods. • Critically read scientific texts adapted for classroom use to determine the central ideas and/or obtain scientific and/or technical information to describe patterns in and/or evidence about the natural and designed world(s). • Integrate qualitative and/or quantitative scientific and/or technical information in written text with that contained in media and visual displays to clarify claims and findings. • Gather, read, and synthesize information from multiple appropriate sources and assess the credibility, accuracy, and possible bias of each publication and methods used, and describe how they are supported or not supported by evidence. • Evaluate data, hypotheses, and/or conclusions in scientific and technical texts in light of competing information or accounts. • Communicate scientific and/or technical information (e.g., about a proposed object, tool, process, system) in writing and/or through oral presentations.	Obtaining, evaluating, and communicating information in 9–12 builds on K–8 experiences and progresses to evaluating the validity and reliability of the claims, methods, and designs. • Critically read scientific literature adapted for classroom use to determine the central ideas or conclusions and/or to obtain scientific and/or technical information to summarize complex evidence, concepts, processes, or information presented in a text by paraphrasing them in simpler but still accurate terms. • Compare, integrate, and evaluate sources of information presented in different media or formats (e.g., visually, quantitatively) as well as in words in order to address a scientific question or solve a problem. • Gather, read, and evaluate scientific and/or technical information from multiple authoritative sources, assessing the evidence and usefulness of each source. • Evaluate the validity and reliability of, and/or synthesize, multiple claims, methods, and/or designs that appear in scientific and technical texts or media reports, verifying the data when possible. • Communicate scientific and/or technical information or ideas (e.g., about phenomena and/or the process of development and the design and performance of a proposed process or system) in multiple formats (i.e., orally, graphically, textually, mathematically).

REFLECTING ON THE PRACTICES OF SCIENCE AND ENGINEERING

Engaging students in the practices of science and engineering outlined in this section is not sufficient for science literacy. It is also important for students to stand back and reflect on how these practices have contributed to their own development and to the accumulation of scientific knowledge and engineering accomplishments over the ages. Accomplishing this is a matter for curriculum and instruction, rather than standards, so specific guidelines are not provided in this document. Nonetheless, this section would not be complete without an acknowledgment that reflection is essential if students are to become aware of themselves as competent and confident learners and doers in the realms of science and engineering.

REFERENCES

Bell, P., Bricker, L., Tzou, C., Lee., T., and Van Horne, K. (2012). Exploring the science framework; Engaging learners in science practices related to obtaining, evaluating, and communicating information. *Science Scope* 36(3):18–22.

Lee, O., Quinn, H., and Valdés, G. (in press). Science and language for English language learners in relation to Next Generation Science Standards and with implications for Common Core State Standards for English language arts and mathematics. *Educational Researcher.*

NRC (National Research Council). (2012). *A framework for K–12 science education: Practices, crosscutting concepts, and core ideas.* Washington, DC: The National Academies Press.

Alternate Arrangement of the Practices Matrix

Science and Engineering Practices	K–2 Condensed Practices	3–5 Condensed Practices	6–8 Condensed Practices	9–12 Condensed Practices
Asking Questions and Defining Problems A practice of science is to ask and refine questions that lead to descriptions and explanations of how the natural and designed world(s) works and which can be empirically tested. Engineering questions clarify problems to determine criteria for successful solutions and identify constraints to solve problems about the designed world. Both scientists and engineers also ask questions to clarify ideas.	Asking questions and defining problems in K–2 builds on prior experiences and progresses to simple descriptive questions that can be tested.	Asking questions and defining problems in 3–5 builds on K–2 experiences and progresses to specifying qualitative relationships.	Asking questions and defining problems in 6–8 builds on K–5 experiences and progresses to specifying relationships between variables and clarifying arguments and models.	Asking questions and defining problems in 9–12 builds on K–8 experiences and progresses to formulating, refining, and evaluating empirically testable questions and design problems using models and simulations.

	• Ask questions based on observations to find more information about the natural and/or designed world(s).	• Ask questions about what would happen if a variable is changed.	• Ask questions
			  o that arise from careful observation of phenomena, models, or unexpected results, to clarify and/or seek additional information.
			  o to identify and/or clarify evidence and/or the premise(s) of an argument.
			  o to determine relationships between independent and dependent variables and relationships in models.
			  o to clarify and/or refine a model, an explanation, or an engineering problem.
				• Ask questions
				  o that arise from careful observation of phenomena, or unexpected results, to clarify and/or seek additional information.
				  o that arise from examining models or a theory, to clarify and/or seek additional information and relationships.
				  o to determine relationships, including quantitative relationships, between independent and dependent variables.
				  o to clarify and refine a model, an explanation, or an engineering problem.

	• Ask and/or identify questions that can be answered by an investigation.	• Identify scientific (testable) and non-scientific (non-testable) questions. • Ask questions that can be investigated and predict reasonable outcomes based on patterns such as cause and effect relationships.	• Ask questions that require sufficient and appropriate empirical evidence to answer. • Ask questions that can be investigated within the scope of the classroom, outdoor environment, and museums and other public facilities with available resources and, when appropriate, frame a hypothesis based on observations and scientific principles.	• Evaluate a question to determine if it is testable and relevant. • Ask questions that can be investigated within the scope of the school laboratory, research facilities, or field (e.g., outdoor environment) with available resources and, when appropriate, frame a hypothesis based on a model or theory.
			• Ask questions that challenge the premise(s) of an argument or the interpretation of a data set.	• Ask and/or evaluate questions that challenge the premise(s) of an argument, the interpretation of a data set, or the suitability of a design.

Alternate Arrangement of the Practices Matrix

Science and Engineering Practices	K–2 Condensed Practices	3–5 Condensed Practices	6–8 Condensed Practices	9–12 Condensed Practices
Asking Questions and Defining Problems (*continued*)	• Define a simple problem that can be solved through the development of a new or improved object or tool.	• Use prior knowledge to describe problems that can be solved. • Define a simple design problem that can be solved through the development of an object, tool, process, or system and includes several criteria for success and constraints on materials, time, or cost.	• Define a design problem that can be solved through the development of an object, tool, process, or system and includes multiple criteria and constraints, including scientific knowledge that may limit possible solutions.	• Define a design problem that involves the development of a process or system with interacting components and criteria and constraints that may include social, technical, and/or environmental considerations. • Analyze complex real-world problems by specifying criteria and constraints for successful solutions.
Developing and Using Models A practice of both science and engineering is to use and construct models as helpful tools for representing ideas and explanations. These tools include diagrams, drawings, physical replicas, mathematical representations, analogies, and computer simulations. Modeling tools are used to develop questions, predictions, and explanations; analyze and identify flaws in systems; and communicate ideas. Models are used to build and revise scientific explanations and proposed engineered systems. Measurements and observations are used to revise models and designs.	Modeling in K–2 builds on prior experiences and progresses to include using and developing models (i.e., diagram, drawing, physical replica, diorama, dramatization, or storyboard) that represent concrete events or design solutions.	Modeling in 3–5 builds on K–2 experiences and progresses to building and revising simple models and using models to represent events and design solutions.	Modeling in 6–8 builds on K–5 experiences and progresses to developing, using, and revising models to describe, test, and predict more abstract phenomena and design systems.	Modeling in 9–12 builds on K–8 experiences and progresses to using, synthesizing, and developing models to predict and show relationships among variables between systems and their components in the natural and designed world(s).
	• Distinguish between a model and the actual object, process, and/or events the model represents. • Compare models to identify common features and differences.	• Identify limitations of models.	• Evaluate limitations of a model for a proposed object or tool.	• Evaluate merits and limitations of two different models of the same proposed tool, process, mechanism, or system in order to select or revise a model that best fits the evidence or design criteria. • Design a test of a model to ascertain its reliability.

Alternate Arrangement of the Practices Matrix

Science and Engineering Practices	K–2 Condensed Practices	3–5 Condensed Practices	6–8 Condensed Practices	9–12 Condensed Practices
Developing and Using Models	• Develop and/or use a model to represent amounts, relationships, relative scales (bigger, smaller), and/or patterns in the natural and designed world(s).	• Collaboratively develop and/or revise a model based on evidence that shows the relationships among variables for frequent and regular occurring events. • Develop a model using an analogy, example, or abstract representation to describe a scientific principle or design solution. • Develop and/or use models to describe and/or predict phenomena.	• Develop or modify a model—based on evidence—to match what happens if a variable or component of a system is changed. • Use and/or develop a model of simple systems with uncertain and less predictable factors. • Develop and/or revise a model to show the relationships among variables, including those that are not observable but predict observable phenomena. • Develop and/or use a model to predict and/or describe phenomena. • Develop a model to describe unobservable mechanisms.	• Develop, revise, and/or use a model based on evidence to illustrate and/or predict the relationships between systems or between components of a system. • Develop and/or use multiple types of models to provide mechanistic accounts and/or predict phenomena, and move flexibly between model types based on merits and limitations.
	• Develop a simple model based on evidence to represent a proposed object or tool.	• Develop a diagram or simple physical prototype to convey a proposed object, tool, or process. • Use a model to test cause and effect relationships or interactions concerning the functioning of a natural or designed system.	• Develop and/or use a model to generate data to test ideas about phenomena in natural or designed systems, including those representing inputs and outputs, and those at unobservable scales.	• Develop a complex model that allows for manipulation and testing of a proposed process or system. • Develop and/or use a model (including mathematical and computational) to generate data to support explanations, predict phenomena, analyze systems, and/or solve problems.

Alternate Arrangement of the Practices Matrix

Science and Engineering Practices	K–2 Condensed Practices	3–5 Condensed Practices	6–8 Condensed Practices	9–12 Condensed Practices
Planning and Carrying Out Investigations Scientists and engineers plan and carry out investigations in the field or laboratory, working collaboratively as well as individually. Their investigations are systematic and require clarifying what counts as data and identifying variables or parameters. Engineering investigations identify the effectiveness, efficiency, and durability of designs under different conditions.	Planning and carrying out investigations to answer questions or test solutions to problems in K–2 builds on prior experiences and progresses to simple investigations, based on fair tests, which provide data to support explanations or design solutions.	Planning and carrying out investigations to answer questions or test solutions to problems in 3–5 builds on K–2 experiences and progresses to include investigations that control variables and provide evidence to support explanations or design solutions.	Planning and carrying out investigations in 6–8 builds on K–5 experiences and progresses to include investigations that use multiple variables and provide evidence to support explanations or solutions.	Planning and carrying out investigations in 9–12 builds on K–8 experiences and progresses to include investigations that provide evidence for and test conceptual, mathematical, physical, and empirical models.
	• With guidance, plan and conduct an investigation in collaboration with peers (for K). • Plan and conduct an investigation collaboratively to produce data to serve as the basis for evidence to answer a question.	• Plan and conduct an investigation collaboratively to produce data to serve as the basis for evidence, using fair tests in which variables are controlled and the number of trials is considered.	Plan an investigation individually and collaboratively, and in the design identify independent and dependent variables and controls, what tools are needed to do the gathering, how measurements will be recorded, and how many data are needed to support a claim. Conduct an investigation and/or evaluate and/or revise the experimental design to produce data to serve as the basis for evidence that meet the goals of the investigation.	• Plan an investigation or test a design individually and collaboratively to produce data to serve as the basis for evidence as part of building and revising models, supporting explanations for phenomena, or testing solutions to problems. Consider possible confounding variables or effects and evaluate the investigation's design to ensure variables are controlled. • Plan and conduct an investigation individually and collaboratively to produce data to serve as the basis for evidence, and in the design decide on types, how much, and accuracy of data needed to produce reliable measurements and consider limitations on the precision of the data (e.g., number of trials, cost, risk, time), and refine the design accordingly. • Plan and conduct an investigation or test a design solution in a safe and ethical manner, including considerations of environmental, social, and personal impacts.
	• Evaluate different ways of observing and/or measuring a phenomenon to determine which way can answer a question.	• Evaluate appropriate methods and/or tools for collecting data.	• Evaluate the accuracy of various methods for collecting data.	• Select appropriate tools to collect, record, analyze, and evaluate data.

Alternate Arrangement of the Practices Matrix

Science and Engineering Practices	K–2 Condensed Practices	3–5 Condensed Practices	6–8 Condensed Practices	9–12 Condensed Practices
Planning and Carrying Out Investigations	• Make observations (firsthand or from media) and/or measurements to collect data that can be used to make comparisons. • Make observations (firsthand or from media) and/or measurements of a proposed object, tool, or solution to determine if it solves a problem or meets a goal. • Make predictions based on prior experiences.	• Make observations and/or measurements to produce data to serve as the basis for evidence for an explanation of a phenomenon or to test a design solution. • Make predictions about what would happen if a variable changes. • Test two different models of the same proposed object, tool, or process to determine which better meets criteria for success.	• Collect data to produce data to serve as the basis for evidence to answer scientific questions or test design solutions under a range of conditions. • Collect data about the performance of a proposed object, tool, process, or system under a range of conditions.	• Make directional hypotheses that specify what happens to a dependent variable when an independent variable is manipulated. • Manipulate variables and collect data about a complex model of a proposed process or system to identify failure points or improve performance relative to criteria for success or other variables.
Analyzing and Interpreting Data Scientific investigations produce data that must be analyzed in order to derive meaning. Because data patterns and trends are not always obvious, scientists use a range of tools—including tabulation, graphical interpretation, visualization, and statistical analysis—to identify the significant features and patterns in the data. Scientists identify sources of error in the investigations and calculate the degree of certainty in the results. Modern technology makes the collection of large data sets much easier, providing secondary sources for analysis.	Analyzing data in K–2 builds on prior experiences and progresses to collecting, recording, and sharing observations.	Analyzing data in 3–5 builds on K–2 experiences and progresses to introducing quantitative approaches to collecting data and conducting multiple trials of qualitative observations. When possible and feasible, digital tools should be used.	Analyzing data in 6–8 builds on K–5 experiences and progresses to extending quantitative analysis to investigations, distinguishing between correlation and causation, and basic statistical techniques of data and error analysis.	Analyzing data in 9–12 builds on K–8 experiences and progresses to introducing more detailed statistical analysis, the comparison of data sets for consistency, and the use of models to generate and analyze data.

Alternate Arrangement of the Practices Matrix

Science and Engineering Practices	K–2 Condensed Practices	3–5 Condensed Practices	6–8 Condensed Practices	9–12 Condensed Practices
Analyzing and Interpreting Data (*continued*) Engineering investigations include analysis of data collected in the tests of designs. This allows comparison of different solutions and determines how well each meets specific design criteria—that is, which design best solves the problem within given constraints. Like scientists, engineers require a range of tools to identify patterns within data and interpret the results. Advances in science make analysis of proposed solutions more efficient and effective.	• Record information (observations, thoughts, and ideas). • Use and share pictures, drawings, and/or writings of observations. • Use observations (firsthand or from media) to describe patterns and/or relationships in the natural and designed world(s) in order to answer scientific questions and solve problems. • Compare predictions (based on prior experiences) to what occurred (observable events).	• Represent data in tables and/or various graphical displays (bar graphs, pictographs, and/or pie charts) to reveal patterns that indicate relationships.	• Construct, analyze, and/or interpret graphical displays of data and/or large data sets to identify linear and nonlinear relationships. • Use graphical displays (e.g., maps, charts, graphs, and/or tables) of large data sets to identify temporal and spatial relationships. • Distinguish between causal and correlational relationships in data. • Analyze and interpret data to provide evidence for phenomena.	• Analyze data using tools, technologies, and/or models (e.g., computational, mathematical) in order to make valid and reliable scientific claims or determine an optimal design solution.
		• Analyze and interpret data to make sense of phenomena, using logical reasoning, mathematics, and/or computation.	• Apply concepts of statistics and probability (including mean, median, mode, and variability) to analyze and characterize data, using digital tools when feasible.	• Apply concepts of statistics and probability (including determining function fits to data, slope, intercept, and correlation coefficient for linear fits) to scientific and engineering questions and problems, using digital tools when feasible.
			• Consider limitations of data analysis (e.g., measurement error) and/or seek to improve precision and accuracy of data with better technological tools and methods (e.g., multiple trials).	• Consider limitations of data analysis (e.g., measurement error, sample selection) when analyzing and interpreting data.
		• Compare and contrast data collected by different groups in order to discuss similarities and differences in their findings.	• Analyze and interpret data to determine similarities and differences in findings.	• Compare and contrast various types of data sets (e.g., self-generated, archival) to examine consistency of measurements and observations.

Alternate Arrangement of the Practices Matrix

Science and Engineering Practices	K–2 Condensed Practices	3–5 Condensed Practices	6–8 Condensed Practices	9–12 Condensed Practices
Analyzing and Interpreting Data	• Analyze data from tests of an object or tool to determine if it works as intended.	• Analyze data to refine a problem statement or the design of a proposed object, tool, or process. • Use data to evaluate and refine design solutions.	• Analyze data to define an optimal operational range for a proposed object, tool, process, or system that best meets criteria for success.	• Evaluate the impact of new data on a working explanation and/or model of a proposed process or system. • Analyze data to identify design features or characteristics of the components of a proposed process or system to optimize it relative to criteria for success.
Using Mathematics and Computational Thinking In both science and engineering, mathematics and computation are fundamental tools for representing physical variables and their relationships. They are used for a range of tasks such as constructing simulations; solving equations exactly or approximately; and recognizing, expressing, and applying quantitative relationships. Mathematical and computational approaches enable scientists and engineers to predict the behavior of systems and test the validity of such predictions.	Mathematical and computational thinking in K–2 builds on prior experience and progresses to recognizing that mathematics can be used to describe the natural and designed world(s).	Mathematical and computational thinking in 3–5 builds on K–2 experiences and progresses to extending quantitative measurements to a variety of physical properties and using computation and mathematics to analyze data and compare alternative design solutions.	Mathematical and computational thinking in 6–8 builds on K–5 experiences and progresses to identifying patterns in large data sets and using mathematical concepts to support explanations and arguments.	Mathematical and computational thinking in 9–12 builds on K–8 and experiences and progresses to using algebraic thinking and analysis, a range of linear and non-linear functions, including trigonometric functions, exponentials and logarithms, and computational tools for statistical analysis to analyze, represent, and model data. Simple computational simulations are created and used based on mathematical models of basic assumptions.
	• Decide when to use qualitative vs. quantitative data.	• Decide if qualitative or quantitative data are best to determine whether a proposed object or tool meets criteria for success.		
	• Use counting and numbers to identify and describe patterns in the natural and designed world(s).	• Organize simple data sets to reveal patterns that suggest relationships.	• Use digital tools (e.g., computers) to analyze very large data sets for patterns and trends.	• Create and/or revise a computational model or simulation of a phenomenon, designed device, process, or system.
	• Describe, measure, and/or compare quantitative attributes of different objects and display the data using simple graphs.	• Describe, measure, estimate, and/or graph quantities such as area, volume, weight, and time to address scientific and engineering questions and problems.	• Use mathematical representations to describe and/or support scientific conclusions and design solutions.	• Use mathematical, computational, and/or algorithmic representations of phenomena or design solutions to describe and/or support claims and/or explanations.

Alternate Arrangement of the Practices Matrix

Science and Engineering Practices	K–2 Condensed Practices	3–5 Condensed Practices	6–8 Condensed Practices	9–12 Condensed Practices
Using Mathematics and Computational Thinking (*continued*)	• Use quantitative data to compare two alternative solutions to a problem.	• Create and/or use graphs and/or charts generated from simple algorithms to compare alternative solutions to an engineering problem.	• Create algorithms (a series of ordered steps) to solve a problem. • Apply mathematical concepts and/or processes (such as ratio, rate, percent, basic operations, and simple algebra) to scientific and engineering questions and problems. • Use digital tools and/or mathematical concepts and arguments to test and compare proposed solutions to an engineering design problem.	• Apply techniques of algebra and functions to represent and solve scientific and engineering problems. • Use simple limit cases to test mathematical expressions, computer programs, algorithms, or simulations of a process or system to see if a model "makes sense" by comparing the outcomes with what is known about the real world. • Apply ratios, rates, percentages, and unit conversions in the context of complicated measurement problems involving quantities with derived or compound units (such as mg/mL, kg/m^3, acre-feet, etc.).
Constructing Explanations and Designing Solutions The end products of science are explanations, and the end products of engineering are solutions. The goal of science is the construction of theories that provide explanatory accounts of the world. A theory becomes accepted when it has multiple lines of empirical evidence and greater explanatory power of phenomena than previous theories.	Constructing explanations and designing solutions in K–2 builds on prior experiences and progresses to the use of evidence and ideas in constructing evidence-based accounts of natural phenomena and designing solutions.	Constructing explanations and designing solutions in 3–5 builds on K–2 experiences and progresses to the use of evidence in constructing explanations that specify variables that describe and predict phenomena and in designing multiple solutions to design problems.	Constructing explanations and designing solutions in 6–8 builds on K–5 experiences and progresses to include constructing explanations and designing solutions supported by multiple sources of evidence consistent with scientific ideas, principles, and theories.	Constructing explanations and designing solutions in 9–12 builds on K–8 experiences and progresses to explanations and designs that are supported by multiple and independent student-generated sources of evidence consistent with scientific ideas, principles, and theories.

Alternate Arrangement of the Practices Matrix

Science and Engineering Practices	K–2 Condensed Practices	3–5 Condensed Practices	6–8 Condensed Practices	9–12 Condensed Practices
Constructing Explanations and Designing Solutions The goal of engineering design is to find a systematic solution to problems that is based on scientific knowledge and models of the material world. Each proposed solution results from a process of balancing competing criteria of desired functions, technical feasibility, cost, safety, aesthetics, and compliance with legal requirements. The optimal choice depends on how well the proposed solutions meet criteria and constraints.	• Use information from observations (firsthand and from media) to construct an evidence-based account for natural phenomena.	• Construct an explanation of observed relationships (e.g., the distribution of plants in a backyard).	• Construct an explanation that includes qualitative or quantitative relationships between variables that predict(s) and/or describe(s) phenomena. • Construct an explanation using models or representations.	• Make a quantitative and/or qualitative claim regarding the relationship between dependent and independent variables.
		• Use evidence (e.g., measurements, observations, patterns) to construct or support an explanation or design a solution to a problem.	• Construct a scientific explanation based on valid and reliable evidence obtained from sources (including students' own experiments) and the assumption that theories and laws that describe the natural world operate today as they did in the past and will continue to do so in the future. • Apply scientific ideas, principles, and/or evidence to construct, revise, and/or use an explanation for real-world phenomena, examples, or events.	• Construct and revise an explanation based on valid and reliable evidence obtained from a variety of sources (including students' own investigations, models, theories, simulations, peer review) and the assumption that theories and laws that describe the natural world operate today as they did in the past and will continue to do so in the future. • Apply scientific ideas, principles, and/or evidence to provide an explanation of phenomena and solve design problems, taking into account possible unanticipated effects.
		• Identify evidence that supports particular points in an explanation.	• Apply scientific reasoning to show why the data or evidence is adequate for the explanation or conclusion.	• Apply scientific reasoning, theory, and/or models to link evidence to claims to assess the extent to which the reasoning and data support the explanation or conclusion.
	• Use tools and/or materials to design and/or build a device that solves a specific problem or a solution to a specific problem. • Generate and/or compare multiple solutions to a problem.	• Apply scientific ideas to solve design problems. • Generate and compare multiple solutions to a problem based on how well they meet the criteria and constraints of the design solution.	• Apply scientific ideas or principles to design, construct, and/or test a design of an object, tool, process, or system. • Undertake a design project, engaging in the design cycle, to construct and/or implement a solution that meets specific design criteria and constraints. • Optimize performance of a design by prioritizing criteria, making tradeoffs, testing, revising, and re-testing.	• Design, evaluate, and/or refine a solution to a complex real-world problem, based on scientific knowledge, student-generated sources of evidence, prioritized criteria, and tradeoff considerations.

Alternate Arrangement of the Practices Matrix

Science and Engineering Practices	K–2 Condensed Practices	3–5 Condensed Practices	6–8 Condensed Practices	9–12 Condensed Practices
Engaging in Argument from Evidence Argumentation is the process by which evidence-based conclusions and solutions are reached. In science and engineering, reasoning and argument based on evidence are essential to identifying the best explanation for a natural phenomenon or the best solution to a design problem. Scientists and engineers use argumentation to listen to, compare, and evaluate competing ideas and methods based on merits. Scientists and engineers engage in argumentation when investigating a phenomenon, testing a design solution, resolving questions about measurements, building data models, and using evidence to evaluate claims.	Engaging in argument from evidence in K–2 builds on prior experiences and progresses to comparing ideas and representations about the natural and designed world(s).	Engaging in argument from evidence in 3–5 builds on K–2 experiences and progresses to critiquing the scientific explanations or solutions proposed by peers by citing relevant evidence about the natural and designed world(s).	Engaging in argument from evidence in 6–8 builds on K–5 experiences and progresses to constructing a convincing argument that supports or refutes claims for either explanations or solutions about the natural and designed world(s).	Engaging in argument from evidence in 9–12 builds on K–8 experiences and progresses to using appropriate and sufficient evidence and scientific reasoning to defend and critique claims and explanations about the natural and designed world(s). Arguments may also come from current scientific or historical episodes in science.
	• Identify arguments that are supported by evidence. • Distinguish between explanations that account for all gathered evidence and those that do not. • Analyze why some evidence is relevant to a scientific question and some is not. • Distinguish between opinions and evidence in one's own explanations.	• Compare and refine arguments based on an evaluation of the evidence presented. • Distinguish among facts, reasoned judgment based on research findings, and speculation in an explanation.	• Compare and critique two arguments on the same topic and analyze whether they emphasize similar or different evidence and/or interpretations of facts.	• Compare and evaluate competing arguments or design solutions in light of currently accepted explanations, new evidence, limitations (e.g., trade-offs), constraints, and ethical issues. • Evaluate the claims, evidence, and/or reasoning behind currently accepted explanations or solutions to determine the merits of arguments.
	• Listen actively to arguments to indicate agreement or disagreement based on evidence and/or to retell the main points of the argument.	• Respectfully provide and receive critiques from peers about a proposed procedure, explanation, or model by citing relevant evidence and posing specific questions.	• Respectfully provide and receive critiques about one's explanations, procedures, models, and questions by citing relevant evidence and posing and responding to questions that elicit pertinent elaboration and detail.	• Respectfully provide and/or receive critiques on scientific arguments by probing reasoning and evidence and challenging ideas and conclusions, responding thoughtfully to diverse perspectives, and determining what additional information is required to resolve contradictions.
	• Construct an argument with evidence to support a claim.	• Construct and/or support an argument with evidence, data, and/or a model. • Use data to evaluate claims about cause and effect.	• Construct, use, and/or present an oral and written argument supported by empirical evidence and scientific reasoning to support or refute an explanation or a model for a phenomenon or a solution to a problem.	• Construct, use, and/or present an oral and written argument or counter-arguments based on data and evidence.

Alternate Arrangement of the Practices Matrix

Science and Engineering Practices	K–2 Condensed Practices	3–5 Condensed Practices	6–8 Condensed Practices	9–12 Condensed Practices
Engaging in Argument from Evidence	• Make a claim about the effectiveness of an object, tool, or solution that is supported by relevant evidence.	• Make a claim about the merit of a solution to a problem by citing relevant evidence about how it meets the criteria and constraints of the problem.	• Make an oral or written argument that supports or refutes the advertised performance of a device, process, or system, based on empirical evidence concerning whether or not the technology meets relevant criteria and constraints. • Evaluate competing design solutions based on jointly developed and agreed-upon design criteria.	• Make and defend a claim based on evidence about the natural world or the effectiveness of a design solution that reflects scientific knowledge and student-generated evidence. • Evaluate competing design solutions to a real-world problem based on scientific ideas and principles, empirical evidence, and/or logical arguments regarding relevant factors (e.g., economic, societal, environmental, ethical considerations).
Obtaining, Evaluating, and Communicating Information Scientists and engineers must be able to communicate clearly and persuasively the ideas and methods they generate. Critiquing and communicating ideas individually and in groups is a critical professional activity.	Obtaining, evaluating, and communicating information in K–2 builds on prior experiences and uses observations and texts to communicate new information.	Obtaining, evaluating, and communicating information in 3–5 builds on K–2 experiences and progresses to evaluating the merit and accuracy of ideas and methods.	Obtaining, evaluating, and communicating information in 6–8 builds on K–5 experiences and progresses to evaluating the merit and validity of ideas and methods.	Obtaining, evaluating, and communicating information in 9–12 builds on K–8 experiences and progresses to evaluating the validity and reliability of claims, methods, and designs.
	• Read grade-appropriate texts and/or use media to obtain scientific and/or technical information to determine patterns in and/or evidence about the natural and designed world(s).	• Read and comprehend grade-appropriate complex texts and/or other reliable media to summarize and obtain scientific and technical ideas and describe how they are supported by evidence. • Compare and/or combine across complex texts and/or other reliable media to support the engagement in other scientific and/or engineering practices.	• Critically read scientific texts adapted for classroom use to determine the central ideas and/or obtain scientific and/or technical information to describe patterns in and/or evidence about the natural and designed world(s).	• Critically read scientific literature adapted for classroom use to determine the central ideas or conclusions and/or to obtain scientific and/or technical information to summarize complex evidence, concepts, processes, or information presented in a text by paraphrasing them in simpler but still accurate terms.
	• Describe how specific images (e.g., a diagram showing how a machine works) support a scientific or engineering idea.	• Combine information in written text with that contained in corresponding tables, diagrams, and/or charts to support the engagement in other scientific and/or engineering practices.	• Integrate qualitative and/or quantitative scientific and/or technical information in written text with that contained in media and visual displays to clarify claims and findings.	• Compare, integrate, and evaluate sources of information presented in different media or formats (e. g., visually, quantitatively) and in words in order to address a scientific question or solve a problem.

Alternate Arrangement of the Practices Matrix

Science and Engineering Practices	K–2 Condensed Practices	3–5 Condensed Practices	6–8 Condensed Practices	9–12 Condensed Practices
Obtaining, Evaluating, and Communicating Information (*continued*) Communicating information and ideas can be done in multiple ways: using tables, diagrams, graphs, models, and equations as well as orally, in writing, and through extended discussions. Scientists and engineers employ multiple sources to obtain information that is used to evaluate the merit and validity of claims, methods, and designs.	• Obtain information using various texts, text features (e.g., headings, tables of contents, glossaries, electronic menus, icons), and other media that will be useful in answering a scientific question and/or supporting a scientific claim.	• Obtain and combine information from books and/or other reliable media to explain phenomena or solutions to a design problem.	• Gather, read, and synthesize information from multiple appropriate sources and assess the credibility, accuracy, and possible bias of each publication and the methods used, and describe how they are supported or not supported by evidence. • Evaluate data, hypotheses, and/or conclusions in scientific and technical texts in light of competing information or accounts.	• Gather, read, and evaluate scientific and/or technical information from multiple authoritative sources, assessing the evidence and usefulness of each source. • Evaluate the validity and reliability of and/or synthesize multiple claims, methods, and/or designs that appear in scientific and technical texts or media reports, verifying the data when possible.
	• Communicate information or design ideas and/or solutions with others in oral and/or written forms using models, drawings, writing, or numbers that provide detail about scientific ideas, practices, and/or design ideas.	• Communicate scientific and/or technical information orally and/or in written formats, including various forms of media as well as tables, diagrams, and charts.	• Communicate scientific and/or technical information (e.g., about a proposed object, tool, process, system) in writing and/or through oral presentations.	• Communicate scientific and/or technical information or ideas (e.g., about phenomena and/or the process of development and the design and performance of a proposed process or system) in multiple formats (including orally, graphically, textually, and mathematically).

APPENDIX G
CROSSCUTTING CONCEPTS IN THE NEXT GENERATION SCIENCE STANDARDS

Crosscutting concepts have value because they provide students with connections and intellectual tools that are related across the differing areas of disciplinary content and can enrich their application of practices and their understanding of core ideas. (NRC, 2012, p. 233)

A Framework for K–12 Science Education: Practices, Crosscutting Concepts, and Core Ideas (*Framework*) recommends science education in grades K–12 be built around three major dimensions: science and engineering practices, crosscutting concepts that unify the study of science and engineering through their common application across fields, and core ideas in the major disciplines of natural science. The purpose of this appendix is to describe the second dimension—crosscutting concepts—and to explain its role in the Next Generation Science Standards (NGSS).

The *Framework* identifies seven crosscutting concepts that bridge disciplinary boundaries, uniting core ideas throughout the fields of science and engineering. Their purpose is to help students deepen their understanding of the disciplinary core ideas (pp. 2 and 8) and develop a coherent and scientifically based view of the world (p. 83). The seven crosscutting concepts presented in Chapter 4 of the *Framework* are as follows:

1. *Patterns*. Observed patterns of forms and events guide organization and classification, and they prompt questions about relationships and the factors that influence them.

2. *Cause and effect: Mechanism and explanation.* Events have causes, sometimes simple, sometimes multi-faceted. A major activity of science is investigating and explaining causal relationships and the mechanisms by which they are mediated. Such mechanisms can then be tested across given contexts and used to predict and explain events in new contexts.

3. *Scale, proportion, and quantity.* In considering phenomena, it is critical to recognize what is relevant at different measures of size, time, and energy and to recognize how changes in scale, proportion, or quantity affect a system's structure or performance.

4. *Systems and system models.* Defining the system under study—specifying its boundaries and making explicit a model of that system—provides tools for understanding and testing ideas that are applicable throughout science and engineering.

5. *Energy and matter: Flows, cycles, and conservation.* Tracking fluxes of energy and matter into, out of, and within systems helps one understand the systems' possibilities and limitations.

6. *Structure and function.* The way in which an object or living thing is shaped and its substructure determine many of its properties and functions.

7. *Stability and change.* For natural and built systems alike, conditions of stability and determinants of rates of change or evolution of a system are critical elements of study.

The *Framework* notes that crosscutting concepts have been featured prominently for the past two decades in other documents about what all students should learn about science. These have been called "themes" in *Science for All Americans* (AAAS, 1989) and *Benchmarks for Science Literacy* (1993), "unifying principles" in *National Science Education Standards* (NRC, 1996), and "crosscutting ideas" the National Science Teachers Association's *Science Anchors Project* (NSTA, 2010). Although these ideas have been consistently included in previous standards documents, the *Framework* recognizes that "students have often been expected to build such knowledge without any explicit instructional support. Hence the purpose of highlighting them as Dimension 2 of the *Framework* is to elevate their role in the development of standards, curricula, instruction, and assessments" (p. 83). The NGSS writing team has continued this commitment by weaving crosscutting concepts into the performance expectations for all students—so they cannot be left out.

GUIDING PRINCIPLES

The *Framework* recommends crosscutting concepts be embedded in the science curriculum beginning in the earliest years of schooling and suggests a number of guiding principles for how they should be used. The development process of the standards provides insights into the crosscutting concepts. These insights are shared in the following guiding principles.

Crosscutting concepts can help students better understand core ideas in science and engineering. When students encounter new phenomena, whether in a science lab, on a field trip, or on their own, they need mental tools to help engage in and come to understand the phenomena from a scientific point of view. Familiarity with crosscutting concepts can provide that perspective. For example, when approaching a complex phenomenon (either a natural phenomenon or a machine), an approach that makes sense is to begin by observing and characterizing the phenomenon in terms of patterns. A next step might be to simplify the phenomenon by thinking of it as a system and modeling its components and how they interact. In some cases it would be useful to study how energy and matter flow through the system or how structure affects function (or malfunction). These preliminary studies may suggest explanations for the phenomena, which could be checked by predicting patterns that might emerge if the explanation is correct, and matching those predictions with those observed in the real world.

Crosscutting concepts can help students better understand science and engineering practices. Because the crosscutting concepts address the fundamental aspects of nature, they also inform the way humans attempt to understand it. Different crosscutting concepts align with different practices, and when students carry out these practices, they are often addressing one of these crosscutting concepts. For example, when students analyze and interpret data, they are often looking for patterns in observations, mathematical or visual. The practice of planning and carrying out an investigation is often aimed at identifying cause and effect relationships: If you poke or prod something, what will happen? The crosscutting concept of "systems and system models" is clearly related to the practice of developing and using models.

Repetition in different contexts will be necessary to build familiarity. Repetition is counter to the guiding principles the NGSS writing team used in creating performance expectations to reflect the core ideas in the science disciplines. In order to reduce the total amount of material students are held accountable to learn, repetition was reduced whenever possible. However, crosscutting concepts are repeated within grades at the elementary level and grade bands at the middle and high school levels so that these concepts "become common and familiar touchstones across the disciplines and grade levels" (p. 83).

Crosscutting concepts should grow in complexity and sophistication across the grades. Repetition alone is not sufficient. As students grow in their understanding of the science disciplines, depth of understanding crosscutting concepts should grow as well. The writing team adapted and added to the ideas expressed in the *Framework* in developing a matrix for use in crafting performance expectations that describe student understanding of the crosscutting concepts. The matrix is found at the end of this section.

Crosscutting concepts can provide a common vocabulary for science and engineering. The practices, disciplinary core ideas, and crosscutting concepts are the same in science and engineering. What is different is how and why they are used—to explain natural phenomena in science and to solve a problem or accomplish a goal in engineering. Students need both types of experiences to develop a deep and flexible understanding of how these terms are applied in each of these closely allied fields. As crosscutting concepts are encountered repeatedly across academic disciplines, familiar vocabulary can enhance engagement and understanding for English language learners, students with language processing difficulties, and students with limited literacy development.

Crosscutting concepts should not be assessed separately from practices or core ideas. Students should not be assessed on their ability to define "pattern," "system," or any other crosscutting concepts as a separate vocabulary word. To capture the vision in the *Framework*, students should be assessed on the extent to which they have achieved a coherent scientific worldview by recognizing similarities among core ideas in science or engineering that may at first seem very different, but are united through crosscutting concepts.

Performance expectations focus on some but not all capabilities associated with a crosscutting concept. As core ideas grow in complexity and sophistication across the grades, it becomes more and more difficult to express them fully in performance expectations. Consequently, most performance expectations reflect only some aspects of a crosscutting concept. These aspects are indicated in the right-hand foundation box in each standard. All aspects of each core idea considered by the writing team can be found in the matrix at the end of this section.

Crosscutting concepts are for all students. Crosscutting concepts raise the bar for students who have not achieved at high levels in academic subjects and who are often assigned to classes that emphasize the "basics," which in science may be taken to provide primarily factual information and lower-order thinking skills. Consequently, it is essential that *all students* engage in using crosscutting concepts, which could result in leveling the playing field and promoting deeper understanding for all students.

Inclusion of nature of science and engineering concepts. Sometimes included in the crosscutting concept foundation boxes are concepts related to materials from the "Nature of Science" or "Science, Technology, Society, and the Environment." These are not to be confused with the "Crosscutting Concepts," but rather represent an organizational structure of the NGSS that recognizes concepts from both the Nature of Science and Science, Technology, Society, and the Environment that extend across all of the sciences. Readers should review Appendixes H and J for further information on these ideas.

PROGRESSION OF CROSSCUTTING CONCEPTS ACROSS THE GRADES

Following is a brief summary of how each crosscutting concept increases in complexity and sophistication across the grades as envisioned in the *Framework*. Examples of performance expectations illustrate how these ideas play out in the NGSS.

1. "**Patterns** exist everywhere—in regularly occurring shapes or structures and in repeating events and relationships. For example, patterns are discernible in the symmetry of flowers and snowflakes, the cycling of the seasons, and the repeated base pairs of DNA" (p. 85).

While there are many patterns in nature, they are not the norm because there is a tendency for disorder to increase (e.g., it is far more likely for a broken glass to scatter than for scattered bits to assemble themselves into a whole glass). In some cases, order seems to emerge from chaos, as when a plant sprouts or a tornado appears amid scattered storm clouds. It is in such examples that patterns exist and the beauty of nature is found. "Noticing patterns is often a first step to organizing phenomena and asking scientific questions about why and how the patterns occur" (p. 85).

"Once patterns and variations have been noted, they lead to questions; scientists seek explanations for observed patterns and for the similarity and diversity within them. Engineers often look for and analyze patterns, too. For example, they may diagnose patterns of failure of a designed system under test in order to improve the design, or they may analyze patterns of daily and seasonal use of power to design a system that can meet the fluctuating needs" (pp. 85–86).

Patterns figure prominently in the science and engineering practice of "Analyzing and Interpreting Data." Recognizing patterns is a large part of working with data. Students might look at geographical patterns on a map, plot data values on a chart or graph, or visually inspect the appearance of an organism or mineral. The crosscutting concept of patterns is also strongly associated with the practice of "Using Mathematics and Computational Thinking." It is often the case that patterns

Crosscutting Concepts: Patterns

Progression Across the Grades	Performance Expectation from the NGSS
In grades K–2, children recognize that patterns in the natural and human designed world can be observed, used to describe phenomena, and used as evidence.	1-ESS1-1. Use observations of the sun, moon, and stars to describe patterns that can be predicted.
In grades 3–5, students identify similarities and differences in order to sort and classify natural objects and designed products. They identify patterns related to time, including simple rates of change and cycles, and use these patterns to make predictions.	4-PS4-1. Develop a model of waves to describe patterns in terms of amplitude and wavelength and that waves can cause objects to move.
In grades 6–8, students recognize that macroscopic patterns are related to the nature of microscopic and atomic-level structure. They identify patterns in rates of change and other numerical relationships that provide information about natural and human designed systems. They use patterns to identify cause and effect relationships, and use graphs and charts to identify patterns in data.	MS-LS4-1. Analyze and interpret data for patterns in the fossil record that document the existence, diversity, extinction, and change of life forms throughout the history of life on Earth under the assumption that natural laws operate today as in the past.
In grades 9–12, students observe patterns in systems at different scales and cite patterns as empirical evidence for causality in supporting their explanations of phenomena. They recognize that classifications or explanations used at one scale may not be useful or may need revision using a different scale, thus requiring improved investigations and experiments. They use mathematical representations to identify certain patterns and analyze patterns of performance in order to reengineer and improve a designed system.	HS-PS1-2. Construct and revise an explanation for the outcome of a simple chemical reaction based on the outermost electron states of atoms, trends in the periodic table, and knowledge of the patterns of chemical properties.

are identified best by using mathematical concepts. As Richard Feynman said, "To those who do not know mathematics it is difficult to get across a real feeling as to the beauty, the deepest beauty, of nature. If you want to learn about nature, to appreciate nature, it is necessary to understand the language that she speaks in."

The human brain is remarkably adept at identifying patterns, and students progressively build on this innate ability throughout their school experiences. The following table lists the guidelines used by the writing team for how this progression plays out across K–12, with examples of performance expectations drawn from the NGSS.

2. Cause and Effect is often the next step in science, after a discovery of patterns or events that occur together with regularity. A search for the underlying cause of a phenomenon has sparked some of the most compelling and productive scientific investigations. "Any tentative answer, or 'hypothesis,' that A causes B requires a model or mechanism for the chain of interactions that connect A and B. For example, the notion that diseases can be transmitted by a person's touch was initially treated with skepticism by the medical profession for lack of a plausible mechanism. Today infectious diseases are well understood as being transmitted by the passing of microscopic organisms (bacteria or viruses) between an infected person and another. A major activity of science is to uncover such causal connections, often with the hope that understanding the mechanisms will enable predictions and, in the case of infectious diseases, the design of preventive measures, treatments, and cures" (p. 87).

"In engineering, the goal is to design a system to cause a desired effect, so cause-and-effect relationships are as much a part of engineering as of science. Indeed, the process of design is a good place to help students begin to think in terms of cause and effect, because they must understand the underlying causal relationships in order to devise and explain a design that can achieve a specified objective" (p. 88).

Crosscutting Concepts: Cause and Effect

Progression Across the Grades	Performance Expectation from the NGSS
In grades K–2, students learn that events have causes that generate observable patterns. They design simple tests to gather evidence to support or refute their own ideas about causes.	1-PS4-3. Plan and conduct an investigation to determine the effect of placing objects made with different materials in the path of a beam of light.
In grades 3–5, students routinely identify and test causal relationships and use these relationships to explain change. They understand events that occur together with regularity might or might not signify a cause and effect relationship.	4-ESS2-1. Make observations and/or measurements to provide evidence of the effects of weathering or the rate of erosion by water, ice, wind, or vegetation.
In grades 6–8, students classify relationships as causal or correlational, and recognize that correlation does not necessarily imply causation. They use cause and effect relationships to predict phenomena in natural or designed systems. They also understand that phenomena may have more than one cause, and some cause and effect relationships in systems can only be described using probability.	MS-PS1-4. Develop a model that predicts and describes changes in particle motion, temperature, and state of a pure substance when thermal energy is added or removed.
In grades 9–12, students understand that empirical evidence is required to differentiate between cause and correlation and to make claims about specific causes and effects. They suggest cause and effect relationships to explain and predict behaviors in complex natural and designed systems. They also propose causal relationships by examining what is known about smaller-scale mechanisms within the system. They recognize changes in systems may have various causes that may not have equal effects.	HS-LS3-2. Make and defend a claim based on evidence that inheritable genetic variations may result from (1) new genetic combinations through meiosis, (2) viable errors occurring during replication, and/or (3) mutations caused by environmental factors.

When students perform the practice of "Planning and Carrying Out Investigations," they often address cause and effect. At early ages, this involves "doing" something to the system of study and then watching to see what happens. At later ages, experiments are set up to test the sensitivity of the parameters involved, and this is accomplished by making a change (cause) to a single component of a system and examining, and often quantifying, the result (effect). Cause and effect is also closely associated with the practice of "Engaging in Argument from Evidence." In scientific practice, deducing the cause of an effect is often difficult, so multiple hypotheses may coexist. For example, though the occurrence (effect) of historical mass extinctions of organisms, such as the dinosaurs, is well established, the reason or reasons for the extinctions (cause) are still debated, and scientists develop and debate their arguments based on different forms of evidence. When students engage in scientific argumentation, it is often centered about identifying the causes of an effect.

Crosscutting Concepts: Scale, Proportion, and Quantity

Progression Across the Grades	Performance Expectation from the NGSS
In grades K–2, students use relative scales (e.g., bigger and smaller; hotter and colder; faster and slower) to describe objects. They use standard units to measure length.	
In grades 3–5, students recognize that natural objects and observable phenomena exist from the very small to the immensely large. They use standard units to measure and describe physical quantities such as weight, time, temperature, and volume.	5-ESS1-1. Support an argument that the apparent brightness of the sun and stars is due to their relative distances from Earth.
In grades 6–8, students observe time, space, and energy phenomena at various scales using models to study systems that are too large or too small. They understand phenomena observed at one scale may not be observable at another scale and that the function of natural and designed systems may change with scale. They use proportional relationships (e.g., speed as the ratio of distance traveled to time taken) to gather information about the magnitude of properties and processes. They represent scientific relationships through the use of algebraic expressions and equations.	MS-LS1-1. Conduct an investigation to provide evidence that living things are made of cells; either one cell or many different numbers and types of cells.
In grades 9–12, students understand that the significance of a phenomenon is dependent on the scale, proportion, and quantity at which it occurs. They recognize that patterns observable at one scale may not be observable or exist at other scales and that some systems can only be studied indirectly as they are too small, too large, too fast, or too slow to observe directly. Students use orders of magnitude to understand how a model at one scale relates to a model at another scale. They use algebraic thinking to examine scientific data and predict the effect of a change in one variable on another (e.g., linear growth vs. exponential growth).	HS-ESS1-4. Use mathematical or computational representations to predict the motion of orbiting objects in the solar system.

3. Scale, Proportion, and Quantity are important in both science and engineering. These are fundamental assessments of dimension that form the foundation of observations about nature. Before an analysis of function or process can be made (the *how or why*), it is necessary to identify the *what*. These concepts are the starting point for scientific understanding, whether it is of a total system or its individual components. Any student who has ever played the game "20 questions" understands this inherently, asking questions such as, "Is it bigger than a bread box?" in order to first determine the object's size.

An understanding of scale involves not only understanding that systems and processes vary in size, time span, and energy, but also that different mechanisms operate at different scales. In engineering, "no structure could be conceived, much less constructed, without the engineer's precise sense of scale. . . . At a basic level, in order to identify something as bigger or smaller than something else—and

how much bigger or smaller—a student must appreciate the units used to measure it and develop a feel for quantity" (p. 90).

"The ideas of ratio and proportionality as used in science can extend and challenge students' mathematical understanding of these concepts. To appreciate the relative magnitude of some properties or processes, it may be necessary to grasp the relationships among different types of quantities—for example, speed as the ratio of distance traveled to time taken, density as a ratio of mass to volume. This use of ratio is quite different than a ratio of numbers describing fractions of a pie. Recognition of such relationships among different quantities is a key step in forming mathematical models that interpret scientific data" (p. 90).

The crosscutting concept of scale, proportion, and quantity figures prominently in the practices of "Using Mathematics and Computational Thinking" and "Analyzing and Interpreting Data." This concept addresses taking measurements of structures and

Crosscutting Concepts: Systems and System Models

Progression Across the Grades	Performance Expectation from the NGSS
In grades K–2, students understand that objects and organisms can be described in terms of their parts and that systems in the natural and designed world have parts that work together.	K-ESS3-1. Use a model to represent the relationship between the needs of different plants or animals (including humans) and the places they live.
In grades 3–5, students understand that a system is a group of related parts that make up a whole and can carry out functions its individual parts cannot. They can also describe a system in terms of its components and their interactions.	3-LS4-4. Make a claim about the merit of a solution to a problem caused when the environment changes and the types of plants and animals that live there may change.
In grades 6–8, students understand that systems may interact with other systems; they may have sub-systems and be a part of larger complex systems. They can use models to represent systems and their interactions—such as inputs, processes, and outputs—and energy, matter, and information flows within systems. They also learn that models are limited in that they only represent certain aspects of the system under study.	MS-PS2-4. Construct and present arguments using evidence to support the claim that gravitational interactions are attractive and depend on the masses of interacting objects.
In grades 9–12, students investigate or analyze a system by defining its boundaries and initial conditions, as well as its inputs and outputs. They use models (e.g., physical, mathematical, computer models) to simulate the flow of energy, matter, and interactions within and between systems at different scales. They also use models and simulations to predict the behavior of a system and recognize that these predictions have limited precision and reliability due to the assumptions and approximations inherent in the models. They also design systems to do specific tasks.	HS-LS2-5. Develop a model to illustrate the role of photosynthesis and cellular respiration in the cycling of carbon among the biosphere, atmosphere, hydrosphere, and geosphere.

phenomena, and these fundamental observations are usually obtained, analyzed, and interpreted quantitatively. This crosscutting concept also figures prominently in the practice of "Developing and Using Models." Scale and proportion are often best understood using models. For example, the relative scales of objects in the solar system or of the components of an atom are difficult to comprehend mathematically (because the numbers involved are either so large or so small), but visual or conceptual models make them much more understandable (e.g., if the solar system were the size of a penny, the Milky Way galaxy would be the size of Texas).

4. Systems and System Models are useful in science and engineering because the world is complex, so it is helpful to isolate a single system and construct a simplified model of it. "To do this, scientists and engineers imagine an artificial boundary between the system in question and everything else. They then examine the system in detail while treating the effects of things outside the boundary as either forces acting on the system or flows of matter and energy across it—for example, the gravitational force due to Earth on a book lying on a table or the carbon dioxide expelled by an organism. Consideration of flows into and out of the system is a crucial element of system design. In the laboratory or even in field research, the extent to which a system under study can be physically isolated or external conditions controlled is an important element of the design of an investigation and interpretation of results. . . . The properties and behavior of the whole system can be very different from those of any of its parts, and large systems may have emergent properties, such as the shape of a tree, that cannot be predicted in detail from knowledge about the components and their interactions" (p. 92).

"Models can be valuable in predicting a system's behaviors or in diagnosing problems or failures in its functioning, regardless of what type of system is being examined. . . . In a simple mechanical system, interactions among the parts are describable in terms of forces among them that cause changes in motion or physical stresses. In more complex systems, it is not always possible or useful

Crosscutting Concepts: Energy and Matter

Progression Across the Grades	Performance Expectation from the NGSS
In grades K–2, students observe that objects may break into smaller pieces, be put together into larger pieces, or change shapes.	2-PS1-3. Make observations to construct an evidence-based account of how an object made of a small set of pieces can be disassembled and made into a new object.
In grades 3–5, students learn matter is made of particles and that energy can be transferred in various ways and between objects. Students observe the conservation of matter by tracking matter flows and cycles before and after processes and by recognizing that the total weight of substances does not change.	5-LS1-1. Support an argument that plants get the materials they need for growth chiefly from air and water.
In grades 6–8, students learn that matter is conserved because atoms are conserved in physical and chemical processes. They also learn within a natural or designed system, the transfer of energy drives the motion and/or cycling of matter. Energy may take different forms (e.g., energy in fields, thermal energy, energy of motion). The transfer of energy can be tracked as energy flows through a designed or natural system.	MS-ESS2-4. Develop a model to describe the cycling of water through Earth's systems driven by energy from the sun and the force of gravity.
In grades 9–12, students learn that the total amount of energy and matter in closed systems is conserved. They can describe changes of energy and matter in a system in terms of energy and matter flows into, out of, and within that system. They also learn that energy cannot be created or destroyed. It only moves between one place and another place, between objects and/or fields, or between systems. Energy drives the cycling of matter within and between systems. In nuclear processes, atoms are not conserved, but the total number of protons plus neutrons is conserved.	HS-PS1-8. Develop models to illustrate changes in the composition of the nucleus of an atom and the energy released during the processes of fission, fusion, and radioactive decay.

to consider interactions at this detailed mechanical level, yet it is equally important to ask what interactions are occurring (e.g., predator-prey relationships in an ecosystem) and to recognize that they all involve transfers of energy, matter, and (in some cases) information among parts of the system. . . . Any model of a system incorporates assumptions and approximations; the key is to be aware of what they are and how they affect the model's reliability and precision. Predictions may be reliable but not precise or, worse, precise but not reliable; the degree of reliability and precision needed depends on the use to which the model will be put" (p. 93).

5. Energy and Matter are essential concepts in all disciplines of science and engineering, often in connection with systems. "The supply of energy and of each needed chemical element restricts a system's operation—for example, without inputs of energy (sunlight) and matter (carbon dioxide and water), a plant cannot

grow. Hence, it is very informative to track the transfers of matter and energy within, into, or out of any system under study.

"In many systems there also are cycles of various types. In some cases, the most readily observable cycling may be of matter—for example, water going back and forth between Earth's atmosphere and its surface and subsurface reservoirs. Any such cycle of matter also involves associated energy transfers at each stage, so to fully understand the water cycle, one must model not only how water moves between parts of the system but also the energy transfer mechanisms that are critical for that motion.

"Consideration of energy and matter inputs, outputs, and flows or transfers within a system or process are equally important for engineering. A major goal in design is to maximize certain types of energy output while minimizing others, in order to minimize the energy inputs needed to achieve a desired task" (p. 95).

Crosscutting Concepts: Structure and Function

Progression Across the Grades	Performance Expectation from the NGSS
In grades K–2, students observe that the shape and stability of structures of natural and designed objects are related to their function(s).	2-LS2-2. Develop a simple model that mimics the function of an animal in dispersing seeds or pollinating plants.
In grades 3–5, students learn that different materials have different substructures, which can sometimes be observed, and substructures have shapes and parts that serve functions.	
In grades 6–8, students model complex and microscopic structures and systems and visualize how their function depends on the shapes, composition, and relationships among its parts. They analyze many complex natural and designed structures and systems to determine how they function. They design structures to serve particular functions by taking into account properties of different materials and how materials can be shaped and used.	MS-PS4-2. Develop and use a model to describe that waves are reflected, absorbed, or transmitted through various materials.
In grades 9–12, students investigate systems by examining the properties of different materials, the structures of different components, and their interconnections to reveal a system's function and/or solve a problem. They infer the functions and properties of natural and designed objects and systems from their overall structure, the way their components are shaped and used, and the molecular substructures of their various materials.	HS-ESS2-5. Plan and conduct an investigation of the properties of water and its effects on Earth materials and surface processes.

6. Structure and Function are complementary properties. "The shape and stability of structures of natural and designed objects are related to their function(s). The functioning of natural and built systems alike depends on the shapes and relationships of certain key parts as well as on the properties of the materials from which they are made. A sense of scale is necessary in order to know what properties and what aspects of shape or material are relevant at a particular magnitude or in investigating particular phenomena—that is, the selection of an appropriate scale depends on the question being asked. For example, the substructures of molecules are not particularly important in understanding the phenomenon of pressure, but they are relevant to understanding why the ratio between temperature and pressure at constant volume is different for different substances.

"Similarly, understanding how a bicycle works is best addressed by examining the structures and their functions at the scale of, say, the frame, wheels, and pedals. However, building a lighter bicycle may require knowledge of the properties (such as rigidity and hardness) of the materials needed for specific parts of the bicycle. In that way, the builder can seek less dense materials with appropriate properties; this pursuit may lead in turn to an examination of the atomic-scale structure of candidate materials. As a result, new parts with the desired properties, possibly made of new materials, can be designed and fabricated" (pp. 96–97).

7. Stability and Change are the primary concerns of many, if not most, scientific and engineering endeavors. "Stability denotes a condition in which some aspects of a system are unchanging, at least at the scale of observation. Stability means that a small disturbance will fade away—that is, the system will stay in, or return to, the stable condition. Such stability can take different forms, with the simplest being a static equilibrium, such as a ladder leaning on a wall. By contrast, a system with steady inflows and outflows (i.e., constant conditions) is said to be in dynamic equilibrium. For example, a dam may be at a constant level with

Crosscutting Concepts: Stability and Change

Progression Across the Grades	Performance Expectation from the NGSS
In grades K–2, students observe that some things stay the same while other things change and that things may change slowly or rapidly.	2-ESS2-1. Compare multiple solutions designed to slow or prevent wind or water from changing the shape of the land.
In grades 3–5, students measure change in terms of differences over time and observe that change may occur at different rates. Students learn that some systems appear stable, but over long periods of time they will eventually change.	
In grades 6–8, students explain stability and change in natural or designed systems by examining changes over time and considering forces at different scales, including the atomic scale. Students learn that changes in one part of a system might cause large changes in another part, systems in dynamic equilibrium are stable due to a balance of feedback mechanisms, and stability might be disturbed by either sudden events or gradual changes that accumulate over time.	MS-LS2-4. Construct an argument supported by empirical evidence that changes to physical or biological components of an ecosystem affect populations.
In grades 9–12, students understand that much of science deals with constructing explanations of how things change and how they remain stable. They quantify and model changes in systems over very short or very long periods of time. They see that some changes are irreversible and that negative feedback can stabilize a system, while positive feedback can destabilize it. They recognize that systems can be designed for greater or lesser stability.	HS-PS1-6. Refine the design of a chemical system by specifying a change in conditions that would produce increased amounts of products at equilibrium.

steady quantities of water coming in and out. . . . A repeating pattern of cyclic change—such as the moon orbiting Earth—can also be seen as a stable situation, even though it is clearly not static.

"An understanding of dynamic equilibrium is crucial to understanding the major issues in any complex system—for example, population dynamics in an ecosystem or the relationship between the level of atmospheric carbon dioxide and Earth's average temperature. Dynamic equilibrium is an equally important concept for understanding the physical forces in matter. Stable matter is a system of atoms in dynamic equilibrium.

"In designing systems for stable operation, the mechanisms of external controls and internal 'feedback' loops are important design elements; feedback is important to understanding natural systems as well. A feedback loop is any mechanism in which a condition triggers some action that causes a change in that same condition, such as the temperature of a room triggering the thermostatic control that turns the room's heater on or off.

"A system can be stable on a small time scale, but on a larger time scale it may be seen to be changing. For example, when looking at a living organism over the course of an hour or a day, it may maintain stability; over longer periods, the organism grows, ages, and eventually dies. For the development of larger systems, such as the variety of living species inhabiting Earth or the formation of a galaxy, the relevant time scales may be very long indeed; such processes occur over millions or even billions of years" (pp. 99–100).

HOW ARE THE CROSSCUTTING CONCEPTS CONNECTED?

Although each of the seven crosscutting concepts can be used to help students recognize deep connections between seemingly disparate topics, it can sometimes be helpful to think of how they are connected to each other. The connections can be envisioned in many different ways. The following is one way to think about their interconnections.

Patterns

Patterns stand alone because patterns are a pervasive aspect of all fields of science and engineering. When first exploring a new phenomenon, children will notice similarities and differences leading to ideas for how they might be classified. The existence of patterns naturally suggests an underlying cause for the pattern. For example, observing that snowflakes are all versions of six-sided symmetrical shapes suggests something about how molecules pack together when water freezes, or when repairing a device, a technician would look for a certain pattern of failures suggesting an underlying cause. Patterns are also helpful when interpreting data, which may supply valuable evidence in support of an explanation or a particular solution to a problem.

Causality

Cause and effect lies at the heart of science. Often the objective of a scientific investigation is to find the cause that underlies a phenomenon, first identified by noticing a pattern. Later, the development of a theory allows for predictions of new patterns, which then provides evidence in support of the theory. For example, Galileo's observation that a ball rolling down an incline gathers speed at a constant rate eventually led to Newton's Second Law of Motion, which in turn provided predictions about regular patterns of planetary motion and a means to guide space probes to their destinations.

Structure and function can be thought of as a special case of cause and effect. Whether the structures in question are living tissue or molecules in the atmosphere, understanding their structure is essential to making causal inferences. Engineers make such inferences when examining structures in nature as inspirations for designs to meet people's needs.

Systems

Systems and system models are used by scientists and engineers to investigate natural and designed systems. The purpose of an investigation might be to explore how the system functions or what may be going wrong. Sometimes investigations are too dangerous or expensive to try out without first experimenting with a model.

Scale, proportion, and quantity are essential considerations when deciding how to model a phenomenon. For example, when testing a scale model of a new airplane wing in a wind tunnel, it is essential to get the proportions right and measure accurately or the results will not be valid. When using a computer simulation of an ecosystem, it is important to use informed estimates of population sizes to make reasonably accurate predictions. Mathematics is essential in both science and engineering.

Energy and matter are basic to any systems model, whether of a natural or a designed system. Systems are described in terms of matter and energy. Often the focus of an investigation is to determine how energy or matter flows through a system or, in the case of engineering, to modify a system, so that a given energy input results in a more useful energy output.

Stability and change are ways of describing how a system functions. Whether studying ecosystems or engineered systems, the question is often to determine how the system is changing over time and which factors are causing the system to become unstable.

CONCLUSION

The purpose of this appendix is to explain the rationale behind integrating crosscutting concepts into the K–12 science curriculum and to illustrate how the seven crosscutting concepts from the *Framework* are integrated into the performance expectations within the NGSS. The crosscutting concepts' utility will be realized when curriculum developers and teachers develop lessons, units, and courses using the crosscutting concepts to tie together the broad diversity of science and engineering core ideas in the curriculum to realize the clear and coherent vision of the *Framework*.

REFERENCES

AAAS (American Association for the Advancement of Science). (1989). *Science for all Americans.* New York: Oxford University Press.

AAAS. (1993). *Benchmarks for science literacy.* New York: Oxford University Press.

Feynman, R. (1965). *The Character of Physical Law.* New York: Modern Library.

NRC (National Research Council). (1996). *National science education standards.* Washington, DC: National Academy Press.

NRC (2012). *A framework for K–12 science education: Practices, cross-cutting concepts, and core ideas.* Washington, DC: The National Academies Press.

NSTA (National Science Teachers Association). (2010). Science Anchors Project. http://www.nsta.org/involved/cse/scienceanchors.aspx.

Performance Expectations Coded to Crosscutting Concepts

	Grades K–2	Grades 3–5	Grades 6–8	Grades 9–12
Patterns	K-LS1-1, K-ESS2-1, 1-LS1-2, 1-LS3-1, 1-ESS1-1, 1-ESS1-2, 2-PS1-1, 2-ESS2-2, 2-ESS2-3	3-PS2-2, 3-LS1-1, 3-LS3-1, 3-ESS2-1, 3-ESS2-2, 4-PS4-1, 4-PS4-3, 4-ESS1-1, 4-ESS2-2, 5-ESS1-2	MS-PS1-2, MS-PS4-1, MS-LS2-2, MS-LS4-1, MS-LS4-2, MS-LS4-3, MS-ESS1-1, MS-ESS2-3, MS-ESS3-2	HS-PS1-1, HS-PS1-2, HS-PS1-3, HS-PS1-5, HS-PS2-4, HS-LS4-1, HS-LS4-3, HS-ESS1-5
Cause and Effect	K-PS2-1, K-PS2-2, K-PS3-1, K-PS3-2, K-ESS3-2, K-ESS3-3, 1-PS4-1, 1-PS4-2, 1-PS4-3, 2-PS1-1, 2-LS2-1	3-PS2-1, 3-PS2-3, 3-LS2-1, 3-LS3-2, 3-LS4-2, 3-LS4-3, 3-ESS3-1, 4-PS4-2, 4-ESS2-1, 4-ESS3-1, 4-ESS3-2, 5-PS1-4, 5-PS2-1	MS-PS1-4, MS-PS2-3, MS-PS2-5, MS-LS1-4, MS-LS1-5, MS-LS2-1, MS-LS3-2, LS4-4, MS-LS4-5, MS-LS4-6, MS-ESS2-5, MS-ESS3-1, MS-ESS3-3, MS-ESS3-4	HS-PS2-4, HS-PS3-5, HS-PS4-1, HS-PS4-4, HS-PS4-5, HS-LS2-8, HS-LS3-1, HS-LS3-2, HS-LS4-2, HS-LS4-4, HS-LS4-5, HS-LS4-6, HS-ESS2-4, HS-ESS3-1
Scale, Proportion, and Quantity		3-LS4-1, 5-PS1-1, 5-PS2-2, 5-PS1-3, 5-ESS1-1, 5-ESS2-2	MS-PS1-1, MS-PS3-1, MS-PS3-4, MS-LS1-1, MS-ESS1-3, MS-ESS1-4, MS-ESS2-2	HS-LS2-1, HS-LS2-2, HS-LS3-3, HS-ESS1-1, HS-ESS1-4
Systems and System Models	K-ESS3-1, K-ESS2-2	3-LS4-4, 4-LS1-1, 5-LS2-1, 5-ESS2-1, 5-ESS3-1	MS-PS2-1, MS-PS2-4, MS-PS3-2, MS-LS1-3, MS-ESS1-2, MS-ESS2-6	HS-PS2-2, HS-PS3-1, HS-PS3-4, HS-PS4-3, HS-LS1-2, HS-LS1-4, HS-LS2-5, HS-ESS3-6
Energy and Matter	2-PS1-3	4-PS3-1, 4-PS3-2, 4-PS3-3, 4-PS3-4, 5-PS3-1, 5-LS1-1	MS-PS1-5, MS-PS1-6, MS-PS3-3, MS-PS3-5, MS-LS1-6, MS-LS1-k, MS-LS1-7, MS-LS2-3, MS-ESS2-4	HS-PS1-4, HS-PS1-7, HS-PS1-8, HS-PS3-2, HS-PS3-3, HS-LS1-5, HS-LS1-6, HS-LS1-7, HS-LS2-3, HS-ESS1-2, HS-ESS1-3, HS-ESS2-3, HS-ESS2-6
Structure and Function	1-LS1-1, 2-LS2-2, K-2-ETS1-2		MS-PS1-5, MS-PS1-6, MS-PS4-a, MS-PS4-2, MS-PS4-3, MS-LS1-6, MS-LS1-7, MS-LS3-1	HS-PS2-6, HS-LS1-1, HS-ESS2-5
Stability and Change	2-ESS1-1, 2-ESS2-1		MS-PS2-2, MS-LS2-4, MS-LS2-5, MS-ESS2-1, MS-ESS3-5	HS-PS1-6, HS-PS4-2, HS-LS1-3, HS-LS2-6, HS-LS2-7, HS-ESS1-6, HS-ESS2-1, HS-ESS2-2, HS-ESS2-7, HS-ESS3-3, HS-ESS3-4, HS-ESS3-5

NGSS Crosscutting Concepts*
Section 2: Crosscutting Concepts Matrix

K–2 Crosscutting Statements	3–5 Crosscutting Statements	6–8 Crosscutting Statements	9–12 Crosscutting Statements
1. Patterns—Observed patterns in nature guide organization and classification and prompt questions about relationships and causes underlying them.			
• Patterns in the natural and human designed world can be observed, used to describe phenomena, and used as evidence.	• Similarities and differences in patterns can be used to sort, classify, communicate, and analyze simple rates of change for natural phenomena and designed products. • Patterns of change can be used to make predictions. • Patterns can be used as evidence to support an explanation.	• Macroscopic patterns are related to the nature of microscopic and atomic-level structure. • Patterns in rates of change and other numerical relationships can provide information about natural and human designed systems. • Patterns can be used to identify cause and effect relationships. • Graphs, charts, and images can be used to identify patterns in data.	• Different patterns may be observed at each of the scales at which a system is studied and can provide evidence for causality in explanations of phenomena. • Classifications or explanations used at one scale may fail or need revision when information from smaller or larger scales is introduced, thus requiring improved investigations and experiments. • Patterns of performance of designed systems can be analyzed and interpreted to reengineer and improve the system. • Mathematical representations are needed to identify some patterns. • Empirical evidence is needed to identify patterns.
2. Cause and Effect: Mechanism and Prediction—Events have causes, sometimes simple, sometimes multi-faceted. Deciphering causal relationships, and the mechanisms by which they are mediated, is a major activity of science and engineering.			
• Events have causes that generate observable patterns. • Simple tests can be designed to gather evidence to support or refute student ideas about causes.	• Cause and effect relationships are routinely identified, tested, and used to explain change. • Events that occur together with regularity might or might not be a cause and effect relationship.	• Relationships can be classified as causal or correlational, and correlation does not necessarily imply causation. • Cause and effect relationships may be used to predict phenomena in natural or designed systems. • Phenomena may have more than one cause, and some cause and effect relationships in systems can only be described using probability.	• Empirical evidence is required to differentiate between cause and correlation and make claims about specific causes and effects. • Cause and effect relationships can be suggested and predicted for complex natural and human designed systems by examining what is known about smaller-scale mechanisms within the system. • Systems can be designed to cause a desired effect. • Changes in systems may have various causes that may not have equal effects.

* Adapted from National Research Council. (2012). *A framework for K–12 science education: Practices, crosscutting concepts, and core ideas.* Washington, DC: The National Academies Press. Chapter 4: Crosscutting Concepts.

K–2 Crosscutting Statements	3–5 Crosscutting Statements	6–8 Crosscutting Statements	9–12 Crosscutting Statements
3. Scale, Proportion, and Quantity—In considering phenomena it is critical to recognize what is relevant at different size, time, and energy scales and the proportional relationships between different quantities as scales change.			
• Relative scales allow objects and events to be compared and described (e.g., bigger and smaller, hotter and colder, faster and slower). • Standard units are used to measure length.	• Natural objects and/or observable phenomena exist from the very small to the immensely large or from very short to very long time periods. • Standard units are used to measure and describe physical quantities such as weight, time, temperature, and volume.	• Time, space, and energy phenomena can be observed at various scales using models to study systems that are too large or too small. • The observed function of natural and designed systems may change with scale. • Proportional relationships (e.g., speed as the ratio of distance traveled to time taken) among different types of quantities provide information about the magnitude of properties and processes. • Scientific relationships can be represented through the use of algebraic expressions and equations. • Phenomena that can be observed at one scale may not be observable at another scale.	• The significance of a phenomenon is dependent on the scale, proportion, and quantity at which it occurs. • Some systems can only be studied indirectly as they are too small, too large, too fast, or too slow to observe directly. • Patterns observable at one scale may not be observable or exist at other scales. • Using the concept of orders of magnitude allows one to understand how a model at one scale relates to a model at another scale. • Algebraic thinking is used to examine scientific data and predict the effect of a change in one variable on another (e.g., linear growth vs. exponential growth).
4. Systems and System Models—A system is an organized group of related objects or components; models can be used for understanding and predicting the behavior of systems.			
• Objects and organisms can be described in terms of their parts. • Systems in the natural and designed world have parts that work together.	• A system is a group of related parts that make up a whole and can carry out functions its individual parts cannot. • A system can be described in terms of its components and their interactions.	• Systems may interact with other systems; they may have sub-systems and be a part of larger complex systems. • Models can be used to represent systems and their interactions—such as inputs, processes, and outputs—and energy, matter, and information flows within systems. • Models are limited in that they only represent certain aspects of the system under study.	• Systems can be designed to do specific tasks. • When investigating or describing a system, the boundaries and initial conditions of the system need to be defined and their inputs and outputs analyzed and described using models. • Models (e.g., physical, mathematical, computer models) can be used to simulate systems and interactions—including energy, matter, and information flows—within and between systems at different scales. • Models can be used to predict the behavior of a system, but these predictions have limited precision and reliability due to the assumptions and approximations inherent in models.

K–2 Crosscutting Statements	3–5 Crosscutting Statements	6–8 Crosscutting Statements	9–12 Crosscutting Statements
5. Energy and Matter: Flows, Cycles, and Conservation—Tracking energy and matter flows into, out of, and within systems helps one understand the system's behavior.			
• Objects may break into smaller pieces, be put together into larger pieces, or change shapes.	• Matter is made of particles. • Matter flows and cycles can be tracked in terms of the weight of the substances before and after a process occurs. The total weight of the substances does not change. This is what is meant by conservation of matter. Matter is transported into, out of, and within systems. • Energy can be transferred in various ways and between objects.	• Matter is conserved because atoms are conserved in physical and chemical processes. • Within a natural or designed system, the transfer of energy drives the motion and/or cycling of matter. • Energy may take different forms (e.g., energy in fields, thermal energy, energy of motion). • The transfer of energy can be tracked as energy flows through a designed or natural system.	• The total amount of energy and matter in closed systems is conserved. • Changes of energy and matter in a system can be described in terms of energy and matter flows into, out of, and within that system. • Energy cannot be created or destroyed— it only moves between one place and another place, between objects and/or fields, or between systems. • Energy drives the cycling of matter within and between systems. • In nuclear processes, atoms are not conserved, but the total number of protons plus neutrons is conserved.
6. Structure and Function—The way an object is shaped or structured determines many of its properties and functions.			
• The shape and stability of structures of natural and designed objects are related to their function(s).	• Different materials have different substructures, which can sometimes be observed. • Substructures have shapes and parts that serve functions.	• Complex and microscopic structures and systems can be visualized, modeled, and used to describe how their function depends on the shapes, composition, and relationships among its parts; therefore, complex natural and designed structures/systems can be analyzed to determine how they function. • Structures can be designed to serve particular functions by taking into account properties of different materials, and how materials can be shaped and used.	• Investigating or designing new systems or structures requires a detailed examination of the properties of different materials, the structures of different components, and connections of components to reveal their function and/or solve a problem. • The functions and properties of natural and designed objects and systems can be inferred from their overall structure, the way their components are shaped and used, and the molecular substructures of their various materials.

K–2 Crosscutting Statements	3–5 Crosscutting Statements	6–8 Crosscutting Statements	9–12 Crosscutting Statements
7. Stability and Change—For both designed and natural systems, conditions that affect stability and factors that control rates of change are critical elements to consider and understand.			
• Some things stay the same while other things change. • Things may change slowly or rapidly.	• Change is measured in terms of differences over time and may occur at different rates. • Some systems appear stable, but over long periods of time will eventually change.	• Explanations of stability and change in natural or designed systems can be constructed by examining changes over time and forces at different scales, including the atomic scale. • Small changes in one part of a system might cause large changes in another part. • Stability might be disturbed either by sudden events or gradual changes that accumulate over time. • Systems in dynamic equilibrium are stable due to a balance of feedback mechanisms.	• Much of science deals with constructing explanations of how things change and how they remain stable. • Change and rates of change can be quantified and modeled over very short or very long periods of time. Some system changes are irreversible. • Feedback (negative or positive) can stabilize or destabilize a system. • Systems can be designed for greater or lesser stability.

UNDERSTANDING THE SCIENTIFIC ENTERPRISE: THE NATURE OF SCIENCE IN THE NEXT GENERATION SCIENCE STANDARDS

Scientists and science teachers agree that science is a way of explaining the natural world. In common parlance, science is both a set of practices and the historical accumulation of knowledge. An essential part of science education is learning science and engineering practices and developing knowledge of the concepts that are foundational to science disciplines. Further, students should develop an understanding of the enterprise of science as a whole—the wondering, investigating, questioning, data collecting, and analyzing. This final statement establishes a connection between the Next Generation Science Standards (NGSS) and the nature of science. Public comments on previous drafts of the NGSS called for more explicit discussion of how students can learn about the nature of science.

This chapter presents perspectives, a rationale, and research supporting an emphasis on the nature of science in the context of the NGSS. Additionally, eight understandings with appropriate grade-level outcomes are included as extensions of the science and engineering practices and crosscutting concepts, not as a fourth dimension of standards. Finally, this chapter discusses how to emphasize the nature of science in school programs.

THE FRAMEWORK FOR K–12 SCIENCE EDUCATION

A Framework for K–12 Science Education: Practices, Crosscutting Concepts, and Core Ideas (*Framework*) (NRC, 2012) acknowledged the importance of the nature of science in the statement "there is a strong consensus about characteristics of the scientific enterprise that should be understood by an educated citizen" (p. 78). The *Framework* reflected on the practices of science and returned

to the nature of science in the following statement: "Epistemic knowledge is knowledge of the constructs and values that are intrinsic to science. Students need to understand what is meant, for example, by an observation, a hypothesis, an inference, a model, a theory, or a claim and be able to distinguish among them" (p. 79). This quotation presents a series of concepts and activities important to understanding the nature of science as a complement to the practices imbedded in investigations, field studies, and experiments.

THE NATURE OF SCIENCE: A PERSPECTIVE FOR THE NGSS

The integration of science and engineering practices, disciplinary core ideas, and crosscutting concepts sets the stage for teaching and learning about the nature of science. That said, learning about the nature of science requires more than engaging in activities and conducting investigations.

When the three dimensions of the science standards are combined, one can ask what is central to the intersection of the science and engineering practices, disciplinary core ideas, and crosscutting concepts? Or, what is the relationship among the three basic elements of the *Framework*? Humans have a need to know and understand the world around them. And they have the need to change their environment using technology in order to accommodate what they understand or desire. In some cases, the need to know originates in satisfying basic needs in the face of potential danger. Sometimes it is a natural curiosity and, in other cases, the promise of a better, more comfortable life. Science is the pursuit of explanations of the natural world, and technology and engineering are means of accommodating human needs, intellectual curiosity, and aspirations.

One fundamental goal for K–12 science education is a scientifically literate person who can understand the nature of scientific knowledge. Indeed, the only consistent characteristic of scientific knowledge across the disciplines is that scientific knowledge itself is open to revision in light of new evidence.

In K–12 classrooms the issue is how to explain both the natural world and what constitutes the formation of adequate, evidence-based scientific explanations. To be clear, this perspective complements but is distinct from students engaging in science and engineering practices in order to enhance their knowledge and understanding of the natural world.

A RATIONALE AND RESEARCH

Addressing the need for students to understand both the concepts and practices of science and the nature of science is not new in American education. For example, the writings of James B. Conant in the 1940s and 1950s argue for a greater understanding of science by citizens (Conant, 1947). In *Science and Common Senses*, Conant (1951) discusses the "bewilderment of laymen" when it comes to understanding what science can and cannot accomplish, in both the detailed context of investigations and the larger perspective of understanding science. Conant says: "The remedy does not lie in a greater dissemination of scientific information among non-scientists. Being well informed about science is not the same thing as understanding science, though the two propositions are not antithetical. What is needed are methods for importing some knowledge of the tactics and strategy of science to those who are not scientists" (Conant, 1951, p. 4). In the context of the discussion here, tactics are analogous to science and engineering practices, as well as to the nature of scientific explanations.

The present discussion recommends the aforementioned "tactics of science and engineering practices and crosscutting concepts" to develop students' understanding of the larger strategies of the scientific enterprise—the nature of scientific explanations. It should be noted that Conant and colleagues went on to develop *Harvard Cases in History of Science* (available at: http://library.wur.nl/WebQuery/clc/382832), a historical approach to understanding science. An extension of the nature of science as a learning goal for education soon followed the original work at Harvard. In the late 1950s, Leo Klopfer adapted the *Harvard Cases* for use in high schools (Klopfer and Cooley, 1963). Work on the nature of science has continued with lines of research by Duschl (1990, 2000, 2008), Lederman (1992), and Lederman and colleagues (2002). One aspect of this research base addresses the teaching of the nature of science (see, e.g., Duschl, 1990; Duschl and Grandy, 2008; Flick and Lederman, 2004; Lederman and Lederman, 2004; McComas, 1998; Osborne et al., 2003).

Further support for teaching about the nature of science can be seen in 40 years of position statements from the National Science Teachers Association. *Science for All Americans* (Rutherford and Ahlgren, 1989), the policy statement *Benchmarks for Science Literacy* (AAAS, 1993), and *National Science Education Standards* (NRC, 1996) clearly set understanding the nature of science as a learning outcome in science education.

Recently, discussions of the *Framework* (NRC, 2012) and implications for teaching science have provided background for instructional strategies that connect specific practices and the nature of scientific explanations (Duschl, 2012; Krajcik and Merritt, 2012; Reiser et al., 2012).

THE NATURE OF SCIENCE AND THE NGSS

The nature of science is included in the NGSS. Here is presented the Nature of Science (NOS) Matrix. The basic understandings about the nature of science are:
* Scientific Investigations Use a Variety of Methods
* Scientific Knowledge Is Based on Empirical Evidence
* Scientific Knowledge Is Open to Revision in Light of New Evidence
* Scientific Models, Laws, Mechanisms, and Theories Explain Natural Phenomena
* Science Is a Way of Knowing
* Scientific Knowledge Assumes an Order and Consistency in Natural Systems
* Science Is a Human Endeavor
* Science Addresses Questions About the Natural and Material World

The first four of these understandings are closely associated with practices and the second four with crosscutting concepts. The NOS Matrix presents specific content for K–2, 3–5, middle school, and high school. Appropriate learning outcomes for the nature of science are expressed in the performance expectations and are presented in either the foundations column for practices or the crosscutting concepts of the disciplinary core ideas standards pages.

Again, it should be noted that inclusion of the nature of science in the NGSS does not constitute a fourth dimension of standards. Rather, the grade-level representations of the eight understandings have been incorporated in the practices and crosscutting concepts, as seen in the performance expectations and represented in the foundation boxes.

Overview

One goal of science education is to help students understand the nature of scientific knowledge. This matrix presents eight major themes and grade-level understandings about the nature of science. Four themes extend the science and engineering practices and four themes extend the crosscutting concepts. The eight themes are presented in the left column. The matrix describes learning outcomes for the themes at grade bands for K–2, 3–5, middle school, and high school. Appropriate learning outcomes are expressed in select performance expectations and are presented in the foundation boxes throughout the standards.

Nature of science understandings most closely associated with practices.

Nature of science understandings most closely associated with crosscutting concepts.

Understandings About the Nature of Science

Categories	K–2	3–5	Middle School	High School
Scientific Investigations Use a Variety of Methods	• Scientific investigations begin with a question. • Scientists use different ways to study the world.	• Scientific methods are determined by questions. • Scientific investigations use a variety of methods, tools, and techniques.	• Scientific investigations use a variety of methods and tools to make measurements and observations. • Scientific investigations are guided by a set of values to ensure accuracy of measurements, observations, and objectivity of findings. • Science depends on evaluating proposed explanations. • Scientific values function as criteria in distinguishing between science and non-science.	• Scientific investigations use diverse methods and do not always use the same set of procedures to obtain data. • New technologies advance scientific knowledge. • Scientific inquiry is characterized by a common set of values that include logical thinking, precision, open-mindedness, objectivity, skepticism, replicability of results, and honest and ethical reporting of findings. • The discourse practices of science are organized around disciplinary domains that share exemplars for making decisions regarding the values, instruments, methods, models, and evidence to adopt and use. • Scientific investigations use a variety of methods, tools, and techniques to revise and produce new knowledge.
Scientific Knowledge Is Based on Empirical Evidence	• Scientists look for patterns and order when making observations about the world.	• Scientific findings are based on recognizing patterns. • Scientists use tools and technologies to make accurate measurements and observations.	• Scientific knowledge is based on logical and conceptual connections between evidence and explanations. • Science disciplines share common rules of obtaining and evaluating empirical evidence.	• Scientific knowledge is based on empirical evidence. • Science disciplines share common rules of evidence used to evaluate explanations about natural systems. • Science includes the process of coordinating patterns of evidence with current theory. • Scientific arguments are strengthened by multiple lines of evidence supporting a single explanation.

Understandings About the Nature of Science				
Categories	**K–2**	**3–5**	**Middle School**	**High School**
Scientific Knowledge Is Open to Revision in Light of New Evidence	• Scientific knowledge can change when new information is found.	• Scientific explanations can change based on new evidence.	• Scientific explanations are subject to revision and improvement in light of new evidence. • The certainty and durability of scientific findings vary. • Scientific findings are frequently revised and/or reinterpreted based on new evidence.	• Scientific explanations can be probabilistic. • Most scientific knowledge is quite durable but, in principle, is subject to change based on new evidence and/or reinterpretation of existing evidence. • Scientific argumentation is a mode of logical discourse used to clarify the strength of relationships between ideas and evidence that may result in revision of an explanation.
Science Models, Laws, Mechanisms, and Theories Explain Natural Phenomena	• Scientists use drawings, sketches, and models as a way to communicate ideas. • Scientists search for cause and effect relationships to explain natural events.	• Scientific theories are based on a body of evidence and many tests. • Scientific explanations describe the mechanisms for natural events.	• Theories are explanations for observable phenomena. • Scientific theories are based on a body of evidence developed over time. • Laws are regularities or mathematical descriptions of natural phenomena. • A hypothesis is used by scientists as an idea that may contribute important new knowledge for the evaluation of a scientific theory. • The term "theory" as used in science is very different from the common use outside science.	• Theories and laws provide explanations in science, but theories do not with time become laws or facts. • A scientific theory is a substantiated explanation of some aspect of the natural world, based on a body of facts that has been repeatedly confirmed through observation and experiment. The science community validates each theory before it is accepted. If new evidence is discovered that a theory does not accommodate, the theory is generally modified in light of new evidence. • Models, mechanisms, and explanations collectively serve as tools in the development of a scientific theory. • Laws are statements or descriptions of the relationships among observable phenomena. • Scientists often use hypotheses to develop and test theories and explanations.

Understandings About the Nature of Science

Categories	K–2	3–5	Middle School	High School
Science Is a Way of Knowing	• Scientific knowledge informs us about the world.	• Science is both a body of knowledge and processes that add new knowledge. • Science is a way of knowing that is used by many people.	• Science is both a body of knowledge and the processes and practices used to add to that body of knowledge. • Scientific knowledge is cumulative and many people from many generations and nations have contributed to scientific knowledge. • Science is a way of knowing used by many people, not just scientists.	• Science is both a body of knowledge that represents a current understanding of natural systems and the processes used to refine, elaborate, revise, and extend this knowledge. • Science is a unique way of knowing, and there are other ways of knowing. • Science distinguishes itself from other ways of knowing through the use of empirical standards, logical arguments, and skeptical review. • Scientific knowledge has a history that includes refinement of, and changes to, theories, ideas, and beliefs over time.
Scientific Knowledge Assumes an Order and Consistency in Natural Systems	• Science assumes natural events happen today as they happened in the past. • Many events are repeated.	• Science assumes consistent patterns in natural systems. • Basic laws of nature are the same everywhere in the universe.	• Science assumes that objects and events in natural systems occur in consistent patterns that are understandable through measurement and observation. • Science carefully considers and evaluates anomalies in data and evidence.	• Scientific knowledge is based on the assumption that natural laws operate today as they did in the past and will continue to do so in the future. • Science assumes the universe is a vast single system in which basic laws are consistent.
Science Is a Human Endeavor	• People have practiced science for a long time. • Men and women of diverse backgrounds are scientists and engineers.	• Men and women from all cultures and backgrounds choose careers as scientists and engineers. • Most scientists and engineers work in teams. • Science affects everyday life. • Creativity and imagination are important to science.	• Men and women from different social, cultural, and ethnic backgrounds work as scientists and engineers. • Scientists and engineers rely on human qualities such as persistence, precision, reasoning, logic, imagination, and creativity. • Scientists and engineers are guided by habits of mind, such as intellectual honesty, tolerance of ambiguity, skepticism, and openness to new ideas. • Advances in technology influence the progress of science, and science has influenced advances in technology.	• Scientific knowledge is a result of human endeavor, imagination, and creativity. • Individuals and teams from many nations and cultures have contributed to science and to advances in engineering. • Scientists' backgrounds, theoretical commitments, and fields of endeavor influence the nature of their findings. • Technological advances have influenced the progress of science, and science has influenced advances in technology. • Science and engineering are influenced by society, and society is influenced by science and engineering.
Science Addresses Questions About the Natural and Material World	• Scientists study the natural and material world.	• Scientific findings are limited to what can be answered with empirical evidence.	• Scientific knowledge is constrained by human capacity, technology, and materials. • Science limits its explanations to systems that lend themselves to observation and empirical evidence. • Scientific knowledge can describe consequences of actions but is not responsible for society's decisions.	• Not all questions can be answered by science. • Science and technology may raise ethical issues for which science, by itself, does not provide answers and solutions. • Scientific knowledge indicates what can happen in natural systems—not what should happen. The latter involves ethics, values, and human decisions about the use of knowledge. • Many decisions are **not** made using science alone, but rely on social and cultural contexts to resolve issues.

IMPLEMENTING INSTRUCTION TO FACILITATE UNDERSTANDING OF THE NATURE OF SCIENCE

Now, the science teacher's question: How do I put the elements of practices and crosscutting concepts together to help students understand the nature of science? Suppose students observe the moon's movements in the sky, changes in seasons, phase changes in water, or life cycles of organisms. One can have them observe patterns and propose explanations of cause and effect. Then, students can develop a model of a system based on their proposed explanation. Next, they design an investigation to test the model. In designing the investigation, they must gather and analyze data. Next, they construct an explanation using an evidence-based argument. These experiences allow students to use their knowledge of the practices and crosscutting concepts to understand the nature of science. This is possible when students have instruction that emphasizes why explanations are based on evidence, that the phenomena they observe are consistent with the way the entire universe continues to operate, and that multiple ways can be used to investigate these phenomena.

The *Framework* emphasizes that students must have the opportunity to stand back and reflect on how the practices contribute to the accumulation of scientific knowledge. This means, for example, that when students carry out an investigation, develop models, articulate questions, or engage in arguments, they should have opportunities to think about what they have done and why. They should be given opportunities to compare their own approaches to those of other students or professional scientists. Through this kind of reflection they come to understand the importance of each practice and develop a nuanced appreciation of the nature of science.

Using examples from the history of science is another method for presenting the nature of science. It is one thing to develop the practices and crosscutting concepts in the context of core disciplinary ideas; it is another aim to develop an understanding of the nature of science within those contexts. The use of case studies from the history of science provides contexts in which to develop students' understanding of the nature of science. In the middle and high school grades, for example, case studies on the following topics might be used to broaden and deepen understanding about the nature of science:

- Copernican Revolution
- Newtonian Mechanics
- Lyell's Study of Patterns of Rocks and Fossils
- Progression from Continental Drift to Plate Tectonics
- Lavoisier–Dalton and Atomic Structure
- Darwin's Theory of Biological Evolution and the Modern Synthesis
- Pasteur and the Germ Theory of Disease
- Watson and Crick and the Molecular Model of Genetics

These explanations could be supplemented with other cases from history. The point is to provide an instructional context that bridges tactics and strategies with practices and the nature of science, through understanding the role of systems, models, patterns, cause and effect, the analysis and interpretation of data, the importance of evidence with scientific arguments, and the construction of scientific explanations of the natural world. Through the use of historical and contemporary case studies, students can understand the nature of explanations in the larger context of scientific models, laws, mechanisms, and theories.

In designing instruction, deliberate choices will need to be made about when it is sufficient to build students' understanding of the scientific enterprise through reflection on their own investigations and when it is necessary and productive to have students analyze historical case studies.

CONCLUSION

This discussion addressed how to support the development of an understanding of the nature of science in the context of the NGSS. The approach centered on eight understandings for the nature of science and the intersection of those understandings with science and engineering practices, disciplinary core ideas, and crosscutting concepts. The nature of the scientific explanations is an idea central to standards-based science programs. Beginning with the practices, disciplinary core ideas, and crosscutting concepts, science teachers can progress to the regularities of laws, the importance of evidence, and the formulation of theories in science. With the addition of historical examples, the nature of scientific explanations assumes a human face and is recognized as an ever-changing enterprise.

REFERENCES

American Association for the Advancement of Science. (1993). *Benchmarks for science literacy*. New York: Oxford University Press.

Conant, J. (1947). *On understanding science: A historical approach.* Cambridge, MA: Harvard University Press.

Conant, J. B. (1951). *Science and common sense.* New Haven, CT: Yale University Press.

Duschl, R. (1990). *Restructuring science education: The role of theories and their importance.* New York: Teachers College Press.

Duschl, R. (2000). Making the nature of science explicit. In R. Millar, J. Leach, and J. Osborne (Eds.), *Improving science education: The contribution of research.* Philadelphia, PA: Open University Press.

Duschl, R. (2008). Science education in 3-part harmony: balancing conceptual, epistemic, and social learning goals. In J. Green, A. Luke, and G. Kelly (Eds.), *Review of Research in Education* 32:268–291. Washington, DC: American Educational Research Association.

Duschl, R. (2012). The second dimension—crosscutting concepts: Understanding *A Framework for K–12 Science Education. The Science Teacher* 79(2):34–38.

Duschl, R., and R. Grandy (Eds.). (2008). *Teaching scientific inquiry: Recommendations for research and implementation.* Rotterdam, Netherlands: Sense Publishers.

Flick, L., and M. Lederman. (2004). *Scientific inquiry and nature of science.* Boston, MA: Kluwer Academic Publishers.

Klopfer, L., and W. Cooley. (1963). The history of science cases for high schools in the development of student understanding of science and scientists. *Journal of Research in Science Teaching* 1(1):33–47.

Krajcik, J., and J. Merritt. (2012). Engaging students in scientific practices: What does constructing and revising models look like in the science classroom? Understanding *A Framework for K–12 Science Education. The Science Teacher* 79(3):38–41.

Lederman, N. G. (1992). Students' and teachers' conceptions of the nature of science: a review of the research. *Journal of Research in Science Teaching* 29(4):331–359.

Lederman, N., and J. Lederman. (2004). Revising instruction to teach nature of science: modifying activities to enhance students' understanding of science. *The Science Teacher* 71(9):36–39.

Lederman, N., F. Abd-El-Khalick, R. L. Bell, and R. S. Schwartz. (2002). View of nature of science questionnaire: Toward valid and meaningful assessment of learners' conceptions of nature of science. *Journal of Research in Science Teaching* 39(6):497–521.

McComas, W. F. (Ed.). (1998). *The nature of science in science education: Rationales and strategies.* Dordrecht, Netherlands: Kluwer Academic Publishers.

National Research Council. (1996). *National science education standards.* Washington, DC: National Academy Press.

National Research Council. (2012). *A framework for K–12 science education: Practices, crosscutting concepts, and core ideas.* Washington, DC: The National Academies Press.

Osborne, J. F., M. Ratcliffe, S. Collins, R. Millar, and R. Duschl. (2003). What "ideas about science" should be taught in school science? A Delphi Study of the "expert" community. *Journal of Research in Science Teaching* 40(7):692–720.

Reiser, B., L. Berland, and L. Kenyon. (2012). Engaging students in the scientific practices of explanation and argumentation: Understanding *A Framework for K–12 Science Education. The Science Teacher* 79(4):8–13.

Rutherford, F. J., and A. Ahlgren. (1989). *Science for all americans.* New York: Oxford University Press.

ENGINEERING DESIGN IN THE NEXT GENERATION SCIENCE STANDARDS

The Next Generation Science Standards (NGSS) represent a commitment to integrate engineering design into the structure of science education by raising engineering design to the same level as scientific inquiry when teaching science disciplines at all levels, from kindergarten to twelfth grade. There are both practical and inspirational reasons for including engineering design as an essential element of science education.

> We anticipate that the insights gained and interests provoked from studying and engaging in the practices of science and engineering during their K–12 schooling should help students see how science and engineering are instrumental in addressing major challenges that confront society today, such as generating sufficient energy, preventing and treating diseases, maintaining supplies of clean water and food, and solving the problems of global environmental change. (NRC, 2012, p. 9)

Providing students a foundation in engineering design allows them to better engage in and aspire to solve the major societal and environmental challenges they will face in the decades ahead.

KEY DEFINITIONS

One of the problems of prior standards has been the lack of clear and consistent definitions of the terms "science," "engineering," and "technology." *A Framework for K–12 Science Education* (*Framework*) defines these terms as follows:

> In the K–12 context, "science" is generally taken to mean the traditional natural sciences: physics, chemistry, biology, and (more recently) earth, space, and environmental sciences. . . . We use the term "engineering" in a very broad sense to mean any engagement in a systematic practice of design to achieve solutions to particular human problems. Likewise, we broadly use the term "technology" to include all types of human-made systems and processes—not in the limited sense often used in schools that equates technology with modern computational and communications devices. Technologies result when engineers apply their understanding of the natural world and of human behavior to design ways to satisfy human needs and wants. (NRC, 2012, pp. 11–12)

The *Framework*'s definitions address two common misconceptions. The first is that engineering design is not just applied science. As described in Appendix F: Science and Engineering Practices in the Next Generation Science Standards, the practices of engineering have much in common with the practices of science, although engineering design has a different purpose and product than scientific inquiry. The second misconception is that technology describes all the ways that people have modified the natural world to meet their needs and wants. Technology does not refer to just computers or electronic devices.

The purpose of defining "engineering" more broadly in the *Framework* and the NGSS is to emphasize engineering design practices that all citizens should learn. For example, students are expected to be able to define problems—situations that people wish to change—by specifying criteria and constraints for acceptable solutions, generating and evaluating multiple solutions, building and testing prototypes, and optimizing a solution. These practices have not been explicitly included in science standards until now.

ENGINEERING DESIGN IN THE *FRAMEWORK*

The term "engineering design" has replaced the older term "technological design," consistent with the definition of engineering as a systematic practice for solving problems, and technology as the result of that practice. According to the *Framework*: "From a teaching and learning point of view, it is the iterative cycle of design that offers the greatest potential for applying science knowledge in the classroom and engaging in engineering practices" (NRC, 2012, pp. 201–202). The *Framework* recommends that students explicitly learn how to engage in engineering design practices to solve problems.

The *Framework* also projects a vision of engineering design in the science curriculum and of what students can accomplish from early school years to high school:

> In some ways, children are natural engineers. They spontaneously build sand castles, dollhouses, and hamster enclosures, and they use a variety of tools and materials for their own playful purposes. . . . Children's capabilities to design structures can then be enhanced by having them pay attention to points of failure and asking them to create and test redesigns of the bridge so that it is stronger. (NRC, 2012, p. 70)

By the time these students leave high school, they can "undertake more complex engineering design projects related to major global, national, or local issues" (NRC, 2012, p. 71). The core idea of engineering design includes three component ideas:

A. Defining and delimiting engineering problems involves stating the problem to be solved as clearly as possible in terms of criteria for success and constraints or limits.

B. Designing solutions to engineering problems begins with generating a number of different possible solutions, then evaluating potential solutions to see which ones best meet the criteria and constraints of the problem.

C. Optimizing the design solution involves a process in which solutions are systematically tested and refined and the final design is improved by trading off less important features for those that are more important.

It is important to point out that these component ideas do not always follow in order, any more than do the "steps" of scientific inquiry. At any stage, a problem solver can redefine the problem or generate new solutions to replace an idea that is just not working out.

ENGINEERING DESIGN IN RELATION TO STUDENT DIVERSITY

The NGSS inclusion of engineering with science has major implications for non-dominant student groups. From a pedagogical perspective, the focus on engineering is inclusive of students who may have traditionally been marginalized in the science classroom or experienced science as not being relevant to their lives or future. By asking questions and solving meaningful problems through engineering in local contexts (e.g., watershed planning, medical equipment, instruments for communication for the deaf), diverse students deepen their science knowledge, come to view science as relevant to their lives and future, and engage in science in socially relevant and transformative ways.

From a global perspective, engineering offers opportunities for "innovation" and "creativity" at the K–12 level. Engineering is a field that is critical to undertaking the world's challenges, and exposure to engineering activities (e.g., robotics and invention competitions) can spark interest in the study of science, technology, engineering, and mathematics and future careers (NSF, 2010). This early engagement is particularly important for students who have traditionally not considered science as a possible career choice, including females and students from multiple languages and cultures.

ENGINEERING DESIGN IN THE NEXT GENERATION SCIENCE STANDARDS

In the NGSS, engineering design is integrated throughout the document. First, a fair number of standards in the three disciplinary areas of life, physical, and earth and space sciences begin with an engineering practice. In these standards, students demonstrate their understanding of science through the application of engineering practices. Second, the NGSS also include separate standards for engineering design at the K–2, 3–5, 6–8, and 9–12 grade levels. This multi-pronged approach, including engineering design both as a set of practices and as a set of core ideas, is consistent with the original intention of the *Framework*.

It is important to point out that the NGSS do not put forward a full set of standards for engineering education, but rather include only practices and ideas about engineering design that are considered necessary for literate citizens. The standards for engineering design reflect the three component ideas of the *Framework* and progress at each grade span.

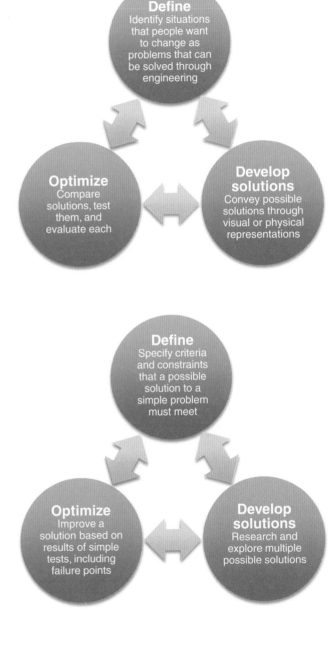

GRADES K–2

Engineering design in the earliest grades introduces students to "problems" as situations that people want to change. They can use tools and materials to solve simple problems, use different representations to convey solutions, and compare different solutions to a problem and determine which is best. Students in all grade levels are not expected to come up with original solutions, although original solutions are always welcome. Emphasis is on thinking through the needs or goals that need to be met and on which solutions best meet those needs and goals.

GRADES 3–5

At the upper elementary grades, engineering design engages students in more formalized problem solving. Students define a problem using criteria for success and constraints or limits of possible solutions. Students research and consider multiple possible solutions to a given problem. Generating and testing solutions also becomes more rigorous as students learn to optimize solutions by revising them several times to obtain the best possible design.

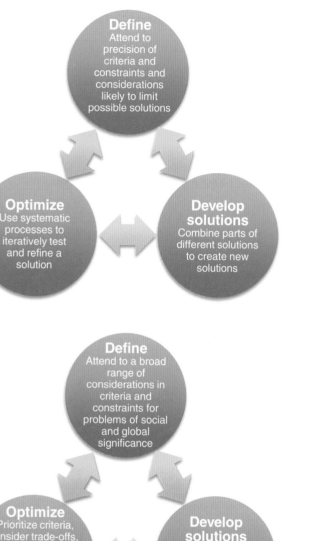

At the middle school level, students learn to sharpen the focus of problems by precisely specifying criteria and constraints of successful solutions, taking into account not only what needs the problem is intended to meet, but also the larger context within which the problem is defined, including limits to possible solutions. Students can identify elements of different solutions and combine them to create new solutions. Students at this level are expected to use systematic methods to compare different solutions to see which best meet criteria and constraints, and to test and revise solutions a number of times in order to arrive at an optimal design.

Engineering design at the high school level engages students in complex problems that include issues of social and global significance. Such problems need to be broken down into simpler problems to be tackled one at a time. Students are also expected to quantify criteria and constraints so that it will be possible to use quantitative methods to compare the potential of different solutions. While creativity in solving problems is valued, emphasis is on identifying the best solution to a problem, which often involves researching how others have solved it before. Students are expected to use mathematics and/or computer simulations to test solutions under different conditions, prioritize criteria, consider tradeoffs, and assess social and environmental impacts.

CONCLUSION

The inclusion of engineering design within the fabric of the NGSS has profound implications for curriculum, teaching, and assessment. All students need opportunities to acquire engineering design practices and concepts alongside the practices and concepts of science.

The decision to integrate engineering design into the science disciplines is not intended either to encourage or discourage development of engineering courses. In recent years, many middle and high schools have introduced engineering courses that build students' engineering skill, engage them in experiences using a variety of technologies, and provide information on a range of engineering careers. The engineering design standards included in the NGSS could certainly be a component of such courses but most likely do not represent the full scope of such courses or an engineering pathway. Rather, the purpose of the NGSS is to emphasize the key knowledge and skills that all students need in order to engage fully as workers, consumers, and citizens in 21st-century society.

REFERENCES

NRC (National Research Council). (2012). *A framework for K–12 science education: Practices, crosscutting concepts, and core ideas.* Washington, DC: The National Academies Press.

NSF (National Science Foundation). (2010). *Preparing the next generation of STEM innovators: Identifying and developing our nation's human capital.* Washington, DC: NSF.

Performance Expectations That Incorporate Engineering Practices

Grade	Physical Sciences	Life Sciences	Earth and Space Sciences	Engineering
K	K-PS2-2 K-PS3-2		K-ESS3-2 K-ESS3-3	K-2-ETS1-1 K-2-ETS1-2 K-2-ETS1-3
1	1-PS4-4	1-LS1-1		
2	2-PS1-2	2-LS2-2	2-ESS2-1	
3	3-PS2-4	3-LS4-4	3-ESS3-1	3-5-ETS1-1 3-5-ETS1-2 3-5-ETS1-3
4	4-PS3-4 4-PS4-3		4-ESS3-2	
5				
6–8	MS-PS1-6 MS-PS2-1 MS-PS3-3	MS-LS2-5		MS-ETS1-1 MS-ETS1-2 MS-ETS1-3 MS-ETS1-4
9–12	HS-PS1-6 HS-PS2-3 HS-PS2-6 HS-PS3-3 HS-PS4-5	HS-LS2-7 HS-LS4-6	HS-ESS3-2 HS-ESS3-4	HS-ETS1-1 HS-ETS1-2 HS-ETS1-3 HS-ETS1-4

SCIENCE, TECHNOLOGY, SOCIETY, AND THE ENVIRONMENT

The goal that all students should learn about the relationships among science, technology, and society (known by the abbreviation STS) came to prominence in the United Kingdom and the United States in the early 1980s. The individual most closely associated with this movement is Robert Yager, who has written extensively on the topic (e.g., Yager, 1996). A study of state standards (Koehler et al., 2007) has shown that STS became common in state science education standards during the first decade of the new millennium, with an increasing focus on environmental issues. Consequently, the core ideas that relate science and technology to society and the natural environment in Chapter 8 of *A Framework for K–12 Science Education* (*Framework*) are consistent with efforts in science education for the past three decades.

IN THE *FRAMEWORK*

The *Framework* specifies two core ideas that relate science, technology, society, and the environment: the interdependence of science, engineering, and technology and the influence of science, engineering, and technology on society and the natural world.

THE INTERDEPENDENCE OF SCIENCE, ENGINEERING, AND TECHNOLOGY

The first core idea is that scientific inquiry, engineering design, and technological development are interdependent:

> The fields of science and engineering are mutually supportive, and scientists and engineers often work together in teams, especially in fields at the borders of science and engineering. Advances in science offer new capabilities, new materials, or new understanding of processes that can be applied through engineering to produce advances in technology. Advances in technology, in turn, provide scientists with new capabilities to probe the natural world at larger or smaller scales; to record, manage, and analyze data; and to model ever more complex systems with greater precision. In addition, engineers' efforts to develop or improve technologies often raise new questions for scientists' investigations. (NRC, 2012, p. 203)

The interdependence of science—with its resulting discoveries and principles—and engineering—with its resulting technologies—includes a number of ideas about how the fields of science and engineering interrelate. One is the idea that scientific discoveries enable engineers to do their work. For example, the discoveries of early explorers of electricity enabled engineers to create a world linked by vast power grids that illuminate cities, enable communications, and accomplish thousands of other tasks. Engineering accomplishments also enable the work of scientists. For example, the development of the Hubble Space Telescope and very sensitive light sensors have made it possible for astronomers to discover our place in the universe, noticing previously unobserved planets and getting even further insight into the origin of stars and galaxies.

The vision projected by the *Framework* is that science and engineering continuously interact and move each other forward, as expressed in the following statement:

> New insights from science often catalyze the emergence of new technologies and their applications, which are developed using engineering design. In turn, new technologies open opportunities for new scientific investigations. (NRC, 2012, p. 210)

This reflects the key roles both science and engineering play in driving each other forward in the research and development cycle.

THE INFLUENCE OF ENGINEERING, TECHNOLOGY, AND SCIENCE ON SOCIETY AND THE NATURAL WORLD

The second core idea focuses on the more traditional STS—theme that scientific and technological advances can have a profound effect on society and the environment.

Together, advances in science, engineering, and technology can have—and indeed have had—profound effects on human society, in such areas as agriculture, transportation, health care, and communication, and on the natural environment. Each system can change significantly when new technologies are introduced, with both desired effects and unexpected outcomes. (NRC, 2012, p. 210).

This idea has two complementary parts. The first is that scientific discoveries and technological decisions affect human society and the natural environment. The second is that people make decisions for social and environmental reasons that ultimately guide the work of scientists and engineers. As expressed in the *Framework*:

From the earliest forms of agriculture to the latest technologies, all human activity has drawn on natural resources and has had both short- and long-term consequences, positive as well negative, for the health of both people and the natural environment. These consequences have grown stronger in recent human history. Society has changed dramatically, and human populations and longevity have increased, as advances in science and engineering have influenced the ways in which people interact with one another and with their surrounding natural environment.

Not only do science and engineering affect society; society's decisions (whether made through market forces or political processes) influence the work of scientists and engineers. These decisions sometimes establish goals and priorities for improving or replacing technologies; at other times they set limits, such as in regulating the extraction of raw materials or in setting allowable levels of pollution from mining, farming, and industry. (NRC, 2012, p. 212)

The first paragraph above refers to the central role that technological changes have had on society and the natural environment. For example, the development of new systems for growing, processing, and distributing food made possible the transition from widely dispersed hunter-gatherer groups to villages and eventually cities. While that change took place over thousands of years, in just the past generation there has been vast growth in the size of cities along with the establishment of new global communications and trade networks. In 1960 the world population was 3 billion. Today it is more than 6 billion, and thanks to advances in medicine and public health, people are living longer. Additionally, the growth of industrialization around the world has increased the rate at which natural resources are being extracted, well beyond what might be expected from a doubling of world population alone.

The second paragraph emphasizes the limits to growth imposed by human society and by the environment, which has limited supplies of certain non-renewable resources. Together, these paragraphs point the way to new science education standards that will help today's children prepare for a world in which technological change, and the consequent impact on society and natural resources, will continue to accelerate.

HOME AND COMMUNITY CONNECTIONS TO SCHOOL SCIENCE FOR STUDENT DIVERSITY

While it has long been recognized that building home-school connections is important for the academic success of non-dominant student groups, in practice this is rarely done in an effective manner. There is a perceived disconnect between the science practices taught in schools and the science supported in the homes and communities of non-dominant student groups. Recent research has identified resources and strengths in the family and home environments of non-dominant student groups (NRC, 2009). Students bring to the science classroom "funds of knowledge" that can serve as resources for academic learning when teachers find ways to validate and activate this prior knowledge (González et al., 2005). Several approaches build connections between home/community and school science: (1) increasing parental involvement in their children's science classrooms and encouraging parents' roles as partners in science learning, (2) engaging students in defining problems and designing solutions of community projects in their neighborhoods (typically engineering), and (3) focusing on science learning in informal environments.

IN THE NEXT GENERATION SCIENCE STANDARDS

There is a broad consensus that these two core ideas belong in the NGSS, but a majority of state teams recommended that these ideas could best be illustrated through their connections to the natural sciences disciplines. There are a number of performance expectations that require students to demonstrate not only their understanding of a core idea in natural science, but also how that idea is supported by evidence derived from certain technological advances. The connection between these core ideas and specific performance expectations is shown in the crosscutting concept foundation box.

The following matrix summarizes how the two core ideas discussed in this appendix progress across the grade levels.

Science, Technology, Society, and the Environment Connections Matrix

1. Interdependence of Science, Engineering, and Technology			
K–2 Connections Statements	3–5 Connections Statements	6–8 Connections Statements	9–12 Connections Statements
• Science and engineering involve the use of tools to observe and measure things.	• Science and technology support each other. • Tools and instruments are used to answer scientific questions, while scientific discoveries lead to the development of new technologies.	• Engineering advances have led to important discoveries in virtually every field of science, and scientific discoveries have led to the development of entire industries and engineered systems. • Science and technology drive each other forward.	• Science and engineering complement each other in the cycle known as research and development (R&D). • Many R&D projects may involve scientists, engineers, and others with wide ranges of expertise.

2. Influence of Engineering, Technology, and Science on Society and the Natural World			
K–2 Connections Statements	3–5 Connections Statements	6–8 Connections Statements	9–12 Connections Statements
• Every human-made product is designed by applying some knowledge of the natural world and is built by using natural materials. • Taking natural materials to make things impacts the environment.	• People's needs and wants change over time, as do their demands for new and improved technologies. • Engineers improve existing technologies or develop new ones to increase their benefits, decrease known risks, and meet societal demands. • When new technologies become available, they can bring about changes in the way people live and interact with one another.	• All human activity draws on natural resources and has both short- and long-term consequences, positive as well as negative, for the health of people and the natural environment. • The uses of technologies and any limitation on their use are driven by individual or societal needs, desires, and values; by the findings of scientific research; and by differences in such factors as climate, natural resources, and economic conditions. Thus, technology use varies from region to region over time.	• Modern civilization depends on major technological systems, such as agriculture, health, water, energy, transportation, manufacturing, construction, and communications. • Engineers continuously modify these systems to increase benefits while decreasing costs and risks. • New technologies can have deep impacts on society and the environment, including some that were not anticipated. • Analysis of costs and benefits is a critical aspect of decisions about technology.

Performance Expectations Related to the Interdependence of Science, Engineering, and Technology

Grade	Physical Sciences	Life Sciences	Earth and Space Sciences	Engineering
K			K-ESS3-2	
1				
2				
3	3-PS2-4	3-LS4-3		
4	4-PS4-3		4-ESS3-1	
5				
6–8	MS-PS1-3	MS-LS1-1 MS-LS4-5	MS-ESS1-3	
9–12	HS-PS4-5		HS-ESS1-2 HS-ESS1-4 HS-ESS2-3	

Performance Expectations Related to the Influence of Engineering, Technology, and Science on Society and the Natural World

Grade	Physical Sciences	Life Sciences	Earth and Space Sciences	Engineering
K			K-ESS3-2	
1	1-PS4-4	1-LS1-1		
2	2-PS1-2		2-ESS2-1	
3			3-ESS3-1	3-5-ETS1-1 3-5-ETS1-2
4	4-PS3-4		4-ESS3-1 4-ESS3-2	
5				
6–8	MS-PS1-3 MS-PS2-1 MS-PS4-3	MS-LS2-5	MS-ESS3-3 MS-ESS3-4	MS-ETS1-1
9–12	HS-PS3-3 HS-PS4-2 HS-PS4-5		HS-ESS2-2 HS-ESS3-1 HS-ESS3-2 HS-ESS3-3 HS-ESS3-4	HS-ETS1-1 HS-ETS1-3

CONCLUSION

In the decades ahead, the continued growth of the world's population along with technological advances and scientific discoveries will continue to impact the lives of students. Whether or not they choose to pursue careers in technical fields, they will be asked to make decisions that influence the development of technologies and the direction of scientific research that cannot be imagined today. Consequently, it is important for teachers to engage their students in learning about the complex interactions among science, technology, society, and the environment.

REFERENCES

González, N., Moll, L. C., and Amanti, C. (2005). *Funds of knowledge: Theorizing practices in households, communities, and classrooms.* Mahwah, NJ: Lawrence Erlbaum Associates.

Koehler, C., Giblin, D., Moss, D., Faraclas, E., and Kazerounian, K. (2007). Are concepts of technical and engineering literacy included in state curriculum standards? A regional overview of the nexus between technical & engineering literacy and state science frameworks. Proceedings of the ASEE Annual Conference and Exposition, Honolulu, HI.

NRC (National Research Council). (2009). *Learning science in informal environments: People, places, and pursuits.* Washington, DC: The National Academies Press.

NRC. (2012). *A framework for K–12 science education: Practices, crosscutting concepts, and core ideas.* Washington, DC: The National Academies Press.

Yager, R. (1996). Science/technology/society: As reform in science education. Albany: State University of New York Press.

MODEL COURSE MAPPING IN MIDDLE AND HIGH SCHOOL FOR THE NEXT GENERATION SCIENCE STANDARDS

REACHING THE POTENTIAL

A Framework for K–12 Science Education (*Framework*) (NRC, 2012) casts a bold vision for science education, and the resulting Next Generation Science Standards (NGSS) have taken a huge leap toward putting this vision into practice, but there is still work to be done as states contemplate adoption and move toward implementation. This appendix focuses on one aspect of this work—organizing the grade-banded performance expectations (PEs) into courses.

The NGSS are organized by grade *level* for kindergarten through grade 5, but as grade-*banded* expectations at the middle school (6–8) and high school (9–12) levels. This arrangement is due to the fact that standards at these levels are handled very differently in different states and because there is no conclusive research that identifies the ideal sequence for student learning.

As states and districts consider implementation of the NGSS, it will be important to thoughtfully consider how to organize these grade-banded standards into courses that best prepare students for post-secondary success in college and careers. Decisions about this organization are handled differently in different states. Sometimes a decision is prescribed by the state education agency, sometimes by a regional office or a local school district, and other times it falls to the lone 6–12 science teacher—who may not only move between two buildings and teach seven different preparations each day, but also is active in school-sponsored extracurricular activities—to determine what science gets taught at what level.

Recognizing the many ways in which decisions about what to teach are made, this appendix provides a tool for guiding this decision-making process. To realize the vision of the *Framework* and the NGSS, courses need to be thoughtfully designed at levels

of complexity that are developmentally appropriate for students to build knowledge both within courses and over the sequence of courses. *It is also important to note that these are merely the first of several models that will be developed.* There are also plans in the works to develop accelerated models to propel students toward Advanced Placement courses earlier in their high school careers as well as models that integrate the NGSS and career technical education pathways, such as engineering and medicine.

FOUNDATIONAL UNDERSTANDINGS FOR THE NGSS MODEL COURSE MAPS

To use these model course maps effectively, it is essential to understand the thought processes that were involved in building them. This section outlines the foundational decisions that were made in the development of all the model course maps and it attempts to clarify the intent for use of the course maps. Each of these six foundational understandings is more fully explained below; they serve as the basis for effective use of these model course maps.

1. Model course maps are starting points, not finished products.
2. Model course map organization is built on the structure of the *Framework*.
3. All standards, all students.
4. Model course maps are not curriculum.
5. All science and engineering practices and all crosscutting concepts in all courses.
6. Engineering for all.

1. Model Course Maps Are Starting Points, Not Finished Products.

States and districts/local education agencies are not expected to adopt these models; rather, they are encouraged to use them as a starting point for developing their own course descriptions and sequences.

The model course maps described here are both models of process for planning courses and sequences *and* models of potential end products. Every attempt has been made to describe the intent and assumptions underlying each model and the process of model development so that states and districts can utilize similar processes to organize the standards in a useful way. These models illustrate *possible* approaches to organizing the content of the NGSS into coherent and rigorous courses that lead to college and career readiness. The word "model" is used here as it is in the *Framework*—as a tool for understanding, not necessarily as an ideal state.

2. Model Course Map Organization Is Built on the Structure of the Framework.

The *Framework* is organized into four major **domains:** the physical sciences; the life sciences; the earth and space sciences; and engineering, technology, and applications of science. Within each domain, the *Framework* describes how a small set of **disciplinary core ideas** was developed using a set of specific criteria (NRC, 2012, p. 31). Each core idea is broken into three or four **component ideas** that provide more organizational development of the core idea. Figure K-1 provides an example of how one core idea, Matter and Its Interactions (PS1), includes three component ideas: PS1.A: Structure and Properties of Matter, PS1.B: Chemical Reactions, and PS1.C: Nuclear Processes.

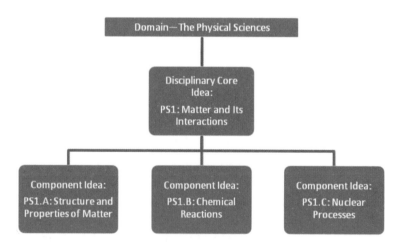

FIGURE K-1 Physical Sciences Core Idea (PS1) and Component Ideas.
NOTE: This in an example from the *Framework* organization to demonstrate the relationship between "domains," "disciplinary core ideas," and "component ideas."

Though the disciplinary core ideas (DCIs) were used as a starting point for building these model course maps, it will be important for coordinated learning that the other dimensions of the *Framework*—science and engineering practices (SEPs) and crosscutting concepts (CCs)—be woven together in classroom instruction (see #5 below). Curriculum designers should consult the *Framework* and the NGSS appendixes for progressions of learning for SEPs and CCs.

3. All Standards, All Students.

All standards are expected of all students. Though this is a foundational commitment of the *Framework* and is discussed at length in Appendix D of the NGSS, it bears repeating here because of its implications for course design. This approach is much more than just a way to refute the common notion that learning physics is only for students in advanced math, or that taking earth and space sciences is only for students who are not on the college track. All standards, all students.

For the 6–8 grade band, this clearly indicates that all of the grade-banded standards should be addressed within the 3-year span and the flexibility of the high school science courses sequence with required and elective courses provides a challenge to ensure that all students are prepared to demonstrate all of the PEs. The model course maps for the 9–12 grade band are all organized into three courses. This decision was made by balancing the "All standards, all students" vision with the reality of the finite amount of time in a school year. It would certainly be recommended that students, especially those considering careers in a science, technology, engineering, and mathematics (STEM)-related field, go beyond these courses to take STEM courses that would enhance their preparation. It should be noted here, however, that an extensive review of the NGSS by college professors of first-year science courses determined that the content in the NGSS does adequately prepare students to be college and career ready in science (see Appendix C). Furthermore, it should also be noted that there is no set amount of time assigned to these courses. Although traditionally these would be considered year-long courses, there is nothing in these models that requires that a course fit into a set amount of time—courses could be spread over a longer time than 3 years, extended to meet student needs, or accelerated. Some modes and settings of instruction—such as proficiency or mastery-based learning, online learning, or alternative learning centers—may even find that structures other than courses are better fits for their situation. Even in these situations, the model course maps and the processes used in their development can help guide curriculum development.

4. Model Course Maps Are Not Curriculum.

The NGSS are student outcomes and are explicitly *not* curriculum. Even though within each NGSS PE the SEPs are partnered with a particular DCI and CC, these intersections *do not predetermine how the three are linked in the curriculum, units, lessons, or instruction*; they simply clarify the expectations of what students will know and be able to do by the end of the grade or grade band. Although considering where PEs will be addressed within courses is an important step in curriculum development, additional work will be needed to create coherent instructional programs that help students achieve these standards.

5. All Science and Engineering Practices and All Crosscutting Concepts in All Courses.

It is the expectation of all the model course maps that *all* SEPs and CCs will be blended into instruction with aspects of the DCIs in every course in the sequence and not just the ones that are outlined in the PEs. The goal is not to teach the PEs, but rather to prepare students to be able to perform them by the end of the grade band course sequence. The PEs are written as grade-band endpoints. Even though a particular PE is placed "in a course," it may not be possible to address the depth of the expectation in its entirety within that course. It may, for example, take repeated exposures to a particular SEP over several courses before a student can achieve the proficiency expected in a given PE, but by the end of the grade band students should be prepared to demonstrate each PE as written.

6. Engineering for All.

As is more carefully detailed in Appendix I, the NGSS represent a commitment to integrate engineering design into the structure of science education by raising engineering design to the same level as scientific inquiry when teaching science disciplines at all levels, from kindergarten to grade 12. Engineering standards have been integrated throughout the science domains of the physical sciences, life sciences, and earth and space sciences. The NGSS also include PEs that focus explicitly on engineering design without a science domain context. Within the range affected by these model course maps, there are four engineering design PEs in the 6–8 grade band and four in the 9–12 grade band. All of the model course maps place the stand-alone engineering PEs with all courses as they help organize and drive instruction of the integrated engineering PEs within each course.

MODEL COURSE MAPS

Three model course maps are included as concrete examples to begin conversations about realizing the vision of the *Framework* and the NGSS. Before reading this section, it is important to read the preceding section, Foundational Understandings for the NGSS Model Course Maps.

Including the three options presented in this section *does not preclude other organizational sequences*. As states, districts, and teachers engage in conversations about the strengths and weaknesses of the model course maps presented here, it is expected that a wider variety of course maps will be collaboratively developed and shared. For example, a curricular and instructional program could be built around the National Academy of Engineering's Grand Challenges for Engineering in the 21st Century or a community-based theme that runs through all the courses and connects the PEs to science, engineering, and technology used in everyday life or could focus on the *Framework*'s CCs or SEPs instead of the DCIs. Furthermore, as was mentioned above, even the term "courses" may be an unnecessarily limiting definition that privileges a time-based system. Some teachers, schools, districts, and states are moving toward a proficiency-based system, but even in such a situation these model course maps can help guide conversations about the connections between PEs and how to begin moving from standards to instruction focused on the NGSS student performance/outcomes.

After the following list, details about each model course map, how it was developed, and ideas for next steps are provided.

1. **Conceptual Progressions Model** (grades 6–8 and 9–12)—The grade-banded PEs are organized so that student understanding of concepts is built progressively throughout the course sequence. This model maps PEs into courses based on what concepts are needed for support without focusing on keeping disciplines separate.

2. **Science Domains Model** (grades 6–8 and 9–12)—The grade-banded PEs are organized into content-specific courses that match the three science domains of the *Framework*: physical sciences, life sciences, and earth and space sciences. Because the engineering domain is mostly integrated into the other three disciplines in the NGSS, it was integrated in these course models rather than presented as a separate course in this sequence. (The four stand-alone engineering PEs in each grade band are connected to all three courses at both levels.)

3. **Modified Science Domains Model** (grades 9–12)—The grade-banded PEs are organized into content-specific courses that match a common high school course sequence of biology, chemistry, and physics. To ensure that all students have access to all standards, the PEs connected to the earth and space sciences domain of the *Framework* are divided among these courses. This model was included as a model for comparison because it is currently a common sequence in high schools across the United States.

Course Map 1—Conceptual Understanding Model (grades 6–8 and 9–12)

Process and Assumptions: How Was This Course Map Developed?

This model course map arranges PEs so that the component ideas of the DCIs in each course progressively build on the skills and knowledge described in courses that precede it. The fifth of the six foundational understandings for using model course maps includes the idea that although all three dimensions described in the *Framework* are specifically integrated within the grade band endpoints, curriculum and instruction will provide students with opportunities to learn the components of the dimensions in a variety of ways to prepare them to perform these endpoints.

Students should have multiple opportunities to engage all of the SEPs and CCs in each course. The premise of this Model Course Map 1, however, is that the DCIs *do* contain content that can be logically sequenced. Creating a logical sequence for the DCI portion of the PEs for this model course map was a multi-stage effort that relied heavily on the *Framework*.

> To develop a thorough understanding of scientific explanations of the world, students need sustained opportunities to work with and develop the underlying ideas and to appreciate those ideas' interconnections during a period of years rather than weeks or months. This sense of development has been conceptualized in the idea of learning progressions. If mastery of a core idea in a science discipline is the ultimate educational destination, then well-designed learning progressions provide a map of the routes that can be taken to reach that destination.
>
> Such progressions describe both how students' understanding of the idea matures over time and the instructional supports and experiences that are needed for them to make progress. Learning progressions may extend all the way from preschool to grade 12 and beyond—indeed, people can continue learning about scientific core ideas their entire lives. Because learning progressions extend over multiple years, they can prompt educators to consider how topics are presented at each grade level so that they build on prior understanding and can support increasingly sophisticated learning. Hence, core ideas and their related learning progressions are key organizing principles for the design of the framework. (NRC, 2012, p. 26)

The first step in this process was separating the core ideas based on their reliance on other core ideas. For example, it is clear just from the titles of the core ideas that to learn about *LS1: From Molecules to Organisms: Structures and Processes*, a student would benefit from an understanding of core idea *PS1: Matter and Its Interactions*. Knowing about atoms, molecules, and how they interact should enhance a student's understanding of how molecules operate in living organisms. This would put core idea PS1 in a course before core idea LS1. Just looking at the titles of the core ideas, however, is not enough to understand the full scope of what content is included in a core idea. Ordering core ideas for this model course map was done by thoroughly comparing the descriptions for each core idea in the *Framework*. Any core ideas that did not have significant reliance on the content in other core ideas were placed in the first course. Core ideas that required support from those in the first course were placed in the second course, and core ideas that required support from core ideas in the second course were placed in the third course. The resulting skeletal sequence based on disciplinary core ideas is shown in Figure K-2. As was discussed in the sixth foundational understanding for all model course maps, there are four PEs in each grade band that focus exclusively on engineering design. Although these PEs are not represented in the figure below, the stand-alone engineering PEs are included in all three courses, as they should help organize and drive instruction of the integrated engineering PEs in all three courses and they will appear in subsequent tables.

Sorting core ideas is a step in the direction of course mapping, but core ideas are at far too big a grain size to be useful for curriculum development. To get closer to a useable grain size, the core ideas were reanalyzed by splitting each one into its component ideas (identified in the *Framework*) and again sorting them into courses to refine their positioning. Essentially, the process used for sorting the DCIs was repeated, but the component ideas disconnected from the core idea and, when appropriate, moved to a different course in the map based on the grade band endpoint descriptions in the *Framework*. For example, although *PS1: Matter and Its Interactions* was originally placed in the first course, its component idea *PS1.C: Nuclear Processes* requires content in both Courses 1 and 2, so it was shifted to Course 3. *PS1.A: Structures and Properties of Matter* and *PS1.B: Chemical*

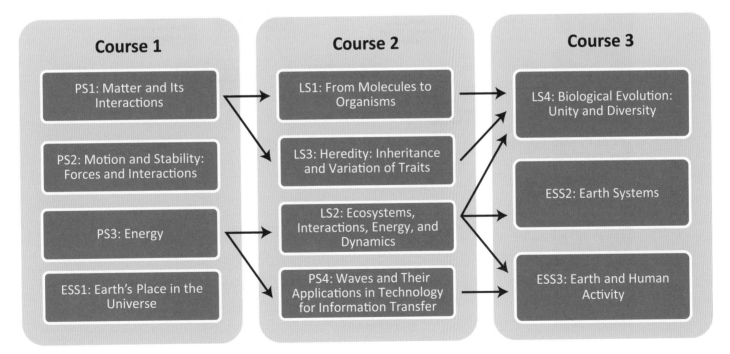

FIGURE K-2 Organization of DCIs for Course Map 1.
NOTE: This figure outlines the first step of organizing the NGSS into courses based on a conceptual progression of the science content outlined in the DCIs in the *Framework*.

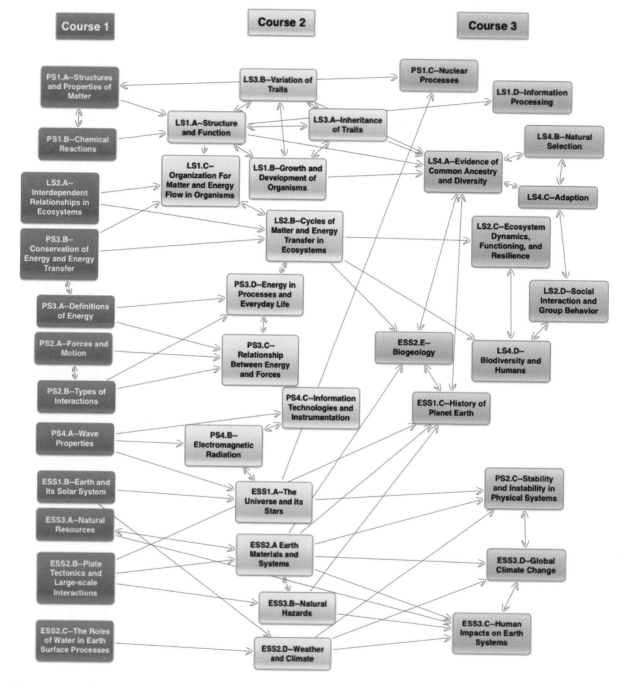

FIGURE K-3 Component idea organization for Model Course Map 1.

NOTE: This figure outlines the result of the second step of mapping the NGSS into courses—refining the arrangement in Figure K-2 by evaluating the DCIs at the finer grain size of the component ideas of which they are made. The arrows illustrate the connections that were used to sort the DCIs into courses, not to determine an order for curriculum.

Reactions remained in course one because they do not require content from other component ideas. Figure K-3 shows the end result of reassigning component ideas to courses. Because this organization is based on the *Framework,* it works for both the 6–8 and 9–12 grade bands.

The final step in the process of building Model Course Map 1 was to reevaluate the organization at the level of the PEs themselves. The tables below outline the first step in this process—connecting the component ideas with their PEs. These tables were built using the information in the NGSS foundation boxes, which document the connections between the PEs and each component idea. Due to the overlapping nature of the content in the component ideas, some PEs are linked to more than one component idea. In these cases, PEs are only listed once in the top section of the table. PE repeats—PEs that are connected to more than one component idea within a course or between courses—and secondary connections are identified in the bottom section of each table.

Next Steps for Course Map 1

It should be clear at this point that this course map will need revision as curricula are developed, but this arrangement should give a good starting point for conversations about what is taught when and why. To help guide these conversations, here are several recommendations and steps that states or districts should consider as they work from this starting point toward developing curricula and instructional unit plans:

1. Revisit the suggested arrangements of DCIs and DCI component ideas to ensure that they progress from course to course in a logical fashion. In this process, make sure to read the descriptions of the core ideas and the component ideas in the *Framework,* rather than only relying on past experiences with those concepts or topics. This may mean ending up with a different arrangement than what is presented here, but collaboratively engaging a broad group of teachers and administrators in this process will result in courses that work for schools, teachers, and students and offers greater buy-in for implementation.

2. As PEs are bundled into curriculum units and lesson plans, it is important to balance this structured arrangement of PEs with

TABLE K-1 Conceptual Progressions Model Course Map—Middle School

COURSE 1

PS1.A	MS-PS1-1.
	MS-PS1-2.
	MS-PS1-3.
	MS-PS1-4.
PS1.B	MS-PS1-5.
	MS-PS1-6.
PS2.A	MS-PS2-1.
	MS-PS2-2.
PS2.B	MS-PS2-3.
	MS-PS2-4.
	MS-PS2-5.
PS3.A	MS-PS3-1.
	MS-PS3-2.
	MS-PS3-3.
	MS-PS3-4.
PS3.B	MS-PS3-5.
PS4.A	MS-PS4-1.
	MS-PS4-2.
LS2.A	MS-LS2-1.
	MS-LS2-2.
ESS1.B	MS-ESS1-1.
	MS-ESS1-2.
	MS-ESS1-3.
ESS2.B	MS-ESS2-3.
ESS2.C	MS-ESS2-2.
	MS-ESS2-4.
	MS-ESS2-5.
	MS-ESS2-6.
ESS3.A	MS-ESS3-1.
ETS1.A	MS-ETS1-1.
ETS1.B	MS-ETS1-2.
	MS-ETS1-3.
	MS-ETS1-4.
ETS1.C	MS-ETS1-3.
	MS-ETS1-4.

COURSE 1 Repeats

PS1.B	MS-PS1-2.
	MS-PS1-3.
PS3.A	*MS-PS1-4.*
PS3.B	MS-PS3-3.
	MS-PS3-4.

COURSE 2

PS4.C	MS-PS4-3.
LS1.A	MS-LS1-1.
	MS-LS1-2.
	MS-LS1-3.
LS1.B	MS-LS1-4.
	MS-LS1-5.
LS1.C	MS-LS1-6.
	MS-LS1-7.
LS2.B	MS-LS2-3.
LS3.A	MS-LS3-1.
	MS-LS3-2.
ESS2.A	MS-ESS2-1.
ESS2.D	MS-ESS2-5.
	MS-ESS2-6.
ESS3.B	MS-ESS3-2.

COURSE 2 Repeats

PS3.C	MS-PS3-2.
PS3.D	*MS-LS1-6.*
	MS-LS1-7.
PS4.B	MS-PS4-2.
LS1.B	*MS-LS3-2.*
LS3.B	MS-LS3-1.
	MS-LS3-2.
ESS1.A	MS-ESS1-1.
	MS-ESS1-2.
ESS2.A	MS-ESS2-2.
ETS1.A	MS-ETS1-1.
ETS1.B	MS-ETS1-2.
	MS-ETS1-3.
	MS-ETS1-4.
ETS1.C	MS-ETS1-3.
	MS-ETS1-4.

COURSE 3

LS1.D	MS-LS1-8.
LS2.C	MS-LS2-4.
	MS-LS2-5.
LS4.A	MS-LS4-1.
	MS-LS4-2.
	MS-LS4-3.
LS4.B	MS-LS4-4.
	MS-LS4-5.
LS4.C	MS-LS4-6.
ESS1.C	MS-ESS1-4.
ESS3.C	MS-ESS3-3.
	MS-ESS3-4.
ESS3.D	MS-ESS3-5.

COURSE 3 Repeats

LS4.D	*MS-LS2-5.*
ESS1.C	*MS-ESS2-3.*
ESS2.D	MS-ESS2-5.
	MS-ESS2-6.
ETS1.A	MS-ETS1-1.
ETS1.B	MS-ETS1-2.
	MS-ETS1-3.
	MS-ETS1-4.
ETS1.C	MS-ETS1-3.
	MS-ETS1-4.

Key to Highlighting

PE appears in two DCIs within the same course
PE is identified in the NGSS as a secondary connection to this component idea
PE is connected to two component ideas between two courses

NOTE: This table connects the middle school NGSS PEs to the component ideas from the *Framework.* These connections are based on the information in the NGSS foundation boxes. In this table the component ideas are arranged into courses based on the organization shown in Figure K-3.

TABLE K-2 Conceptual Progression Model Course Map—High School

COURSE 1

PS1.A	HS-PS1-1.
	HS-PS1-2.
	HS-PS1-3.
	HS-PS1-4.
PS1.B	HS-PS1-5.
	HS-PS1-6.
	HS-PS1-7.
PS2.A	HS-PS2-1.
	HS-PS2-2.
	HS-PS2-3.
PS2.B	HS-PS2-4.
	HS-PS2-5.
	HS-PS2-6.
PS3.A	HS-PS3-2.
	HS-PS3-3.
PS3.B	HS-PS3-1.
	HS-PS3-4.
PS4.A	HS-PS4-1.
	HS-PS4-2.
	HS-PS4-3.
	HS-PS4-5.
LS2.A	HS-LS2-1.
	HS-LS2-2.
ESS1.B	HS-ESS1-4.
ESS2.B	HS-ESS2-1.
	HS-ESS2-3.
ESS2.C	HS-ESS2-5.
ESS3.A	HS-ESS3-2.
ETS1.A	HS-ETS1-1
ETS1.B	HS-ETS1-3
	HS-ETS1-4
ETS1.C	HS-ETS1-2

COURSE 1 Repeats

PS1.B	HS-PS1-2.
	HS-PS1-4.
PS2.B	HS-PS1-1.
	HS-PS1-3.
PS3.A	HS-PS2-5.
PS3.B	HS-PS3-1.
PS4.A	HS-ESS2-3.
ESS1.B	HS-ESS2-4.
ESS2.B	HS-ESS1-5.

COURSE 2

PS3.C	HS-PS3-5.
PS4.B	HS-PS4-4.
LS1.A	HS-LS1-1.
	HS-LS1-2.
	HS-LS1-3.
LS1.B	HS-LS1-4.
	HS-LS1-5.
LS1.C	HS-LS1-6.
	HS-LS1-7.
LS2.B	HS-LS2-3.
	HS-LS2-4.
	HS-LS2-5.
LS3.A	HS-LS3-1.
LS3.B	HS-LS3-2.
	HS-LS3-3.
ESS1.A	HS-ESS1-1.
	HS-ESS1-2.
	HS-ESS1-3.
ESS2.A	HS-ESS2-1.
	HS-ESS2-2.
	HS-ESS2-3.
	HS-ESS2-4.
ESS2.D	HS-ESS2-6.
ESS3.B	HS-ESS3-1.

COURSE 2 Repeats

PS3.D	HS-PS3-3.
	HS-PS3-4.
	HS-PS4-5.
	HS-LS2-5.
	HS-ESS1-1.
PS4.B	HS-PS4-3.
	HS-PS4-5.
	HS-ESS1-2.
PS4.C	HS-PS4-5.
ESS2.A	HS-ESS2-1.
	HS-ESS2-3.
ETS1.A	HS-ETS1-1
ETS1.B	HS-ETS1-3
	HS-ETS1-4
ETS1.C	HS-ETS1-2

COURSE 3

PS1.C	HS-PS1-8.
LS2.C	HS-LS2-6.
	HS-LS2-7.
LS2.D	HS-LS2-8.
LS4.A	HS-LS4-1.
LS4.B	HS-LS4-2.
	HS-LS4-3.
LS4.C	HS-LS4-4.
	HS-LS4-5.
LS4.D	HS-LS4-6.
ESS1.C	HS-ESS1-5.
	HS-ESS1-6.
ESS2.E	HS-ESS2-7.
ESS3.C	HS-ESS3-3.
	HS-ESS3-4.
ESS3.D	HS-ESS3-5.
	HS-ESS3-6.

COURSE 3 Repeats

PS1.C	HS-ESS1-5.
	HS-ESS1-6.
LS2.C	HS-LS2-2.
LS4.C	HS-LS4-2.
	HS-LS4-3.
	HS-LS4-6.
ESS2.D	HS-ESS2-4.
	HS-ESS2-7.
	HS-ESS3-6.
ESS3.A	HS-ESS3-1.
ETS1.A	HS-ETS1-1
ETS1.B	HS-ETS1-3
	HS-ETS1-4
ETS1.C	HS-ETS1-2

Key to Highlighting

PE appears in two DCIs within the same course
PE is identified in the NGSS as a secondary connection to this component idea
PE is connected to two component ideas between two courses

NOTE: This table connects the high school NGSS PEs to the component ideas from the *Framework* on which they were based. These connections are based on the information in the NGSS foundation boxes. In this table the component ideas are arranged into courses based on the organization shown in Figure K-3.

creating courses and units that flow well and engage students in learning. Use the final PE arrangement that is developed (or the one provided by Model Course Map 1) as a *starting point* for building instructional units. As the student outcomes described in the PEs are bundled into meaningful units to build flow within and between courses, PEs may well be pulled from different courses in the map to make this happen. The course map is there to make sure that when PEs are moved from one course to another, instruction is moved accordingly; it is not meant to be a prescriptive, static document. For example, one might decide to connect HS-ESS2-3 ("Develop a model based on evidence of Earth's interior to describe the cycling of matter by thermal convection.") and HS-PS3-2 ("Develop and use models to illustrate that energy at the macroscopic scale can be accounted for as either motions of particles or energy stored in fields.") from Course 1 with HS-PS3-3 from Course 2 ("Design, build, and refine a device that works within given constraints to convert one form of energy into another form of energy.") in an instructional unit that has students engaging in argumentation about sources of energy (gas, electric, geothermal, solar, etc.) for heating and cooling homes as a part of Course 1.

3. As PEs are bundled into instructional units and these units are tied together into courses, units may need to be moved from one course to another to make sure that courses are balanced. This does not necessarily mean that the courses have the same number of PEs. Curriculum units with fewer PEs may take longer than those with more PEs, depending on how those PEs are addressed in the lesson plans. It is recommended to pay particular attention to the repeat PEs listed in the tables in this process. PEs that are connected to more than one component idea may bundle better with the PEs in just one course rather than being represented in two courses.

4. When rearranging PEs and building instructional units, remember that the PEs are *grade-banded* student outcomes and to map out student course expectations appropriately. It may be that, although a PE is placed in a course, students may not be ready to perform all aspects of that PE by the end of the course. For example, a PE may be placed in the first course because the DCI dimension is determined to be foundational to a PE in the second course, but the depth of the SEP described

in the PE may not be reached until the third year. The curriculum will need to be designed in a way that accounts for this reality. In other words, although the expectation is that all SEPs will be in all courses, it would make sense for students in grade 6 to engage differently from those in grade 8; one needs to deliberately build complexity of practices over the middle school sequence. Model Course Map 1 attempts to organize PEs in a way that scaffolds the content from course to course, but as these are rearranged for curriculum development, it may be that some core ideas in PEs may need scaffolding within a course to prepare students to learn the content.

5. The math and English language arts (ELA) NGSS connections boxes and their supporting appendixes (Math—Appendix L; ELA—Appendix M) should be consulted to make sure that courses are not expecting math or ELA content or practices before they are expected in the science sequence. At the high school level, the Common Core State Standards (CCSS) also have grade-banded expectations, so this discussion will need to occur at the state, district, and building levels to make sure that the course map for science does not demand math and ELA performances before they are expected in those curricula. At the middle school level, there are two PEs (MS-PS3-1 and MS-PS4-1) that are presented in the course map before they are expected in the CCSS. This issue is addressed at length in the middle school revision below.

6. It also may be determined that getting all students prepared for all PEs requires more than three courses at the high school level. Organizing the standards into four science courses would simply mean repeating the process as described above, but sorting into four courses instead of three. In order for this to still align with the vision of the *Framework* of all PEs being for all students, all four courses would need to be required for all students. Alternatively, some education systems—especially those heading toward a proficiency-based system—could address some of the PEs in other course structures such as career and technical education, agriculture education, elective science courses, integrated mathematics or STEM courses, alternative education, or online modules.

NEXT STEPS EXAMPLE: MIDDLE SCHOOL REVISION

With work left to do on these models, it might seem overwhelming and difficult to move forward, so this section provides an example of the types of decisions that might be made to advance a revision. In this case the focus is on revising the Conceptual Progressions Model Course Map described in Table K-1. This revision pulls from several of the suggested next steps described above to provide an example of a result of this revision process.

Unsure about whether the Conceptual Progressions Model Course Map would work in their middle school, John, Deb, and Carmen—the only grade 6, 7, and 8 science teachers for Randolph Middle School—decide to dig into the middle school course map and see how it looks after they do a bit of rearranging. In a local-option state that has recently adopted the NGSS, the decision for what will happen with the grade-banded middle and high school standards ends up at the district level and John, Deb, and Carmen are the district's middle school teachers. They had been teaching middle school science courses that were discipline specific as John likes biology, Carmen likes the physical sciences, and Deb has always enjoyed the earth and space sciences. But following a recent K–12 district science meeting in which they took a stab at sorting the disciplinary core ideas into courses, both the middle and high school teachers walked out of the meeting seriously considering using Model Course Map 1. At their next in-service day, John, Deb, and Carmen were able to schedule a half day to work on what their courses might look like next year.

Not sure where to start, Deb suggests beginning with the suggestions in the next steps section for Model Course Map 1. After reading through the steps, the three teachers decide that they still do not have a good sense of what this course map might look like in the classroom, so their starting point is to look for related component ideas that could be bundled for coordinated instruction. Maybe by looking for related PEs and organizing them into units of instruction, they will get a better sense of what it would mean to teach more interdisciplinary courses. In performing this analysis, they notice that several component ideas had only a few PEs and they did not seem to relate too closely to the other component ideas in that course. Whenever the three teachers found what they started calling "orphan PEs," the component idea and attached PEs were moved to a course that had related ideas, as long as the repositioning did not alter the concept flow. For example, John noticed that LS2.B Cycles of Energy and Matter Transfer in Ecosystems in Course 2 had only one PE directly linked to it (see Table K-1). Although there were other life sciences PEs in Course 2, Carmen suggested they move LS2.B and its orphan PE to Course 1 because it would bundle nicely with LS2.A Interdependent Relationships in Ecosystems. John was initially unsure about moving the component idea to another course because it also had some connection to component ideas in Course 2 until Deb pointed out that LS2.A (and its two PEs) was the only life sciences PE in Course 1 and that adding another life sciences PE not only found a home for the orphan PE, but also made Course 1 more coherent. They quickly reviewed the math and ELA connections and did not discover any reason not to move this component idea to Course 1 at the middle school level. A similar line of logic led the group to move ESS2.D Weather and Climate from Course 2 to Course 1—there was only one PE connected to the component idea—and a closer examination of the PEs revealed that it bundled well with ESS1.A Universe and Its Stars and ESS2.C The Roles of Water in Earth Surface Processes.

As the three teachers more closely examined the PEs (their previous work was with the *Framework*), they had concerns that some PEs were not in the right course based on the cognitive complexity demanded. Sometimes the aspect of the component idea emphasized in a PE at the middle school level seemed different than what they remembered from conversations with their high school colleagues at the K–12 district meeting. For example, at the middle school level, *ESS1.A Universe and Its Stars* focuses on the motions of the solar system. Deb suggested that they move this component idea to Course 1 because it fits well with component idea *ESS1.B Earth and Its Solar System*. (At the high school level, *ESS1.A* includes ideas about the Big Bang theory—a better fit with *PS4.B Electromagnetic Radiation* in Course 2). By comparing Tables K-1 and K-2, John picked up on another difference between middle school and high school: Several component ideas do not have PEs at the middle school level, so they eliminated the following component ideas from their middle school course

map: *PS1.C Nuclear Processes, LS2.D Social Interaction and Group Behavior, ESS2.E Biogeology,* and *PS2.C Stability and Instability in Physical Systems*—all of which were placed in Course 3 in the original component idea organization.

Having moved several component ideas from Course 2 to Course 1 and having eliminated a number of component ideas from Course 3, the group had a growing concern about courses becoming unbalanced, so they changed their approach and each looked at their content area specialties for component ideas that might be a good fit to move. Deb nominated *PS3.B Conservation of Energy and Energy Transfer* as a good candidate to move from Course 1 to Course 2. She explained that there was only one PE unique to this component idea and it had good connections with other chemistry PEs in the second course; *PS3.B* was moved to the second course. John suggested moving *LS3.A Inheritance of Traits* and *LS3.B Variation of Traits* to Course 3—both PEs tie in well with the LS4 component ideas that focus on natural selection and evolution— and Carmen proposed moving *ESS3.A Natural Resources* to Course 3 because it fits well with the PEs from *ESS3.A Natural Hazards* and *ESS1.C History of Planet Earth*.

Thinking that they were getting close to something that might work, the three teachers turned their thoughts to what they could make work in their school. They realized that with the room arrangement at Randolph Middle School and the differences in schedules between grades 6 and 7, it simply would not work to have *PS1.B Chemical Reactions* at the grade 6 level. They just did not have the chemistry lab space, safety equipment, or supplies available to make it happen. They decided that advocating for any big changes in room arrangements or schedules was not where they wanted to spend their energy, and so they moved *PS1.B* to Course 2. In looking closely at *PS1.B*, Carmen noticed that a couple of PEs were connected to both *PS1.A* (still in Course 1) and *PS1.B* (now in Course 2). Rather than having these PEs listed in both courses, the teachers decided to evaluate MS-PS1-2 and MS-PS1-3 to determine which course was better to bundle with other PEs. After comparing the PEs, they decided to list MS-PS1-2 with *PS1.B* in Course 2 and MS-PS1-3 with *PS1.A* in Course 1.

Feeling like they had now successfully arranged the science content into a conceptual progression that could work for their school, the three teachers decided to double-check that the model course map they had developed did not require mastery of a level of mathematics that students did not yet have. By examining the NGSS mathematics connections boxes and Appendix L: Connections to CCSS—Mathematics, it became apparent that a couple of PEs needed to be reconsidered. MS-PS3-1—*Construct and interpret graphical displays of data to describe the relationships of kinetic energy to the mass of an object and to the speed of an object*—was of concern because the concept of squares (as would be found in the graphical analysis of kinetic energy) and the graphical analysis of lines are not expected until grade 8 in the CCSS. In their current arrangement (and the one listed above in Table K-1), this PE (which is connected to component idea *PS3.A Definitions of Energy*) was placed in Course 1. Rather than moving this isolated PE to the third course, the teachers decided to move the entire component idea to Course 3 (where it is in Figure K-4), but they were concerned about how exactly it would fit in this course. They decided to talk with their school's math teachers about developing a cross-disciplinary unit. If the math teachers were amenable, the concept of kinetic energy would remain in Course 1, where it bundles well with related PEs. They would also then collaboratively develop a unit for grade 8, in which the math teachers would build on this conceptual foundation by using the science concept of kinetic energy as a context for teaching about squares and graphical analysis. Then when these students reached the grade 8, the science teachers would loan some equipment (and a bit of science knowledge) to the math teachers so that they could collect data in their math classes and use the analysis of these data to teach the mathematics components of the PE—preparing the students to be able to perform the PE by the end of the grade band. MS-PS4-1—*Use mathematical representations to describe a simple model for waves that includes how the amplitude of a wave is related to the energy in a wave*—requires math that would not be expected until the grade 7 and this PE was also housed in Course 1. In this case it was decided to move the PE to Course 2. There it bundles nicely with the component ideas *PS4.B Electromagnetic Radiation* and *PS4.C Information Technologies and Instrumentation*.

John, Deb, and Carmen's revisions are by no means exhaustive—more could be done along these same lines to truly adapt this model course map to local realities, and the decisions they made may not fit another's reality—but continuing to engage in similar processes and collaborating on course map development within and between schools, districts, and states, along with continued research on the relative effectiveness of the implementation of different course maps, will better inform the next round of standards revision.

The revised middle school course map showing all of these changes can be found in Figure K-4, a component idea concept map, and also in Table K-3.

NEXT STEPS EXAMPLE: MIDDLE SCHOOL REVISION 2, STATE SPECIFIC MODEL

As mentioned in the introductory section, the middle school and high school standards are grade banded due to the fact that standards at these levels are handled differently in different states. As states move forward toward adoption these models should be referenced for guidance on how to arrange the PEs. States are encouraged to edit the sample models and turn them into state specific models to reflect an organization that works best for the state. There are many unique factors that may influence a state's decision to arrange the PEs in a particular way.

The following is an example of a state revision where the focus is on revising the Conceptual Progressions Course Map described in Table K-1. This revision was developed by California's Science Expert Panel (SEP), a group comprised of kindergarten through grade 12 teachers, scientists, educators, business industry representatives, and informal science educators.

The SEP used the following criteria to arrange the PEs for middle school grades six, seven, and eight:

1. PEs were placed at each grade level so that they support content articulation across grade levels (from fifth through eighth grade) and provide the opportunity for content integration within each grade level.

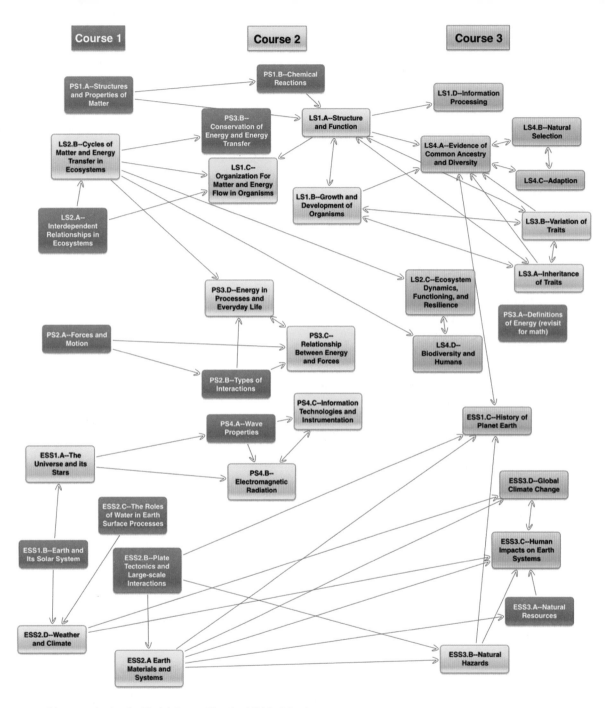

FIGURE K-4 Revised component idea organization for Model Course Map 1—Middle School.

NOTE: This figure outlines the result of refining the arrangement in Figure K-3 using the process described in the Next Steps Example: Middle School Revision.

TABLE K-3 REVISED Conceptual Progressions Model Course Map—Middle School

Course 1

PS1.A	MS-PS1-1.
	MS-PS1-3.
	MS-PS1-4.
PS2.A	MS-PS2-1.
	MS-PS2-2.
LS2.A	MS-LS2-1.
	MS-LS2-2.
LS2.B	MS-LS2-3.
ESS1.A	MS-ESS1-1.
	MS-ESS1-2.
ESS1.B	MS-ESS1-3.
ESS2.A	MS-ESS2-1.
	MS-ESS2-2.
ESS2.B	MS-ESS2-3.
ESS2.C	MS-ESS2-4.
ESS2.C	MS-ESS2-5.
	MS-ESS2-6.
ETS1.A	MS-ETS1-1.
ETS1.B	MS-ETS1-2.
	MS-ETS1-3.
	MS-ETS1-4.
ETS1.C	MS-ETS1-3.
	MS-ETS1-4.

COURSE 1 Repeats

ESS1.B	MS-ESS1-1.
	MS-ESS1-2.
ESS2.C	MS-ESS2-2.
ESS2.D	MS-ESS2-5.
	MS-ESS2-6.

Course 2

PS1.B	MS-PS1-2.
	MS-PS1-5.
	MS-PS1-6.
PS2.B	MS-PS2-3.
	MS-PS2-4.
	MS-PS2-5.
PS3.B	MS-PS3-3.
	MS-PS3-4.
	MS-PS3-5.
PS3.C	MS-PS3-2.
PS4.A	MS-PS4-1.
	MS-PS4-2.
PS4.C	MS-PS4-3.
LS1.A	MS-LS1-1.
	MS-LS1-2.
	MS-LS1-3.
LS1.B	MS-LS1-4.
	MS-LS1-5.
LS1.C	MS-LS1-6.
	MS-LS1-7.

COURSE 2 Repeats

PS3.D	MS-LS1-6.
	MS-LS1-7.
PS4.B	MS-PS4-2.
LS1.B	MS-LS3-2.
ETS1.A	MS-ETS1-1.
ETS1.B	MS-ETS1-2.
	MS-ETS1-3.
	MS-ETS1-4.
ETS1.C	MS-ETS1-3.
	MS-ETS1-4.

Course 3

PS3.A	MS-PS3-1.
LS1.D	MS-LS1-8.
LS2.C	MS-LS2-4.
	MS-LS2-5.
LS3.A	MS-LS3-1.
	MS-LS3-2.
LS4.A	MS-LS4-1.
	MS-LS4-2.
	MS-LS4-3.
LS4.B	MS-LS4-4.
	MS-LS4-5.
LS4.C	MS-LS4-6.
ESS1.C	MS-ESS1-4.
ESS3.A	MS-ESS3-1.
ESS3.B	MS-ESS3-2.
ESS3.C	MS-ESS3-3.
	MS-ESS3-4.
ESS3.D	MS-ESS3-5.

COURSE 3 Repeats

PS3.A	MS-PS3-2.
	MS-PS3-3.
	MS-PS3-4.
	MS-PS1-4.
LS3.B	MS-LS3-1.
	MS-LS3-2.
LS4.D	MS-LS2-5.
ESS1.C	MS-ESS2-3.
ETS1.A	MS-ETS1-1.
	MS-ETS1-2.
ETS1.B	MS-ETS1-3.
	MS-ETS1-4.
ETS1.C	MS-ETS1-3.
	MS-ETS1-4.

Key to Highlighting

PE appears in two DCIs within the same course
PE is identified in the NGSS as a secondary connection to this component idea
PE is connected to two component ideas between two courses

NOTE: This table connects the middle school NGSS PEs to the component ideas from the *Framework*. These connections are taken from the information in the NGSS foundation boxes. In this table the component ideas are arranged into courses based on the revised organization described above and shown in Figure K-4.

2. Performance expectations were aligned with the CCSS in ELA and Mathematics so that science learning would not be dependent on math skills not yet acquired.
3. The final arrangement of PEs reflected a balance both in content complexity and number at each grade level with human impact and engineering PEs appropriately integrated.

In addition to these criteria, the SEP worked to ensure that the PEs could be bundled together in various ways to facilitate curriculum development.

Course Map 2—Science Domains Model (grades 6–8 and 9–12)

Process and Assumptions: How Was This Course Map Developed?

This model course map was built by placing the NGSS PEs into a course structure defined by the science domains outlined in the *Framework*: One course is assigned to each science domain of the *Framework*—life sciences, physical sciences, and earth and space sciences. A fourth course is not included for the fourth domain of the *Framework*—engineering—as most of the NGSS PEs connected to engineering are integrated into the science domains through the SEPs and CCs. The NGSS do include four PEs in both the middle and high school grade bands that focus exclusively on core idea *ETS1: Engineering Design*. As noted in the sixth foundational understanding, these stand-alone engineering PEs are included with all three courses as they help organize and drive instruction of the integrated engineering PEs.

This model does not assume a particular order for these three courses. There is no conclusive research at this point to recommend one sequence over another, and there are a variety of factors that may affect the order determined for these courses if this model course map is selected as a starting point. Ideas for guiding this conversation are included in the next steps section following the presentation of the model.

This model course map is significantly less complicated in development relative to the Conceptual Progressions Model Course Map. The organization was essentially taken straight from the organization of the *Framework*. All component ideas from a given domain

TABLE K-3A California Integrated Learning Progressions Model—Middle School

Course 1

Component Idea	PE
PS3.A	MS-PS3-3.
	MS-PS3-4.
PS3.B	MS-PS3-5.
LS1.A	MS-LS1-1.
	MS-LS1-2.
	MS-LS1-3.
LS1.B	MS-LS1-4.
	MS-LS1-5.
LS1.D	MS-LS1-8.
LS3.A	MS-LS3-2.
ESS2.C	MS-ESS2-4.
	MS-ESS2-5.
	MS-ESS2-6.
ESS3.C	MS-ESS3-3.
ESS3.D	MS-ESS3-5.
ETS1.A	MS-ETS1-1.
ETS1.B	MS-ETS1-2.
	MS-ETS1-3.
	MS-ETS1-4.
ETS1.C	MS-ETS1-3.
	MS-ETS1-4.

COURSE 1 Repeats

Component Idea	PE
PS3.B	MS-PS3-3.
	MS-PS3-4.
LS1.B	MS-LS3-2.
LS3.B	MS-LS3-2.
ESS2.D	MS-ESS2-5.
	MS-ESS2-6.

Key to Highlighting

PE appears in two DCIs within the same course
PE is identified in the NGSS as a secondary connection to this component idea
PE is connected to two component ideas between two courses

Course 2

Component Idea	PE
PS1.A	MS-PS1-1.
	MS-PS1-2.
	MS-PS1-3.
	MS-PS1-4.
PS1.B	MS-PS1-5.
	MS-PS1-6.
LS1.C	MS-LS1-6.
	MS-LS1-7.
LS2.A	MS-LS2-1.
	MS-LS2-2.
LS2.B	MS-LS2-3.
LS2.C	MS-LS2-4.
	MS-LS2-5.
ESS2.A	MS-ESS2-1.
	MS-ESS2-2.
ESS2.B	MS-ESS2-3.
ESS3.A	MS-ESS3-1.
ESS3.B	MS-ESS3-2

COURSE 2 Repeats

Component Idea	PE
PS1.B	MS-PS1-2.
	MS-PS1-3.
PS3.A	MS-PS1-4.
PS3.D	MS-LS1-6.
	MS-LS1-7.
LS4.D	MS-LS2-5.
ESS2.C	MS-ESS2-2.
ETS1.A	MS-ETS1-1.
ETS1.B	MS-ETS1-2.
	MS-ETS1-3.
	MS-ETS1-4.
ETS1.C	MS-ETS1-3.
	MS-ETS1-4.

Course 3

Component Idea	PE
PS2.A	MS-PS2-1.
	MS-PS2-2.
	MS-PS2-3.
PS2.B	MS-PS2-4.
	MS-PS2-5.
PS3.A	MS-PS3-1.
	MS-PS3-2.
PS4.A	MS-PS4-1.
	MS-PS4-2.
PS4.C	MS-PS4-3.
LS3.A	MS-LS3-1.
LS4.A	MS-LS4-1.
	MS-LS4-2.
	MS-LS4-3.
LS4.B	MS-LS4-4.
	MS-LS4-5.
LS4.C	MS-LS4-6.
ESS1.A	MS-ESS1-1.
	MS-ESS1-2.
ESS1.B	MS-ESS1-3.
ESS1.C	MS-ESS1-4.
ESS3.C	MS-ESS3-4.

COURSE 3 Repeats

Component Idea	PE
PS3.C	MS-PS3-2.
PS4.B	MS-PS4-2.
LS3.B	MS-LS3-1.
ESS1.B	MS-ESS1-1.
	MS-ESS1-2.
ETS1.A	MS-ETS1-1.
	MS-ETS1-2.
ETS1.B	MS-ETS1-3.
	MS-ETS1-4.
ETS1.C	MS-ETS1-3.
	MS-ETS1-4.

NOTE: This table connects the middle school NGSS performance expectations to the component ideas from the *Framework*. These connections are taken from the information in the NGSS foundation boxes. In this table, the component ideas are arranged into courses based on California's revised organization.

and all of the PEs connected to each of those component ideas (as noted in the NGSS foundation boxes) were compiled to define each course. Tables K-4 and K-5 display the resulting organization of courses based on the domains model.

Next Steps for Model Course Map 2

Because the courses were effectively designed based on the parameters of the domains of science defined in the *Framework*, any significant shuffling of PEs between courses would, in some sense, void the initial premise of this model, but getting to this point was mainly about taking a first step toward curriculum, so there are several things to be considered in refining the model. As mentioned in the next steps section for Model Course Map 1, it is important to balance this structured arrangement of PEs with creating courses and units that flow well and engage students in learning. This model course map is another potential *starting point* for building instructional units. When bundling student outcomes into meaningful units to build the flow for courses, PEs may still be pulled from different courses in the map to make this work.

1. The order in which these courses would be offered was not pre-determined by the course map, so a decision on how to sequence the courses will need to be made before proceeding with curriculum development. It is important to not sequence courses based only on current courses, but to also look in detail at the PEs mapped to each course (including what is required for math and ELA to accomplish the PEs) and to sequence courses to best benefit student learning. Figure K-3 and Tables K-1 and K-2 from Model Course Map 1 provide insight about the interconnected nature of the component ideas and how they support each other in a progression of content. A close examination of these resources and the next steps suggested for the first model course map are very relevant to this decision-making process. Additionally, the math and ELA connections boxes and their supporting appendixes (Math—Appendix L; ELA—Appendix M) should be consulted to make sure that courses are not requiring math or ELA content or practices before they are expected in the CCSS.

2. Regardless of the final sequence of courses, it is likely that some component ideas from other domains will need to be brought into each course. For example, if the life sciences course is taught before the physical sciences course, some

TABLE K-4 Science Domains Model—Middle School

Physical Sciences

PS1.A	MS-PS1-1.
	MS-PS1-2.
	MS-PS1-3.
	MS-PS1-4.
PS1.B	MS-PS1-5.
	MS-PS1-6.
PS2.A	MS-PS2-1.
	MS-PS2-2.
PS2.B	MS-PS2-3.
	MS-PS2-4.
	MS-PS2-5.
PS3.A	MS-PS3-1.
	MS-PS3-2.
	MS-PS3-3.
	MS-PS3-4.
PS3.B	MS-PS3-5.
PS4.A	MS-PS4-1.
	MS-PS4-2.
PS4.C	MS-PS4-3.
ETS1.A	MS-ETS1-1.
ETS1.B	MS-ETS1-2.
	MS-ETS1-3.
	MS-ETS1-4.
ETS1.C	MS-ETS1-3.
	MS-ETS1-4.

Physical Sciences Repeats

PS1.B	MS-PS1-2.
	MS-PS1-3.
PS3.A	*MS-PS1-4.*
PS3.B	MS-PS3-3.
	MS-PS3-4.
PS3.C	MS-PS3-2.
PS3.D	*MS-LS1-6.*
	MS-LS1-7.
PS4.B	MS-PS4-2.

Life Sciences

LS1.A	MS-LS1-1.
	MS-LS1-2.
	MS-LS1-3.
LS1.B	MS-LS1-4.
	MS-LS1-5.
LS1.C	MS-LS1-6.
	MS-LS1-7.
LS1.D	MS-LS1-8.
LS2.A	MS-LS2-1.
	MS-LS2-2.
LS2.B	MS-LS2-3.
LS2.C	MS-LS2-4.
	MS-LS2-5.
LS3.A	MS-LS3-1.
	MS-LS3-2.
LS4.A	MS-LS4-1.
	MS-LS4-2.
	MS-LS4-3.
LS4.B	MS-LS4-4.
	MS-LS4-5.
LS4.C	MS-LS4-6.

Life Sciences Repeats

LS1.B	*MS-LS3-2.*
LS3.B	MS-LS3-1.
	MS-LS3-2.
LS4.D	*MS-LS2-5.*
ETS1.A	MS-ETS1-1.
	MS-ETS1-2.
ETS1.B	MS-ETS1-3.
	MS-ETS1-4.
ETS1.C	MS-ETS1-3.
	MS-ETS1-4.

Earth and Space Sciences

ESS1.A	MS-ESS1-1.
	MS-ESS1-2.
ESS1.B	MS-ESS1-3.
ESS1.C	MS-ESS1-4.
ESS2.A	MS-ESS2-1.
	MS-ESS2-2.
ESS2.B	MS-ESS2-3.
	MS-ESS2-4.
ESS2.C	MS-ESS2-5.
	MS-ESS2-6.
ESS3.A	MS-ESS3-1.
ESS3.B	MS-ESS3-2.
ESS3.C	MS-ESS3-3.
	MS-ESS3-4.
ESS3.D	MS-ESS3-5.

Earth and Space Sciences Repeats

ESS1.B	MS-ESS1-1.
	MS-ESS1-2.
ESS1.C	*MS-ESS2-3.*
ESS2.C	MS-ESS2-2.
ESS2.D	MS-ESS2-5.
	MS-ESS2-6.
ETS1.A	MS-ETS1-1.
ETS1.B	MS-ETS1-2.
	MS-ETS1-3.
	MS-ETS1-4.
ETS1.C	MS-ETS1-3.
	MS-ETS1-4.

Key to Highlighting

PE appears in two DCIs within the same course
PE is identified in the NGSS as a secondary connection to this component idea
PE is connected to two component ideas between two courses

NOTE: This table connects the middle school NGSS PEs to the component ideas from the *Framework* on which they were based. These connections are based on information in the NGSS foundation boxes. In this table the component ideas are arranged into courses based on the organization described as the Science Domains Model—one course is assigned to each sciences domain of the *Framework*—life sciences, physical sciences, and earth and space sciences.

content from the physical sciences will need to be included in the life sciences course as prerequisite understandings for biological processes. As PEs are bundled into curriculum units and lesson plans it is important to balance this structured arrangement of PEs with creating courses and units that flow well and engage students in learning. The model course map can be used as a *starting point* for building instructional units. When bundling these student outcomes into meaningful units to build the flow for courses, PEs may be pulled from different courses in the map to make this work. The course map is not meant to be a prescriptive, static document; it is meant to provide structure for decision making

3. While rearranging PEs and building instructional units, it is important to remember that the PEs are *grade-banded* student outcomes and to map student course expectations appropriately. It may be that although a PE is placed in a certain course, students may not be ready to perform all aspects of the PE by the end of the course. For example, it could be that a PE is placed in the first course because the DCI dimension is determined to be foundational to a PE in the second course, but the depth of the SEP described in the PE may not be reached until the third year. The curriculum will need to be designed in a way that accounts for this reality. In other words, although the expectation is that all SEPs will be in all courses, it would make sense for students in grade 6 to engage in these differently than those in grade 8. Deliberately building complexity of practices over the middle school sequence is needed.

4. If, during the implementation process, restricting the 9–12 grade band to three courses does not meet local needs, a fourth course could be developed. If all four courses are required, a course map variation like this could still meet the vision of the NGSS and the *Framework*. Because the three domains fit fairly well into courses, there is no obvious way to siphon PEs into a fourth course, but an examination of Course Map Model 1 could provide direction to this process. Because the third course in that sequence contains PEs that are most dependent on content from other PEs, this would be a good starting point in determining which PEs should be considered for being a part of a fourth course.

Physical Sciences

DCI	PE
PS1.A	HS-PS1-1.
	HS-PS1-2.
	HS-PS1-3.
	HS-PS1-4.
PS1.B	HS-PS1-5.
	HS-PS1-6.
	HS-PS1-7.
PS1.C	HS-PS1-8.
PS2.A	HS-PS2-1.
	HS-PS2-2.
	HS-PS2-3.
PS2.B	HS-PS2-4.
	HS-PS2-5.
	HS-PS2-6.
PS3.A	HS-PS3-1.
	HS-PS3-2.
	HS-PS3-3.
PS3.B	HS-PS3-4.
PS3.C	HS-PS3-5.
PS4.A	HS-PS4-1.
	HS-PS4-2.
	HS-PS4-3.
	HS-PS4-5.
PS4.B	HS-PS4-4.
ETS1.A	HS-ETS1-1.
ETS1.B	HS-ETS1-3.
	HS-ETS1-4.
ETS1.C	HS-ETS1-2.

Physical Sciences Repeats

DCI	PE
PS1.B	HS-PS1-2.
	HS-PS1-4.
PS1.C	HS-ESS1-5.
	HS-ESS1-6.
PS2.B	HS-PS1-1.
	HS-PS1-3.
PS3.A	HS-PS2-5.
PS3.B	HS-PS3-1.
PS3.D	HS-PS3-3.
	HS-PS3-4.
	HS-PS4-5.
	HS-LS2-5.
	HS-ESS1-1.
PS4.A	HS-ESS2-3.
PS4.B	HS-PS4-3.
	HS-PS4-5.
	HS-ESS1-2.
PS4.C	HS-PS4-5.

Life Sciences

DCI	PE
LS1.A	HS-LS1-1.
	HS-LS1-2.
	HS-LS1-3.
LS1.B	HS-LS1-4.
LS1.C	HS-LS1-5.
	HS-LS1-6.
	HS-LS1-7.
LS2.A	HS-LS2-1.
	HS-LS2-2.
LS2.B	HS-LS2-3.
	HS-LS2-4.
	HS-LS2-5.
LS2.C	HS-LS2-6.
	HS-LS2-7.
LS2.D	HS-LS2-8.
LS3.A	HS-LS3-1.
LS3.B	HS-LS3-2.
	HS-LS3-3.
LS4.A	HS-LS4-1.
LS4.B	HS-LS4-2.
	HS-LS4-3.
LS4.C	HS-LS4-4.
	HS-LS4-5.
	HS-LS4-6.

Life Sciences Repeats

DCI	PE
LS2.C	HS-LS2-2.
LS4.C	HS-LS4-2.
	HS-LS4-3.
LS4.D	HS-LS4-6.
ETS1.A	HS-ETS1-1.
ETS1.B	HS-ETS1-3.
	HS-ETS1-4.
ETS1.C	HS-ETS1-2.

Earth and Space Sciences

DCI	PE
ESS1.A	HS-ESS1-1.
	HS-ESS1-2.
	HS-ESS1-3.
ESS1.B	HS-ESS1-4.
ESS1.C	HS-ESS1-5.
	HS-ESS1-6.
ESS2.A	HS-ESS2-1.
	HS-ESS2-2.
	HS-ESS2-3.
	HS-ESS2-4.
ESS2.C	HS-ESS2-5.
ESS2.D	HS-ESS2-6.
	HS-ESS2-7.
ESS3.A	HS-ESS3-1.
	HS-ESS3-2.
ESS3.C	HS-ESS3-3.
	HS-ESS3-4.
ESS3.D	HS-ESS3-5.
	HS-ESS3-6.

Earth and Space Sciences Repeats

DCI	PE
ESS1.B	HS-ESS2-4.
ESS2.B	HS-ESS1-5.
	HS-ESS2-1.
	HS-ESS2-3.
ESS2.D	HS-ESS2-4.
	HS-ESS3-6.
ESS2.E	HS-ESS2-7.
ESS3.B	HS-ESS3-1.
ETS1.A	HS-ETS1-1.
ETS1.B	HS-ETS1-3.
	HS-ETS1-4.
ETS1.C	HS-ETS1-2.

Key to Highlighting

PE appears in two DCIs within the same course
PE is identified in the NGSS as a secondary connection to this component idea
PE is connected to two component ideas between two courses

NOTE: This table connects the high school NGSS PEs to the component ideas from the *Framework* on which they were based. These connections are based on the information in the NGSS foundation boxes. In this table the component ideas are arranged into courses based on the organization described as the Science Domains Model—one course is assigned to each sciences domain of the *Framework*—life sciences, physical sciences, and earth and space sciences.

Course Map 3—Modified Science Domains Model (grades 9–12)

Process and Assumptions: How Was This Course Map Developed?

The model course maps presented here attempt to organize the 9–12 grade band PEs based on the frequently taught courses of biology, chemistry, and physics. These courses represent a very common course distribution across many states—either through legislation, regulation, or tradition—so these examples are presented as tools for evaluating how this commonly used course sequence overlays with the expectations of the NGSS. The challenge of this model course map was to also address the earth and space sciences because they are a domain outlined in the *Framework*, but do not have a course of their own in this organization. A fundamental understanding of the NGSS and all of the model course maps is that all PEs are for all students. Because few states currently require four high school science courses, this model examined how the earth and space sciences PEs could be distributed among the three courses already described.

Most of the NGSS engineering PEs are integrated into the other domains; however, in the final draft of the NGSS there are four PEs in each grade band that focus exclusively on engineering design. These stand-alone engineering PEs are included in all three courses because they should help organize and drive instruction of the integrated engineering PEs in all three courses.

The first step in mapping PEs to courses was to examine the component idea level of the DCIs and decide with which course the component ideas best aligned, along with the associated PEs (as noted in the foundation boxes of the NGSS). These decisions were made through a careful reading of the text describing the grade-band endpoints for each component idea in the *Framework*. This was easiest for the life sciences component ideas as they all ended up in biology. It was a more difficult step for the physical sciences component ideas as they had to be split between chemistry and physics courses.

The most challenging domain to organize into these three courses was the earth and space sciences as these PEs did not have a course of their own. Because a fundamental assumption of all of the

model course maps is that all of the PEs of the NGSS are for all students and many states do not require four courses of science for high school graduation, the decision was made to attempt to distribute the earth and space sciences in a logical fashion across the biology, chemistry, and physics courses. This was done in a two-step process: First the 12 earth and space sciences DCI component ideas were assigned to a course based on their best conceptual fit; then the individual earth sciences PEs were sorted by their alignment to those component ideas. This was done using the alignment of PEs to component ideas in the DCI foundation boxes of the NGSS.

As with Model Course Map 2, no course sequence has been assumed in this model.

The assignment of the life sciences DCIs to biology is self-evident based on conventional course descriptions, as is the assignment of the earth sciences DCI component idea *ESS2.E Biogeology*. The component idea of *ESS3.B Natural Hazards* is placed in biology because it offers an opportunity to examine the impact of earth systems on organisms. Conversely, *ESS3.C Human Impacts* is attached to biology so that students can examine the impact of the human organism on other organisms and Earth systems. *ESS1.C History of the Earth* is included because of the interdependent nature of the co-evolution of the Earth system and living organisms.

The DCI component idea *ESS3.A Natural Resources* is included in chemistry because of the important role of many natural resources in chemical reactions that are crucial to modern human society. *ESS3.A Global Climate Change* is connected to chemistry because many Earth-based and atmospheric chemical processes drive systems that affect climate. Addressing *ESS2.D Weather and Climate* is then a logical progression once students better understand its driving mechanisms. *ESS2.C Water in Earth's Surface Processes* is included because many of the geologic effects of water are a result of its molecular structure and chemical properties.

Forces, interactions, waves and electromagnetic radiation, and energy are historically all components of a physics course. The DCI component ideas *ESS1.A The Universe and Stars* and *ESS1.B The Earth and the Solar System* find their home in physics because of the understanding of motion and forces needed to explain their interactions. Similarly, understanding energy flow and the interactions of forces helps explain the mechanisms described in *ESS2.A Earth Materials and Systems* and also in *ESS2.B Plate Tectonics*.

Next Steps for Course Map 3

Course Map 3 lies in between Course Maps 1 and 2 in terms of needed refinement. The courses in this map were primarily driven by the domains of science defined in the *Framework*, but they are designed within the constraint of having biology, chemistry, and physics courses, with the earth and space sciences PEs split among courses. As was mentioned in the next steps sections for the previous two model course maps, it is important to balance this structured arrangement of PEs with creating courses and instructional units that flow well and engage students in learning. This PE arrangement can be used as a *starting point* for building instructional units. While bundling student outcomes into meaningful units to build flow for courses, PEs may be pulled from different courses in the map to make this work.

There are several other considerations when revising this model:

1. Much like Model Course Map 2, the sequence of courses is not predetermined, so deciding on an order would be one of the first decisions to make. It is important to not sequence courses based only on current courses, but to look in detail at the PEs mapped to each course (including what is required for math and ELA to accomplish the PEs) and to then sequence courses so as to best benefit student learning. Figure K-3 and Tables K-1 and K-2 from Model Course Map 1 provide insight about the interconnected nature of the component ideas and how they support each other in a progression of content. A close examination of these resources and the next steps suggested for the first model course map will support this decision-making process. Additionally, the math and ELA connections boxes and their supporting appendixes (Math—Appendix L; ELA—Appendix M) should be consulted to ensure that courses are not requiring math or ELA content or practices before the grade level indicated in the CCSS.

2. The split of earth and space sciences PEs also needs close examination to make sure that the PEs have been effectively arranged and that they fit the expectations of state or local courses. The sequence of courses may have a significant impact on which earth and space sciences PEs are placed in which course.

3. Table K-6, which outlines how the PEs are organized in this model course map, makes it clear that this map has an imbalance of PEs in each course. This deserves examination as PEs are bundled into instructional units to determine if any PEs (or even entire component ideas) should shift courses. The earth and space sciences PEs would be ready candidates for this move, but it might also be that a component idea, such as *LS1.C Organization for Matter and Energy Flow in Organisms*, might be moved from biology (which has the most PEs) to chemistry (which has the least). This move would also make sense because the content of *LS1.C* ties in nicely with some of the chemistry concepts. It should be noted here that simply counting the number of PEs in a course does not necessarily give a good sense of the time it will take to prepare students to be able to perform what is expected—this is better determined by the length of time needed for the instructional units that are developed.

4. While rearranging PEs and building instructional units remember that the PEs are *grade-banded* student outcomes and map student course expectations appropriately. It may be that, although a PE is placed in a course, students may not be ready to perform all aspects of the PE by the end of the course. For example, it could be that a PE is placed in the first course because the DCI dimension is determined to be foundational to a PE in the second course, but the depth of the SEPs described in the PE may not be reached until the third year. The curriculum will need to be designed in a way that accounts for this reality. In other words, although the expectation is that all SEPs will be in all courses, it would make sense for students in grade 6 to engage in these differently than those in grade 8. Deliberately building complexity of practices over the middle school sequence is needed.

5. Another solution to mesh the NGSS with an existing course sequence that includes biology, chemistry, and physics courses would be to add a fourth course—earth and space sciences—to the sequence. If all four courses are required, this variation would still meet the vision of the *Framework* that all PEs are

TABLE K-6 Modified Science Domains Model—High School

Biology

LS1.A	HS-LS1-1.
	HS-LS1-2.
	HS-LS1-3.
LS1.B	HS-LS1-4.
LS1.C	HS-LS1-5.
	HS-LS1-6.
	HS-LS1-7.
LS2.A	HS-LS2-1.
	HS-LS2-2.
LS2.B	HS-LS2-3.
	HS-LS2-4.
	HS-LS2-5.
LS2.C	HS-LS2-6.
	HS-LS2-7.
LS2.D	HS-LS2-8.
LS3.A	HS-LS3-1.
LS3.B	HS-LS3-2.
	HS-LS3-3.
LS4.A	HS-LS4-1.
LS4.B	HS-LS4-2.
	HS-LS4-3.
LS4.C	HS-LS4-4.
	HS-LS4-5.
	HS-LS4-6.
ESS1.C	HS-ESS1-5.
	HS-ESS1-6.
ESS2.E	HS-ESS2-7.
ESS3.B	HS-ESS3-1.
ESS3.C	HS-ESS3-3.
	HS-ESS3-4.
ETS1.A	HS-ETS1-1.
ETS1.B	HS-ETS1-3.
	HS-ETS1-4.
ETS1.C	HS-ETS1-2.

Biology Repeats

LS2.C	HS-LS2-2.
LS4.C	HS-LS4-2.
	HS-LS4-3.
LS4.D	HS-LS4-6.

Chemistry

PS1.A	HS-PS1-1.
	HS-PS1-2.
	HS-PS1-3.
	HS-PS1-4.
PS1.B	HS-PS1-5.
	HS-PS1-6.
	HS-PS1-7.
PS1.C	HS-PS1-8.
PS3.B	HS-PS3-1.
	HS-PS3-4.
PS3.D	HS-PS3-3.
ESS2.C	HS-ESS2-5.
ESS2.D	HS-ESS2-4.
	HS-ESS2-6.
ESS3.A	HS-ESS3-2.
ESS3.D	HS-ESS3-5.
	HS-ESS3-6.

Chemistry Repeats

PS1.B	HS-PS1-2.
	HS-PS1-4.
PS1.C	*HS-ESS1-5.*
	HS-ESS1-6.
PS3.D	HS-PS3-4.
	HS-PS4-5.
	HS-LS2-5.
	HS-ESS1-1.
ESS2.D	HS-ESS2-7.
	HS-ESS3-6.
ESS3.A	HS-ESS3-1.
ETS1.A	HS-ETS1-1.
ETS1.B	HS-ETS1-3.
	HS-ETS1-4.
ETS1.C	HS-ETS1-2.

Physics

PS2.A	HS-PS2-1.
	HS-PS2-2.
	HS-PS2-3.
PS2.B	HS-PS2-4.
	HS-PS2-5.
	HS-PS2-6.
PS3.A	HS-PS3-2.
PS3.C	HS-PS3-5.
PS4.A	HS-PS4-1.
	HS-PS4-2.
	HS-PS4-3.
	HS-PS4-5.
PS4.B	HS-PS4-4.
ESS1.A	HS-ESS1-1.
	HS-ESS1-2.
	HS-ESS1-3.
ESS1.B	HS-ESS1-4.
ESS2.A	HS-ESS2-1.
	HS-ESS2-2.
	HS-ESS2-3.

Physics Repeats

PS2.B	*HS-PS1-1.*
	HS-PS1-3.
PS3.A	HS-PS3-1.
	HS-PS3-3.
	HS-PS2-5.
PS3.B	HS-PS3-1.
	HS-PS3-4.
PS4.A	*HS-ESS2-3.*
PS4.B	HS-PS4-3.
	HS-PS4-5.
	HS-ESS1-2.
ESS1.B	*HS-ESS2-4.*
ESS2.A	HS-ESS2-4.
ESS2.B	*HS-ESS1-5.*
	HS-ESS2-1.
	HS-ESS2-3.
ETS1.A	HS-ETS1-1.
ETS1.B	HS-ETS1-3.
	HS-ETS1-4.
ETS1.C	HS-ETS1-2.

Key to Highlighting

PE appears in two DCIs within the same course
PE is identified in the NGSS as a secondary connection to this component idea
PE is connected to two component ideas between two courses

NOTE: In this table the component ideas are arranged into courses based on the organization described as the Modified Science Domains Model—biology, chemistry, and physics. The table uses the information in the NGSS foundation boxes to connect the high school NGSS PEs to the component ideas from the *Framework*.

expected for all students. Remember that these "courses" do not have a defined length of time—four courses does not necessarily mean 4 years.

NEXT STEPS EXAMPLE: REVISING THE MODIFIED SCIENCE DOMAINS MODEL—FOUR COURSES

The following vignette describes an experience that a high school might have in deciding to use the science domains model, but with revisions to make it a four-course model.

A school district decides that the Modified Science Domains Model will be the easiest to implement because it aligns with the teacher licensure system in the state/district and there is no flexibility in modifying qualified admissions criteria within the state university system. In this state, teacher licensure is restricted to particular content areas (there is no general science endorsement area) and it is particularly difficult to add areas of endorsement. The admissions criteria for state universities specify successful completion of a course called "biology." The organization that regulates these admissions criteria has historically been resistant to make any changes to these criteria. The district is swayed by the vision of the *Framework* and the NGSS and has decided to move forward quickly with implementation for the betterment of its students, but it sees these barriers as insurmountable in the short term and or beyond its control. The K–12 science team has decided that the Modified Science Domains Model will be its starting point and that it will re-evaluate this decision in 5 years based on its effectiveness, any new research that evaluates the course maps at a larger scale, and any changes made to the licensure and admissions criteria—which the team perceives as barriers to using the other model course maps as starting points.

As the K–12 science team evaluates the Modified Science Domains Model team members are unable to come to terms with how the earth and space sciences PEs are to be divided across courses. Unable to propose a different arrangement that they find accept-able, they make a decision to pull out the earth and space sciences component ideas into a separate fourth course. To ensure that this arrangement is robust, the K–12 science team assembles a strategic stakeholder team of local teachers, professors, science-related business and industry representatives, a local school board member who has an interest in science education, and the educator for the local science children's museum to organize the NGSS into four courses. The science team members know that in order to still meet the vision of the NGSS of all standards for all students, they will have to change the graduation criteria for their high school, which currently require only biology and two other science electives. There is a strong relationship between the K–12 science team and the local school board, and especially with the inclusion of a liaison to the board on the team, the team members are hopeful that this is possible—they at least perceive this to be within their realm of potential influence. This local-control state has state graduation requirements, but local modifications are allowed if they exceed the state requirements.

Through discussions of this strategic stakeholder team, the science team decides to keep essentially the same content distribution of the life sciences and physical sciences PEs as they are in the Modified Course Domains Model, but pull the earth and space sciences PEs into the team's own course. In addition to separating the PEs into four courses, the team's revised model course map also follows the example suggested in the third recommended next step (above) and moves LS1.C from biology to chemistry. The science team agrees that even though this is a life sciences component idea, the content has a fair amount of crossover with chemistry and this better balances the courses.

After determining the arrangement of PEs for its course map (see Table K-7), the science team decides to outline a 4-year tentative implementation plan to highlight all necessary changes to curriculum, instruction, professional learning opportunities, and local graduation requirements. The K–12 science team, with the endorsement of the science team, presents the course sequence and implementation plan to the local school board as a part of its request to increase high school graduation requirements to include all four science courses.

TABLE K-7 REVISED Modified Science Domains Model—Four Courses High School

Biology

LS1.A	HS-LS1-1.
	HS-LS1-2.
	HS-LS1-3.
LS1.B	HS-LS1-4.
LS1.C*	HS-LS1-5.
	HS-LS1-6.
	HS-LS1-7.
LS2.A	HS-LS2-1.
	HS-LS2-2.
LS2.B	HS-LS2-3.
	HS-LS2-4.
	HS-LS2-5.
LS2.C	HS-LS2-6.
	HS-LS2-7.
LS2.D	HS-LS2-8.
LS3.A	HS-LS3-1.
LS3.B	HS-LS3-2.
	HS-LS3-3.
LS4.A	HS-LS4-1.
LS4.B	HS-LS4-2.
	HS-LS4-3.
LS4.C	HS-LS4-4.
	HS-LS4-5.
	HS-LS4-6.
ETS1.A	HS-ETS1-1.
ETS1.B	HS-ETS1-3.
	HS-ETS1-4.
ETS1.C	HS-ETS1-2.

Biology Repeats

LS2.C	HS-LS2-2.
LS4.C	HS-LS4-2.
	HS-LS4-3.
LS4.D	HS-LS4-6.

Chemistry

PS1.A	HS-PS1-1.
	HS-PS1-2.
	HS-PS1-3.
	HS-PS1-4.
PS1.B	HS-PS1-5.
	HS-PS1-6.
	HS-PS1-7.
PS3.B	HS-PS3-1.
	HS-PS3-4.
PS3.D	HS-PS3-3.

LS1.C moved from Biology

LS1.C*	HS-LS1-5.
	HS-LS1-6.
	HS-LS1-7.

Chemistry Repeats

PS1.B	HS-PS1-2.
	HS-PS1-4.
PS3.D	HS-PS4-5.
	HS-LS2-5.
	HS-ESS1-1.
	HS-PS3-4.
ETS1.A	HS-ETS1-1.
ETS1.B	HS-ETS1-3.
	HS-ETS1-4.
ETS1.C	HS-ETS1-2.

Physics

PS2.A	HS-PS2-1.
	HS-PS2-2.
	HS-PS2-3.
PS2.B	HS-PS2-4.
	HS-PS2-5.
	HS-PS2-6.
PS1.C	HS-PS1-8.
PS3.A	HS-PS3-2.
PS3.C	HS-PS3-5.
PS4.A	HS-PS4-1.
	HS-PS4-2.
	HS-PS4-3.
	HS-PS4-5.
PS4.B	HS-PS4-4.

Physics Repeats

PS2.B	HS-PS1-1.
	HS-PS1-3.
PS3.A	HS-PS3-1.
	HS-PS3-3.
	HS-PS2-5.
PS3.B	HS-PS3-1.
	HS-PS3-4.
PS4.A	HS-ESS2-3.
PS4.B	HS-PS4-3.
	HS-PS4-5.
	HS-ESS1-2.
ETS1.A	HS-ETS1-1.
ETS1.B	HS-ETS1-3.
	HS-ETS1-4.
ETS1.C	HS-ETS1-2.

Earth and Space Sciences

ESS1.A	HS-ESS1-1.
	HS-ESS1-2.
	HS-ESS1-3.
ESS1.B	HS-ESS1-4.
ESS1.C	HS-ESS1-5.
	HS-ESS1-6.
ESS2.A	HS-ESS2-1.
	HS-ESS2-2.
	HS-ESS2-3.
	HS-ESS2-4.
ESS2.C	HS-ESS2-5.
ESS2.D	HS-ESS2-6.
	HS-ESS2-7.
ESS3.A	HS-ESS3-1.
	HS-ESS3-2.
ESS3.C	HS-ESS3-3.
	HS-ESS3-4.
ESS3.D	HS-ESS3-5.
	HS-ESS3-6.

Earth and Space Sciences Repeats

ESS1.B	HS-ESS2-4
ESS2.B	HS-ESS1-5.
	HS-ESS2-1.
	HS-ESS2-3.
ESS2.D	HS-ESS2-4.
	HS-ESS3-6.
ESS2.E	HS-ESS2-7.
ESS3.B	HS-ESS3-1.
ETS1.A	HS-ETS1-1.
ETS1.B	HS-ETS1-3.
	HS-ETS1-4.
ETS1.C	HS-ETS1-2.

Key to Highlighting

PE appears in two DCIs within the same course
PE is identified in the NGSS as a secondary connection to this component idea
PE is connected to two component ideas between two courses

NOTE: In this table the component ideas are arranged into courses based on the organization described as the Modified Science Domains Model—biology, chemistry, and physics—with a fourth course added for the earth and space sciences. The table uses the information in the NGSS foundation boxes to connect the high school NGSS PEs to the component ideas from the *Framework*.
*LS1.C moved from Biology to Chemistry.

COURSE MAPS AND IMPLEMENTATION

Choosing a Course Map

These course maps are not end products; they are models of processes for mapping PEs onto courses and starting points for continued work. They are by no means the only arrangements possible, but are intended to be concrete examples to start conversations about the direction of science education at the building, district, and state levels. This section highlights factors to consider in making a decision to use one, more than one (at different grade bands), or none of the model course maps presented.

Any course map will have benefits and challenges linked to the underlying assumptions and processes that were involved in making them and to the local situation where they are to be implemented. Of course, "benefits" and "challenges" depend on one's perspective. Something identified as a "challenge" may actually be a primary reason for selecting a model if the challenge is one that is determined to be in the students' best interest. For example, if a state education agency is already planning a redesign of teacher licensure criteria, then selecting a model course map that does not fit well with the existing teacher licensure system would not necessarily be a barrier to selecting that course map—it might even be a reason for selection because it aligns with the direction of the licensure redesign process. Likewise, what some may consider a "benefit," others may see as a reason not to select a course map. Some may start with a particular course map because it contains courses that are very similar to what is currently offered, but others may see this as more of a drawback as it may result in teachers being less convinced they need to make any changes—making it difficult to ensure a complete and coherent implementation of the vision of the *Framework*. The realities and needs in states and local education agencies (LEAs) are quite different; therefore, outlined below are factors to consider in deciding how to map the grade-banded PEs onto courses for the NGSS.

Factors for Consideration

1. **Are the performance expectations organized in a way to maximize student learning?**
   Course Map 1, Conceptual Understanding, was the only model that was consciously designed with this in mind. DCI component ideas and their related PEs are deliberately sequenced to allow students to build knowledge in a logical progression. This model supports students' engagement in SEPs and applies CCs to deepen students' understanding of the core ideas in the physical sciences, life sciences, and earth and space sciences over multiple years (NRC, 2012, p. 8). According to the *Framework*, "By the end of the 12th grade, students should have gained sufficient knowledge of the practices, crosscutting concepts, and core ideas of science and engineering to engage in public discussions on science-related issues, to be critical consumers of scientific information related to their everyday lives, and to continue to learn about science throughout their lives" (NRC, 2012, p. 9).

   This does not mean that, through effective curriculum planning and lesson plan development, the other models course maps could not be developed in a way that would also maximize student learning, but their infrastructure was not designed with this as a focus. With an organizational structure built directly from the domains of the *Framework* (Course Map 2) or traditional scientific divisions (Course Map 3), it will take a concerted effort to ensure that there are opportunities to build conceptual knowledge over time, especially for concepts that are cross-disciplinary.

2. **Are the performance expectations organized in a way that increases efficiency in instruction?**
   Among the many recommendations for improving the coherence and effectiveness of the K–12 curriculum, *Designs for Science Literacy* (AAAS, 2001) is a cross-disciplinary organization that eliminates the unnecessary repetition of topics—the same ideas in the same contexts, often with the same activities and the same questions. A common student complaint is that the same topics are presented in successive grades, often in the same way. Similarly, a common teacher complaint is that students did not receive instruction in important topics in prior

grades and so these topics then have to be taught in the present grade, thus perpetuating an instructional gap for the following grades (AAAS, 2001).

In Course Map 1 the thoughtful sequence of DCI component ideas and PEs limits unnecessary repetition while still providing students with the requisite knowledge for success in subsequent science courses. Course Maps 2 and 3 were not designed with this in mind, and although the order that courses are sequenced within either model could alleviate some of this, there are PEs within every course that expect students to know concepts that are being addressed in other courses. If this is addressed thoughtfully in curriculum design, it could provide opportunities for cross-disciplinary connections, but in terms of instruction efficiency, it does mean that there will be times that teachers will have to allot class time to bring students up to speed on the background concepts necessary to progress to the concepts intended to be addressed in any given course.

3. **Are the performance expectations organized in a way that represents the interconnectedness of science?**
The organization of scientific research has become more complex and has evolved from the Committee of Ten's constructs of 1893, which organized K–12 science education around astronomy, meteorology, botany, zoology, physiology, anatomy, hygiene, chemistry, and physics. The cross-disciplinary organization of Course Map 1 makes natural connections across the science domains of the *Framework* more evident to teachers and students and provides for a more flexible, coherent, and realistic pathway to developing deep understandings of science. Course Maps 2 and 3 were not designed with this in mind, although careful curriculum and lesson plan development could create these connections.

4. **How does the course map align with current state guidelines/ legislation/policies for course titles, course sequences, teacher licensure, credits for graduation, and college admissions expectations?**
States vary in terms of how these policies are created and the processes that are involved in changing them, but these are all important factors for consideration in selecting or developing a course map. For example, some states require only two science

credits for graduation, but the NGSS PEs are written for all students and none of the model course maps include fewer than three courses. "Credit" and "courses" do not describe what students know or are able to do; the system of PEs in the NGSS, all of which are for all students, detail what is to be achieved.

5. **What are the implications for teaching positions?**
Any of the course map models (depending on the realities of current teacher preparation and licensure policies, current course offerings, graduation requirements, course sequences, etc., and any changes that are proposed) may have a significant impact on the number of teachers prepared to teach courses. This could also be affected by the proposed sequencing of courses in Course Maps 2 and 3. For example, switching from a biology–chemistry–physics sequence in a state where biology is the only "required" science in a sequence of three required for graduation to using Course Map 2 and sequencing physical sciences–life sciences–earth sciences courses will put different demands on the system to provide teachers qualified to teach these courses. This would also potentially impact teacher certification/licensure policies, teacher preparation, and professional learning opportunities.

6. **How do these course maps affect the focus of pre-service teacher preparation and professional learning opportunities?**
Transitioning from current state science standards to the NGSS provides significant opportunities to support advancing science instruction regardless of the course map that is utilized. Teachers of science will need intensive, ongoing, and job-embedded professional development in order for their students to meet the challenges of the PEs defined in the NGSS. Teachers will need to wrestle with questions such as:

- What do we want students to learn?
- How will we know what students are learning?
- How will we respond when they do not learn?

The cross-disciplinary approach of Course Map 1 is somewhat different than common current practice in teacher preparation and professional development. Pre-service teachers are less likely to have experienced an explicitly cross-disciplinary course in their own courses, which will mean that those responsible for preparing them to be teachers will have to explicitly incorporate this into teaching and learning experiences. Many teachers already in the field are very passionate about the particular domain they are teaching. They may have accumulated a significant amount of knowledge of practices and core ideas within a content area and may have less experience outside their preferred domain. If Course Map 1 is used, professional learning opportunities will need to be carefully crafted to value this expertise and support teachers in making any transition.

Course Map 2 does not require a specific focus for teacher preparation or professional learning other than the focuses called for in transitioning to the NGSS.

Course Map 3 would also require a specific focus on teacher preparation and professional learning opportunities. Incorporation of the earth and space sciences PEs across biology, chemistry, and physics courses may not align with current practice. Teacher preparation and professional learning opportunities will need to be explicitly designed to support teachers in this transition.

7. **Does the course map affect any plans for communicating about science education with stakeholders?**
In adopting the NGSS (an assumed step if now choosing a course map of these standards), communication with key stakeholders—students, parents, teachers, administrators, school boards, business and industry, etc.—will be important to support effective implementation. The course map model that is used may require additional specific communication with messaging targeted for stakeholder groups, particularly if the course map requires significant system changes.

8. **How is the chosen course map impacted by resource availability?**
Existing resources, such as textbooks, workbooks, and even online resources, often sort information based on content in a way that is more similar to Course Maps 2 and 3. For states or districts that focus curriculum on a particular textbook, this may affect the decision of how to map courses, but for others that pull from a variety of resources and already use textbooks as a support for curriculum rather than as the curriculum, this may be irrelevant. As new resources are written and existing resources are rewritten for the NGSS, they might be more

frequently designed with one course map or another in mind, but this too may be less of a concern due to the development of more flexible resources, such as open education resources and editable digital textbook formats.

CONCLUSIONS

It may seem a forgone conclusion that the course map specifically designed to coherently build student conceptual understanding over time, maximize efficient use of class time, and prepare students for the cross-disciplinary reality of science research will be the one that everyone selects, but there may be good reasons for choosing a different model (including "none of the above"). In fact, engineering an effective learning program is a complex and challenging task that depends on instructor knowledge of the content and pedagogy, materials that support good instruction, determination and implementation of learning progressions, assessments for formative and summative purposes, and even school climate—issues much beyond the goals of this appendix. Hopefully the factors described above will result in meaningful conversations in states and districts about their science education systems. Adopting the NGSS will require systemic changes to implement them with fidelity to the vision of the *Framework*. It is a great opportunity for deliberate decision making about whether or not a school system is designed in a way that gives students the best opportunities possible to realize this vision. Deciding on a course map is just one of the important decisions in this process, but it requires careful consideration because of the potential impacts across the system.

This situation of many states and districts utilizing the same standards, but with different course maps also has significant potential to inform our understanding of how students learn science. As mentioned in the beginning of this chapter, the reason all educators implementing the NGSS even have to juggle the idea of multiple course maps is that there is insufficient research to recommend a particular sequence. With 50 different sets of state standards, it has been difficult to determine if one sequence is more effective than another, but with many states considering adoption of these standards, there is fertile ground for historic research to move our understanding forward.

Developing a New Course Map

It might be that none of the course maps presented here meet the needs of a particular state or LEA. If this is the case, it would definitely make sense to design a new, individual course map model rather than simply refine what has been provided. The multi-dimensionality of the NGSS would certainly allow for a course map based on something other than just DCIs—either by one of the other dimensions or a combination of the three. These and other reasons for developing alternative course map models are certainly valid, but hopefully there is enough in the descriptions above to make this process a bit smoother. Examining the underlying assumptions of these course maps, reviewing the processes that were used to create the course maps, and weighing all this with the factors for consideration described above provides a framework to jump-start the development of new course maps that meet the needs of the students in an LEA or state.

Refining a Course Map

Selecting one of the course maps provided here does not mean the work is done; it is the first step in a journey. The course map will need further refinement to meet local needs. Then the real work begins to develop curricula and lessons based on the course map, and necessary professional learning opportunities will need to be accessed or developed to support implementation with fidelity. Additionally, as with all scientific endeavors, it will be necessary to plan how it will be determined whether efforts are successful. What types of data will be used to determine whether or not the new arrangement has worked? What processes will be put in place to refine a course map to increase its effectiveness? Even once these questions have been answered, as curriculum units and lesson plans are designed and refined in the classroom, it is likely that further refinement of the course map will be necessary.

Recommendations for refining each course map are provided at the end of each model description above, but more significant revisions may be in order if the underlying assumptions described in the beginning of this chaper are not acceptable. For example, if a state requires four courses in science and there is no intention to change this, then a three-course sequence for high school may not what is needed. This may mean that the models presented here will need to be refined—perhaps simply re-sorting PEs in Course Map Model 1 into four courses or using Course Map Model 3 with a separate earth and space sciences course rather than splitting the earth and space sciences PEs across biology, chemistry, and physics—or it may mean starting from scratch.

Additional work will need to be done locally to consider the mathematics expected by the PEs in both middle school and high school grade bands. As local mathematics courses may differ, especially at the high school level, it will be important to have cross-disciplinary conversations to make sure that students are receiving complementary instruction across content areas. The connections boxes in the NGSS should inform this conversation.

REFERENCES

AAAS (American Association for the Advancement of Science). (2001). *Designs for science literacy.* New York: Oxford University Press.

NRC (National Research Council). (2012). *A framework for K–12 science education: Practices, crosscutting concepts, and core ideas.* Washington, DC: The National Academies Press.

CONNECTIONS TO THE COMMON CORE STATE STANDARDS FOR MATHEMATICS

CONSISTENCY WITH THE COMMON CORE STATE STANDARDS FOR MATHEMATICS

Science is a quantitative discipline, so it is important for educators to ensure that students' science learning coheres well with their learning in mathematics.[1,2] To achieve this alignment, the Next Generation Science Standards (NGSS) development team worked with the Common Core State Standards for Mathematics (CCSSM) writing team to ensure the NGSS do not outpace or otherwise misalign to the grade-by-grade standards in the CCSSM. Every effort has been made to ensure consistency. It is essential that the NGSS always be interpreted, and implemented, in such a way that the math does not outpace or misalign to the grade-by-grade standards in the CCSSM (this includes the development of NGSS-aligned instructional materials and assessments).

For convenience, Table L-1 shows CCSSM grade placements for key topics relevant to science. This table can help science educators ensure that students' work in science does not require them to meet the indicated CCSSM standards before the grade level in which they appear.

- For additional information on representing and interpreting data in grades K–5, see the *Progressions* document available at: http://commoncoretools.files.wordpress.com/2011/06/ccss_progression_md_k5_2011_06_20.pdf.
- For additional information on measurement in grades K–5, see the *Progressions* document available at: http://commoncoretools.files.wordpress.com/2012/07/ccss_progression_gm_k5_2012_07_21.pdf.

TABLE L-1 Key Topics Relevant to Science and the Grade at Which They Are First Expected in the CCSSM

Number and Operations	Grade First Expected
Multiplication and division of whole numbers	3
Concept of a fraction a/b	3
Beginning fraction arithmetic	4
Coordinate plane	5
Ratios, rates (e.g., speed), proportional relationships	6
Simple percent problems	6
Rational number system/signed numbers—concepts	6
Rational number system/signed numbers—arithmetic	7
Measurement	**Grade First Expected**
Standard length units (inch, centimeter, etc.)	2
Area	3
Convert from a larger unit to a smaller in the same system	4
Convert units within a given measurement system	5
Volume	5
Convert units across measurement systems (e.g., inches to centimeters)	6
Statistics and Probability	**Grade First Expected**
Statistical distributions (including center, variation, clumping, outliers, mean, median, mode, range, quartiles) and statistical associations or trends (including two-way tables, bivariate measurement data, scatter plots, trend line, line of best fit, correlation)	6–8
Probability, including chance, likely outcomes, probability models	7

NOTE: See the CCSSM for exact Statements of Expectations.

---

[1] For more on this point, see page 17 of the *K–8 Publishers' Criteria for the Common Core State Standards for Mathematics* and page 15 of the *High School Publishers' Criteria for the Common Core State Standards for Mathematics*, both available at: www.corestandards.org.

[2] For example, concepts of physical measurement are intertwined with students' developing understanding of arithmetic in the elementary grades; see the *Progressions* document available at: http://commoncoretools.files.wordpress.com/2012/07/ccss_progression_gm_k5_2012_07_21.pdf and the brief essay "Units, a Unifying Idea in Measurement, Fractions, and Base Ten" available at: http://commoncoretools.me/2013/04/19/units-a-unifying-idea.

During the middle school and high school years, students develop a number of powerful quantitative tools, from rates and proportional relationships, to basic algebra and functions, to basic statistics and probability. Such tools are applicable far beyond the mathematics classroom. Such tools can also be better understood, and more securely mastered, by applying them in a variety of contexts. Fortunately, the National Research Council (NRC) report *A Framework for K–12 Science Education* (*Framework*) makes clear in its science and engineering practices (Analyzing and Interpreting Data, Using Mathematics and Computational Thinking) that statistics and mathematics have a prominent role in science. The NGSS aim to give middle school and high school science educators a clear road map to prepare their students for the quantitative demands of college and careers, where students need to apply quantitative tools in an applied or scientific context.[3] For all these reasons, the NGSS require key tools for grades 6–8 and the high school Common Core State Standards (CCSS) to be integrated into middle school and high school science instructional materials and assessments.

For additional detail, see Table L-2, as well as the NGSS Condensed Practices (Appendix F) and the CCSS connections boxes that appear throughout the NGSS.

CONNECTIONS TO CCSSM STANDARDS FOR MATHEMATICAL PRACTICE

Some general connections to the CCSSM can be found among CCSSM's Standards for Mathematical Practice. The three CCSSM practice standards most directly relevant to science are:
- MP.2. Reason abstractly and quantitatively.
- MP.4. Model with mathematics.
- MP.5. Use appropriate tools strategically.

Mathematical practice standards MP.2 and MP.4 are both about using mathematics in context. The first practice standard, MP.2, is about the back and forth between (1) manipulating symbols abstractly and (2) attending to the meaning of those symbols

TABLE L-2 Middle School and High School Science and Engineering Practices That Require Integrating the CCSSM Math/Statistics Tools into the NGSS-Aligned Instructional Materials and Assessments

Science and Engineering Practices	6–8 Condensed Practices (subset requiring integration)	9–12 Condensed Practices (subset requiring integration)
Analyzing and Intepreting Data	Apply concepts of statistics and probability from the CCCSS (found in grades 6-8.SP) to scientific and engineering questions and problems, using digital tools when feasible.	Apply concepts of statistics and probability from the high school CCCSS (found in S) to scientific and engineering questions and problems, using digital tools when feasible.
Using Mathematics and Computational Thinking	Apply concepts of ratio, rate, percent, basic operations, and simple algebra to scientific and engineering questions and problems. (See grades 6-7.RP, 6-8.NS, and 6-8.EE in the CCSS.)	Apply techniques of algebra and functions to represent and solve scientific and engineering problems. (See A and F in the CCSS.) Apply key takeaways from grades 6–8 mathematics, such as applying ratios, rates, percentages, and unit conversions (e.g., in the context of complicated measurement problems involving quantities with derived or compound units, such as mg/mL, kg/m^3, acre-feet, etc.).[a]

NOTE: Refer to the NGSS Science and Engineering Practices for context and to the CCSSM for information about the standards notation: http://www.corestandards.org/Math.
[a] See Table 1 of the *High School Publishers' Criteria for the Common Core State Standards for Mathematics*, available at: www.corestandards.org/resources.

---

[3] Table 1 of the *High School Publishers' Criteria for the Common Core State Standards for Mathematics* shows widely applicable prerequisites for college and careers available at: www.corestandards.org.

while doing so. For example, a kindergarten student might connect a symbolic statement like "6 > 4" to the fact that there are more objects in one given set than in another. A middle school student might rewrite the equation $d = 65t$ for the motion of a car in the equivalent form $d/t = 65$, recognizing that the new equation abstractly expresses the steps in a computation of the car's speed. A high school student might connect the 2 in the equation $N = 2^n$ to the fact that each dividing cell gives rise to two daughter cells.

The second practice standard, MP.4, is also about applying mathematics, but with more of a focus on results and less on the mental processes involved:

- In grades K–2, modeling with mathematics typically means diagramming a situation mathematically, and/or solving a one-step addition/subtraction word problem.
- In grades 3–5, modeling with mathematics typically means representing and/or solving a one-step or multi-step word problem.
- In grades 6–8, modeling with mathematics typically means representing and/or solving a one-step or multi-step word problem, possibly one in which certain assumptions necessary to formulate the problem mathematically are not specified for the student.
- In high school, modeling with mathematics typically includes the kinds of problems seen in grades 6–8 as well as "full models"—that is, problems that include more of the steps of the modeling cycle. (National Governors Association Center for Best Practices, Council of Chief State School Officers, 2010, pp. 72–73)

Finally, the third practice standard, MP.5, refers not only to technological tools, but also to such strategies as drawing diagrams from kindergarten onward and, in later grades, using well-known formulas and powerful representation schemes like the coordinate plane. These tools, and the skill and judgment to use them well, are important for quantitative work in science.

About CCSSM practice standard MP.3: None of the connections boxes include a link to CCSSM practice standard MP.3, which reads, "Make viable arguments and critique the reasoning of others." The lack of a connection to MP.3 might appear surprising, given that science too involves making arguments and critiquing them. However, there is a difference between mathematical arguments and scientific arguments—a difference so fundamental that it would be misleading to connect any of the standards to MP.3

here. The difference is that *scientific arguments are always based on evidence, whereas mathematical arguments never are*. It is this difference that renders the findings of science provisional and the findings of mathematics eternal. As Isaac Asimov wrote in the Foreword to *A History of Mathematics*, "Ptolemy may have developed an erroneous picture of the planetary system, but the system of trigonometry he worked out to help him with his calculations remains correct forever" (Boyer and Merzbach, 1991, pp. vii–viii). Blurring the distinction between mathematical and scientific arguments leads to a misunderstanding of what science is about. For more information about argumentation in science, see the NGSS science and engineering practice "Engaging in argument from evidence."

For more information on the standards for mathematical practice in general, see CCSSM, pp. 6–8. Also see pp. 72–73 for information on modeling in particular.

The rest of this appendix presents the remaining connections from the connections boxes. Illustrative science examples are provided for a number of the connections, along with alignment notes in select cases.

K-PS2 MOTION AND STABILITY: FORCES AND INTERACTIONS

As part of this work, teachers should give students opportunities to **use direct measurement:**

K.MD.A.1. Describe measurable attributes of objects, such as length or weight. Describe several measurable attributes of a single object.

K.MD.A.2. Directly compare two objects with a measurable attribute in common to see which object has more of/less of the attribute and describe the difference. *For example, directly compare the heights of two children and describe one child as taller/shorter.* **Science examples: Students make a simple pulley that uses one object to lift a second object. They describe one of the objects as heavier than the other. They try to predict which will rise and which will fall. In consecutive trials that vary the weight of the first object (keeping the second object the same), students conclude that a heavier object will lift a given target object faster.**

Alignment notes: (1) Data displays such as picture graphs and bar graphs are not expected until grade 2. (2) Standard length units such as centimeters or inches are not expected until grade 2. Informal units (e.g., a paper clip used as a length unit) are not expected until grade 1.

K-PS3 ENERGY

As part of this work, teachers should give students opportunities to **use direct measurement:**

K.MD.A.2. Directly compare two objects with a measurable attribute in common to see which object has more of/less of the attribute and describe the difference. *For example, directly compare the heights of two children and describe one child as taller/shorter.* **Science example: Directly compare a stone left in the sun with a stone left in the shade and describe one of the stones as warmer/cooler than the other.**

K-LS1 FROM MOLECULES TO ORGANISMS: STRUCTURES AND PROCESSES

As part of this work, teachers should give students opportunities to **use direct measurement:**

K.MD.A.2. Directly compare two objects with a measurable attribute in common to see which object has more of/less of the attribute and describe the difference. *For example, directly compare the heights of two children and describe one child as taller/shorter.* **Science example: Directly compare a sunflower grown in the shade with a sunflower grown in the sun. Which flower is taller? Observe that these plants need light to thrive.**

Alignment notes: (1) Data displays such as picture graphs and bar graphs are not expected until grade 2. (2) Standard length units such as centimeters or inches are not expected until grade 2.

K-ESS2 EARTH'S SYSTEMS

As part of this work, teachers should give students opportunities to **use numbers, counting, direct measurement, and classification:**

K.CC.A.[4] Know number names and the count sequence. **Science example: Students write the number of sunny or rainy days in the previous month.**

K.MD.A.1. Describe measurable attributes of objects, such as length or weight. Describe several measurable attributes of a single object. **Science example: Describe a beaker of water as being heavy and cold.**

K.MD.B.3. Classify objects into given categories; count the number of objects in each category and sort the categories by count. **Science example: Build a tally chart showing the number of rainy or sunny days as the month progresses. Count the number of sunny or rainy days in the previous month (see K.CC.B). Were there more rainy days or sunny days (see K.CC.C)?**

Alignment notes: (1) Data displays such as picture graphs and bar graphs are not expected until grade 2. (2) Standard length units such as centimeters or inches are not expected until grade 2.

K-ESS3 EARTH AND HUMAN ACTIVITY

As part of this work, teachers should give students opportunities to **count and compare numbers** (see K.CC). **Science examples: (1) Count the number of trees in each of two photographs. In which photograph are there more trees? In which place might you find more squirrels? (2) Keep a tally of the number of severe weather days (forecast and actual). Count the number of severe weather days at the end of the year.**

1-PS4 WAVES AND THEIR APPLICATIONS IN TECHNOLOGIES FOR INFORMATION TRANSFER

As part of this work, teachers should give students opportunities to **measure with non-standard units:**

1.MD.A.1. Order three objects by length; compare the lengths of two objects indirectly by using a third object. **Science example: The class makes string phones. Maria's string is longer than Sue's and Sue's string is longer than Tia's, so without measuring directly we know that Maria's string is longer than Tia's.**

---

[4] The capital letter "A" in "K.CC.A" refers to the *first* cluster heading in domain K.CC. See p. 11 of the CCSSM, available at: http://www.corestandards.org/assets/CCSSI_Math%20Standards.pdf.

1.MD.A.2. Express the length of an object as a whole number of length units, by layering multiple copies of a shorter object (the length unit) end to end. Understand that the length measurement of an object is the number of same-size length units that span it with no gaps or overlaps. *Limit to contexts where the object being measured is spanned by a whole number of length units with no gaps or overlaps.* **Science example: Using a shoe as the length unit, the string for Sue's string phone is 11 units long.**

Alignment note: Standard length units such as centimeters or inches are not expected until grade 2.

1-LS1 FROM MOLECULES TO ORGANISMS: STRUCTURES AND PROCESSES

As part of this work, teachers should give students opportunities to **work with 2-digit numbers:**

1.NBT.B.3. Compare two 2-digit numbers based on the meanings of the tens and ones digits, recording the results of comparisons with the symbols >, =, and <.

1.NBT.C.4. Add within 100, including adding a 2-digit number and a 1-digit number, and adding a 2-digit number and a multiple of 10, using concrete models or drawings and strategies based on place value, properties of operations, and/or the relationship between addition and subtraction. Relate the strategy to a written method and explain the reasoning uses. Understand that in adding 2-digit numbers, one adds tens and tens, ones and ones; and sometimes it is necessary to compose a ten.

1.NBT.C.5. Given a 2-digit number, mentally find 10 more or 10 less than the number, without having to count. Explain the reasoning used.

1.NBT.C.6. Subtract multiples of 10 in the range 10–90 from multiples of 10 in the range 10–90 (positive or zero differences), using concrete models or drawings and strategies based on place value, properties of operations, and/or the relationship between addition and subtraction. Relate the strategy to a written method and explain the reasoning used.

Science examples: (1) A mother wolf spider is carrying 40 baby spiders on her back. There were 50 eggs in the egg sac. How many of the hatchlings is the mother spider not caring for?

(2) During the breeding season, a female cottontail rabbit has litters of five, six, five, and four bunnies. How many bunnies did the rabbit have during this time?

1-LS3 HEREDITY: INHERITANCE AND VARIATION OF TRAITS

As part of this work, teachers should give students opportunities to **measure with non-standard units** and **use indirect measurement:**

1.MD.A.1. Order three objects by length and compare the lengths of two objects indirectly by using a third object. **Science example: Every sunflower is taller than the ruler and every daisy is shorter than the ruler, so without measuring directly we know that every sunflower is taller than every daisy. The sunflowers and daisies are not exactly like the plants from which they grew, but they resemble the plants from which they grew in being generally tall or generally short.**

Alignment note: Standard length units such as centimeters or inches are not expected until grade 2.

1-ESS1 EARTH'S PLACE IN THE UNIVERSE

As part of this work, teachers should give students opportunities to **practice addition and subtraction** and **represent and interpret data:**

1.OA.A.1. Use addition and subtraction within 20 to solve word problems involving situations of adding to, taking from, putting together, taking apart, and comparing, with unknowns in all positions (e.g., by using objects, drawings, and equations to represent the problem). **Science example: There were 16 hours of daylight yesterday. On December 21, there were 8 hours of daylight. How many more hours of daylight were there yesterday?**

1.MD.C.4. Organize, represent, and interpret data with up to three categories. Ask and answer questions about the total number of data points, how many are in each category, and how many more or less are in one category than in another. **Science example: Based on the data collected so far and posted on the bulletin board, which day has been the longest of the year so far? Which day has been the shortest?**

Alignment notes: (1) Students in this grade are expected to be fluent in adding and subtracting within 10. (2) Picture graphs and bar graphs are not expected until grade 2. (3) Line plots are not expected until grade 2. (4) The coordinate plane is not expected until grade 5.

2-PS1 MATTER AND ITS INTERACTIONS

As part of this work, teachers should give students opportunities to **represent and interpret categorical data:**

2.MD.D.10. Draw a picture graph and a bar graph (with a single-unit scale) to represent a data set with up to four categories. Solve simple put-together, take-apart, and compare problems[5] using information presented in a bar graph. **Science examples: (1) Make a bar graph with a single-unit scale showing how many samples in a mineral collection are red, green, purple, or various other colors. Based on the graph, how many samples are represented in all? (2) As part of an investigation of which materials are best for different intended uses, make a picture graph with a single-unit scale showing how many tools in a toolbox are made of metal, wood, rubber/plastic, or a combination. Based on the graph, how many tools are represented in all?**

Alignment notes: (1) Scaled bar graphs are not expected until grade 3. (2) Multiplication and division of whole numbers are not expected until grade 3.

2-LS2 ECOSYSTEMS: INTERACTIONS, ENERGY, AND DYNAMICS

As part of this work, teachers should give students opportunities to **represent and interpret categorical data:**

2.MD.D.10. Draw a picture graph and a bar graph (with a single-unit scale) to represent a data set with up to four categories. Solve simple put-together, take-apart, and compare problems[6] using information presented in a bar graph. **Science example:**

Make a bar graph with a single-unit scale showing the number of seedlings that sprout with and without watering.

Alignment notes: (1) Scaled bar graphs are not expected until Grade 3. (2) Multiplication and division of whole numbers are not expected until Grade 3.

2-LS4 BIOLOGICAL EVOLUTION: UNITY AND DIVERSITY

As part of this work, teachers should give students opportunities to **represent and interpret categorical data:**

2.MD.D.10. Draw a picture graph and a bar graph (with a single-unit scale) to represent a data set with up to four categories. Solve simple put-together, take-apart, and compare problems[7] using information presented in a bar graph. **Science example: Make a picture graph with a single-unit scale showing the number of plant species, vertebrate animal species, and invertebrate animal species observed during a field trip or in a nature photograph. How many more plant species were observed than animal species?**

Alignment notes: (1) Scaled bar graphs are not expected until grade 3. (2) Multiplication and division of whole numbers are not expected until grade 3.

2-ESS1 EARTH'S PLACE IN THE UNIVERSE

As part of this work, teachers should give students opportunities to **work with numbers to 1,000:**

2.NBT.A.[8] Understand place value. **Science example: As part of comprehending media to identify the varying timescales on which Earth events can occur, students understand that a period of thousands of years is much longer than a period of hundreds of years, which in turn is much longer than a period of tens of years.**

Alignment note: Rounding is not expected until grade 3.

---

[5] See Glossary on p. 85 and Table 1 on p. 88 in the CCSSM, available at: http://www.corestandards.org/assets/CCSSI_Math%20Standards.pdf.
[6] Ibid.

[7] Ibid.
[8] The capital letter "A" in "2.NBT.A" refers to the *first* cluster heading in domain 2.NBT. See p. 19 of the CCSSM, available at: http://www.corestandards.org/assets/CCSSI_Math%20Standards.pdf.

2-ESS2 EARTH'S SYSTEMS

As part of this work, teachers should give students opportunities to **work with numbers to 1,000, to use standard units for length, and to relate addition and subtraction to length:**

2.NBT.A.3. Read and write numbers to 1,000 using base-ten numerals, number names, and expanded form. **Science example: Students write about a lake that is 550 feet deep, a river that is 687 miles long, a forest that began growing about 200 years ago, and so on.**

2.MD.B.5. Use addition and subtraction within 100 to solve word problems involving lengths that are given in the same units (e.g., by using drawings [such as drawings of rulers] and equations with a symbol for the unknown number to represent the problem). **Science example: A gulley was 17 inches deep before a rainstorm and 42 inches deep after a rainstorm. How much deeper did it get during the rainstorm?**

Alignment note: Students in this grade are expected to be fluent in mentally adding and subtracting within 20, knowing single-digit sums from memory by the end of grade 2; and are expected to be fluent in adding and subtracting within 100 using strategies based on place value, properties of operations, and/or the relationship between addition and subtraction.

K-2-ETS1 ENGINEERING DESIGN

As part of this work, teachers should give students opportunities to **represent and interpret categorical data:**

2.MD.D.10. Draw a picture graph and a bar graph (with a single-unit scale) to represent a data set with up to four categories. Solve simple put-together, take-apart, and compare problems[9] using information presented in a bar graph. **Science example: Make a bar graph with a single-unit scale showing the number of seeds dispersed by two or three different design solutions for seed dispersal.**

Alignment notes: (1) Scaled bar graphs are not expected until grade 3. (2) Multiplication and division of whole numbers are not expected until grade 3.

3-PS2 MOTION AND STABILITY: FORCES AND INTERACTIONS

As part of this work, teachers should give students opportunities to **work with continuous quantities:**

3.MD.A.2. Measure and estimate liquid volumes and masses of objects using standard units such as grams (g), kilograms (kg), and liters (l).[10] Add, subtract, multiply, or divide to solve one-step word problems involving masses or volumes that are given in the same units (e.g., by using drawings [such as a beaker with a measurement scale] to represent the problem).[11] **Science example: Estimate, then measure, the masses of two objects being used in an investigation of the effect of forces. Observe that the change of motion due to an unbalanced force is larger for the smaller mass. (Students need not explain or quantify this observation in terms of Newton's Laws of Motion.)**

3-LS1 FROM MOLECULES TO ORGANISMS: STRUCTURES AND PROCESSES

As part of this work, teachers should give students opportunities to **be quantitative in giving descriptions:**

3.NF. Number and Operations—Fractions
3.NBT. Number and Operations in Base Ten
Science example: Be quantitative when describing the life cycles of organisms, such as their varying life spans (e.g., ranging from a fraction of a year up to thousands of years) and their varying reproductive capacity (e.g., ranging from a handful of offspring to thousands).

---

[9] See Glossary on p. 85 and Table 1 on p. 88 in the CCSSM, available at: http://www.corestandards.org/assets/CCSSI_Math%20Standards.pdf.

[10] Excludes compound units such as cubic centimeters (cm^3) and finding the geometric volume of a container. See p. 25 of the CCSSM, available at: http://www.corestandards.org/assets/CCSSI_Math%20Standards.pdf.

[11] Excludes multiplicative comparison problems (problems involving notions of "times as much"). See Glossary on p. 85 and Table 2 on p. 89 in the CCSSM, available at: http://www.corestandards.org/assets/CCSSI_Math%20Standards.pdf.

3-LS2 ECOSYSTEMS: INTERACTIONS, ENERGY, AND DYNAMICS

As part of this work, teachers should give students opportunities to **be quantitative in giving descriptions**:

3.NBT. Number and Operations in Base Ten. **Science example: Be quantitative when describing the group behaviors of animals (e.g., describe groups ranging in size from a handful up to thousands of animals).**

3-LS3 HEREDITY: INHERITANCE AND VARIATION OF TRAITS

As part of this work, teachers should give students opportunities to **represent and interpret data**:

3.MD.B.4. Generate measurement data by measuring lengths using rulers marked with halves and fourths of an inch. Show the data by making a line plot, where the horizontal scale is marked off in appropriate units—whole numbers, halves, or quarters. **Science examples: (1) Make a line plot to show the height of each of a number of plants grown from a single parent. Observe that not all of the offspring are the same size. Compare the sizes of the offspring to the size of the parent. (2) Make a similar plot for plants grown with insufficient water.**

3-LS4 BIOLOGICAL EVOLUTION: UNITY AND DIVERSITY

As part of this work, teachers should give students opportunities to **represent and interpret data**:

3.MD.B.3. Draw a scaled picture or bar graph to represent a data set with several categories. Solve one- and two-step "how many more" and "how many less" problems using information presented in scaled bar graphs. *For example, draw a bar graph in which each square in the bar graph might represent five pets.* **Science examples: (1) Given a bar graph showing the number of flower species found in several different habitats, determine how many more flower species were found in a grassy meadow than in a dense forest. Would flower species be affected if a forest were to spread into its habitat? (2) Make a scaled bar graph to show the number of surviving individuals with and without an advantageous trait. How**

many more of the individuals with the advantageous trait survived?

3.MD.B.4. Generate measurement data by measuring lengths using rulers marked with halves and fourths of an inch. Show the data by making a line plot, where the horizontal scale is marked off in appropriate units—whole numbers, halves, or quarters. **Science example: Make a line plot to show the length of each fossil that is visible in a piece of shale. Do any of the fossils resemble modern organisms except for their size?**

3-ESS2 EARTH'S SYSTEMS

As part of this work, teachers should give students opportunities to **work with continuous quantities** and **represent and interpret categorical data**:

3.MD.A.2. Measure and estimate liquid volumes and masses of objects using standard units of grams (g), kilograms (kg), and liters (l).[12] Add, subtract, multiply, or divide to solve one-step word problems involving masses or volumes that are given in the same units (e.g., by using drawings [such as a beaker with a measurement scale] to represent the problem).[13] **Science examples: (1) Estimate the mass of a large hailstone that damaged a car on a used-car lot. (2) Measure the volume of water in liters collected during a rainstorm.**

3.MD.B.3. Draw a scaled picture graph and a scaled bar graph to represent a data set with several categories. Solve one- and two-step "how many more" and "how many less" problems using information presented in bar graphs. **Science example: Make a picture graph or bar graph to show the number of days with high temperatures below freezing in December, January, February, and March. How many days were below freezing this winter?**

---

[12] Excludes compound units such as cubic centimeters (cm^3) and finding the geometric volume of a container. See p. 25 of the CCSSM, available at: http://www.corestandards.org/assets/CCSSI_Math%20Standards.pdf.

[13] Excludes multiplicative comparison problems (problems involving notions of "times as much"). See Glossary on p. 85 and Table 2 on p. 89 in the CCSSM, available at: http://www.corestandards.org/assets/CCSSI_Math%20Standards.pdf.

Alignment notes: (1) Students are not expected to understand statistical ideas such as average, mean, and median until grade 6. (2) Graphing in the coordinate plane is not expected until grade 5.

3-ESS3 EARTH AND HUMAN ACTIVITY

As part of this work, teachers should give students opportunities to **work with continuous quantities, including area:**

3.MD.A.2. Measure and estimate liquid volumes and masses of objects using standard units of grams (g), kilograms (kg), and liters (l).[14] Add, subtract, multiply, or divide to solve one-step word problems involving masses or volumes that are given in the same units (e.g., by using drawings [such as a beaker with a measurement scale] to represent the problem).[15]

3.MD.C.5. Recognize area as an attribute of plane figures and understand concepts of area measurement.

a. A square with a side length of one unit, called "a unit square," is said to have "one square unit" of area and can be used to measure area.

b. A plane figure that can be covered without gaps or overlaps by n unit squares is said to have an area of n square units.

3.MD.C.6. Measure areas by counting unit squares (square centimeters, square meters, square inches, square feet, and improvised units).

Science example: In Hawaii some houses are raised on stilts to reduce the impact of a tsunami. The force of a tsunami on an object is greater if the object presents greater area to an incoming wave. Based on a diagram of a stilt house, determine how much area the stilts present to an incoming wave. How much area would the house present to an incoming wave if it were not on stilts?

4-PS3 ENERGY

As part of this work, teachers should give students opportunities to **use the four operations with whole numbers to solve problems:**

4.OA.A.3. Solve multi-step word problems posed with whole numbers and having whole-number answers using the four operations, including problems in which remainders must be interpreted. Represent these problems using equations with a letter standing for the unknown quantity. Assess the reasonableness of answers using mental computation and estimation strategies, including rounding. **Science example: The class has 144 rubber bands with which to make rubber-band cars. If each car uses six rubber bands, how many cars can be made? If there are 28 students, at most how many rubber bands can each car have (if every car has the same number of rubber bands)?**

Alignment note: Grade 4 students are expected to fluently add and subtract multi-digit whole numbers, multiply a number of up to four digits by a 1-digit whole number, multiply two 2-digit numbers, and find whole-number quotients and remainders with up to 4-digit dividends and 1-digit divisors.

4-PS4 WAVES AND THEIR APPLICATION IN TECHNOLOGIES FOR INFORMATION TRANSFER

As part of this work, teachers should give students opportunities to **draw and identify lines and angles:**

4.G.A.1. Draw points, lines, line segments, rays, angles (right, acute, obtuse), and perpendicular and parallel lines. Identify these in two-dimensional figures. **Science example: Identify rays and angles in drawings of wave propagation.**

4-LS1 FROM MOLECULES TO ORGANISMS: STRUCTURES AND PROCESSES

As part of this work, teachers should give students opportunities to **recognize symmetry:**

4.G.A.3. Recognize a line of symmetry for a two-dimensional figure as a line across the figure such that the figure can be folded across the line into matching parts. Identify line-symmetric figures and draw lines of symmetry. **Science example: Recognize**

---

[14] Excludes compound units such as cubic centimeters (cm³) and finding the geometric volume of a container. See p. 25 of the CCSSM, available at: http://www.corestandards.org/assets/CCSSI_Math%20Standards.pdf.
[15] Excludes multiplicative comparison problems (problems involving notions of "times as much"). See Glossary on p. 85 and Table 2 on p. 89 in the CCSSM, available at: http://www.corestandards.org/assets/CCSSI_Math%20Standards.pdf.

symmetry, or lack of symmetry, in the internal and external structures of plants and animals. Does the symmetry or lack thereof contribute to the function of the organism? (For example, bilateral symmetry is a signal of reproductive fitness in many animals; the asymmetry in an owl's face helps it pinpoint the location of prey.)

4-ESS1 EARTH'S PLACE IN THE UNIVERSE

As part of this work, teachers should give students opportunities to **solve problems involving measurement:**

4.MD.A.1. Know relative sizes of measurement units within one system of units, including km, m, and cm; kg and g; lb and oz; l, mL; and hr, min, and sec. Within a single system of measurement, express measurements in a larger unit in terms of a smaller unit. Record measurement equivalents in a two-column table. For example, know that 1 ft is 12 times as long as 1 in. Express the length of a 4 ft snake as 48 in. Generate a conversion table for feet and inches listing the number pairs (1, 12), (2, 24), (3, 36). **Science example: A limestone layer with many marine fossils is visible in the Grand Canyon. One reference book lists this layer as being 300 feet thick. Another reference book lists this layer as being 100 yards thick. Are the two references consistent?**

Alignment note: Expressing measurements in a smaller unit in terms of a larger unit within the same system of measurement is not expected until grade 5.

4-ESS2 EARTH'S SYSTEMS

As part of this work, teachers should give students opportunities to **solve problems involving measurement:**

4.MD.A.1. Know relative sizes of measurement units within one system of units, including km, m, and cm; kg and g; lb and oz; l, mL; and hr, min, and sec. Within a single system of measurement, express measurements in a larger unit in terms of a smaller unit. Record measurement equivalents in a two-column table. For example, know that 1 ft is 12 times as long as 1 in. Express the length of a 4 ft snake as 48 in. Generate a conversion table for feet and inches listing the number pairs (1, 12),

(2, 24), (3, 36). **Science example: One map shows that a particular point in the ocean is 1,600 meters deep, while another map shows the same point as being 1.5 kilometers deep. Are the two maps consistent?**

4.MD.A.2. Use the four operations to solve word problems involving distances, intervals of time, liquid volumes, masses of objects, and money, including problems involving simple fractions or decimals and problems that require expressing measurements given in a larger unit in terms of a smaller unit. Represent measurement quantities using diagrams such as number line diagrams that feature a measurement scale. **Science example: A coastline is reduced by an average of 4 feet per year. In an 18-month period, approximately how much of the coastline has been lost?**

Alignment note: Expressing measurements in a smaller unit in terms of a larger unit within the same system of measurement is not expected until grade 5.

4-ESS3 EARTH AND HUMAN ACTIVITY

As part of this work, teachers should give students opportunities to **be quantitative in descriptions:**

4.OA.A.1. Interpret a multiplication equation as a comparison; for example, interpret $35 = 5 \times 7$ as a statement that 35 is 5 times as many as 7 and 7 times as many as 5. Represent verbal statements of multiplicative comparisons as multiplication equations. **Science example: Be quantitative when discussing environmental effects. For example, say not only that a particular oil spill was "large," but also that 5 million gallons was spilled or that the oil spill was 40 times larger than the next-worst oil spill.**

5-PS1 MATTER AND ITS INTERACTIONS

As part of this work, teachers should give students opportunities to **relate very large and very small quantities to place value and division, convert measurement units, and work with volume:**

5.NBT.A.1. Explain patterns in the number of zeros of a product when multiplying a number by powers of 10, and explain patterns in the placement of the decimal point when a decimal is multiplied or divided by a power of 10. Use whole-number exponents to denote powers of 10.

5.NF.B.7. Apply and extend previous understandings of division to divide unit fractions by whole numbers and whole numbers by unit fractions.[16]

a. Interpret division of a unit fraction by a non-zero whole number and compute such quotients. *For example, create a story context for (1/3) ÷ 4, and use a visual fraction model to show the quotient. Use the relationship between multiplication and division to explain that (1/3) ÷ 4 = 1/12 because (1/12) × 4 = 13.*

b. Interpret division of a whole number by a unit fraction and compute such quotients. *For example, create a story context for 4 ÷ (1/5), and use a visual fraction model to show the quotient. Use the relationship between multiplication and division to explain that 4 ÷ (1/5) = 20 because 20 × (1/5) = 4.*

c. Solve real-world problems involving the division of unit fractions by non-zero whole numbers and the division of whole numbers by unit fractions (e.g., by using visual fraction models and equations to represent the problem). *For example, how much chocolate will each person get if three people share 1/2 lb of chocolate equally? How many 1/3 cup servings are in 2 cups of raisins?*

Science examples: (1) If you split a salt grain with a weight of 1 mg into 10 equal parts, find the weight of each part. (Answer in milligrams.) If you next divide each of the parts into 10 equal parts, find the weight of one of the new parts. (Answer in milligrams.) How many parts are there in the end? (2) Suppose a salt grain with a weight of 1 mg is split into 10 equal parts, and each of those parts is split into 10 equal parts, and so on, until there are 10^8 parts. What is the weight of one of these tiny parts? Write the number of these tiny parts as a whole number without using exponents.

5.MD.A.1. Convert among different-sized standard measurement units within a given measurement system (e.g., convert 5 cm to 0.05 m), and use these conversions in solving multi-step, real-world problems. **Science example: When 100 g of sugar is dissolved in 0.5 kg of water, what is the total weight of the system? Answer in grams; then answer again in kilograms. After the water evaporates, see how much the sugar residue weighs.**

5.MD.C.3. Recognize volume as an attribute of solid figures and understand concepts of volume measurement.

a. A cube with a side length of one unit, called a "unit cube," is said to have "one cubic unit" of volume and can be used to measure volume.

b. A solid figure that can be packed without gaps or overlaps using *n* unit cubes is said to have a volume of *n* cubic units.

5.MD.C.4. Measure volumes by counting unit cubes, using cubic centimeters, cubic inches, cubic feet, and improvised units.

Science example: Compress the air in a cylinder to half its volume. Draw a picture of the volume before and after, and explain how you know that the new volume is half of the old volume. Can you compress the volume by half again? Why is it difficult to do?

Alignment notes: (1) Ratios are not expected until grade 6.
(2) Scientific notation is not expected until grade 8.

5-PS2 MOTION AND STABILITY: FORCES AND INTERACTION

N/A

5-PS3 ENERGY

N/A

5-LS1 FROM MOLECULES TO ORGANISMS: STRUCTURES AND PROCESSES

As part of this work, teachers should give students opportunities to **convert measurement units:**

5.MD.A.1. Convert among different-sized standard measurement units within a given measurement system (e.g., convert 5 cm to 0.05 m), and use these conversions in solving multi-step, real-world problems. **Science example: In an experiment to rule out soil as a source of plant food, Sue weighed the soil using units**

---

[16] Students able to multiply fractions can generally develop strategies to divide fractions by reasoning about the relationship between multiplication and division. But division of a fraction by a fraction is not a requirement at this grade. See p. 36 in the CCSSM, available at: http://www.corestandards.org/Math/Content/5/NF.

of grams, but Katya weighed the plant using units of kilograms. The soil lost 4 grams, while the plant gained 0.1 kilograms. Did the plant gain much more than the soil lost? Much less? About the same? (A good way to begin is to express both figures in grams.)

Alignment notes: (1) Converting between measurement systems (e.g., centimeters to inches) is not expected until grade 6. (2) Rate quantities, such as annual rates of ecosystem production, are not expected until grade 6. (3) Grade 5 students are expected to read, write, and compare decimals to thousandths and to perform decimal arithmetic to hundredths.

5-LS2 ECOSYSTEMS: INTERACTIONS, ENERGY, AND DYNAMICS

As part of this work, teachers should give students opportunities to **be quantitative in giving descriptions. Science example: In a diagram showing matter flowing in a system, assign values to the arrows in a diagram to show the flows quantitatively.**

5-ESS1 EARTH'S PLACE IN THE UNIVERSE

As part of this work, teachers should give students opportunities to **relate very large and very small quantities to place value and to use the coordinate plane:**

5.NBT.A.2. Explain patterns in the number of zeros of a product when multiplying a number by powers of 10, and explain patterns in the placement of the decimal point when a decimal is multiplied or divided by a power of 10. Use whole-number exponents to denote powers of 10. **Science example: The sun is about 10^{11} meters from Earth. Sirius, another star, is about 10^{17} meters from Earth. Write these two numbers without exponents; position the numbers directly below the other, aligning on the 1. How many times farther away from Earth is Sirius compared to the sun?**

5.G.A.2. Represent real-world and mathematical problems by graphing points in the first quadrant of the coordinate plane, and interpret coordinate values of points in the context of the situation. **Science examples: (1) Over the course of a year, students compile data for the length of the day over the course of

the year. What pattern is observed when the data are graphed on a coordinate plane? How can a model of the sun and Earth explain the pattern? (2) Students are given (x, y) coordinates for the Earth at six equally spaced times during its orbit around the sun (with the sun at the origin). Students graph the points to show snapshots of Earth's motion through space.**

Alignment note: Scientific notation is not expected until grade 8.

5-ESS2 EARTH'S SYSTEMS

As part of this work, teachers should give students opportunities to **use the coordinate plane:**

5.G.A.2. Represent real-world and mathematical problems by graphing points in the first quadrant of the coordinate plane, and interpret coordinate values of points in the context of the situation. **Science example: Plot monthly data for high and low temperatures in two locations, one coastal and one inland (e.g., San Francisco County and Sacramento). What patterns are seen? How can the influence of the ocean be seen in the observed patterns?**

Alignment notes: (1) Percentages are not expected until grade 6. (2) Trends in scatterplots and patterns of association in two-way tables are not expected until grade 8.

5-ESS3 EARTH AND HUMAN ACTIVITY

As part of this work, teachers should give students opportunities to **be quantitative in giving descriptions. Science example: In describing ways that individual communities use science ideas to protect Earth's resources and environment, provide quantitative information, such as the amount of energy saved and the cost of the approach.**

3-5-ETS1 ENGINEERING DESIGN

As part of this work, teachers should give students opportunities to **use the four operations to solve problems:**

OA: Operations and Algebraic Thinking (representing and solving problems using the four operations; see each grade in the CCSSM for detailed expectations). **Science example: Analyze** constraints on materials, time, or cost to draw implications for design solutions. For example, if a design calls for 20 screws and screws are sold in boxes of 150, how many copies of the design could be made?

MS-PS1 MATTER AND ITS INTERACTIONS

As part of this work, teachers should give students opportunities to **work with ratios and proportional relationships, use signed numbers, write and solve equations, and use order-of-magnitude thinking and basic statistics:**

Ratios and Proportional Relationships (6-7.RP). **Science examples: (1) A pile of salt has a mass of 100 mg. How much chlorine is in it? Answer in milligrams. What would the answer be for a 500 mg pile of salt? (2) Twice as much water is twice as heavy. Explain why twice as much water is not twice as dense. (3) Based on a model of a water molecule, recognize that any sample of water has a 2:1 ratio of hydrogen atoms to oxygen atoms. (4) Measure the mass and volume of a sample of reactant and compute its density. (5) Compare a measured/computed density to a nominal/textbook value, converting units as necessary. Determine the percent difference between the two.**

The Number System (6-8.NS). **Science examples: (1) Use positive and negative quantities to represent temperature changes in a chemical reaction (signs of energy released or absorbed). (2) For grade 7 or 8: Solve a simple equation for an unknown signed number. For example, a solution was initially at room temperature. After the first reaction, the temperature change was −8°C. After the second reaction, the temperature was 3°C below room temperature. Find the temperature change during the second reaction. Was energy released or absorbed in the second reaction? Show all of the given information on a number line/thermometer scale. Also represent the problem by an equation.**

Expressions and Equations (6-8.EE). **Science examples: (1) For grade 8: With substantial scaffolding, use algebra and quantitative thinking to determine the interatomic spacing in a salt crystal. (2) For grade 8: Use scientific notation for atomic masses, large numbers of atoms, and other quantities much**

less than or much greater than 1. Also use convenient units such as unified atomic mass units.

Statistics and Probability (6-8.SP). **Science example: Compile all of the boiling point measurements from the students into a line plot and discuss the distribution in terms of clustering and outliers. Why were not all of the measured values equal? How close is the average value to the nominal/textbook value? Show the average value and the nominal value on the line plot.**

MS-PS2 MOTION AND STABILITY: FORCES AND INTERACTIONS

As part of this work, teachers should give students opportunities to **work with signed numbers** and interpret expressions:

The Number System (6-8.NS). **Science examples: (1) Represent a third-law pair of forces as a +100 N force on one object and a −100 N force on the other object. (2) Represent balanced forces on a single object as equal and opposite numbers ±5 N. (3) Represent the net result of two or more forces as a sum of signed numbers. For example, given a large force and an oppositely directed small force, represent the net force as (+100 N) + (−5 N) = +95 N. Relate the number sentence to the fact that the net effect on the motion is approximately what it would have been with only the large force.**

Expressions and Equations (6-8.EE). **Science example: Interpret an expression in terms of a physical context. For example, interpret the expression $F_1 + F_2$ in a diagram as representing the net force on an object.**

MS-PS3 ENERGY

As part of this work, teachers should give students opportunities to **work with ratios and proportional relationships and basic statistics:**

Ratios and Proportional Relationships (6-7.RP) and Functions (8.F). **Science examples: (1) Analyze an idealized set of bivariate measurement data for kinetic energy versus mass (holding speed constant). Decide whether the two quantities are in a proportional relationship (e.g., by testing for equivalent ratios or graphing on a coordinate plane and observing whether the** graph is a straight line through the origin). (2) Do the same for an idealized set of data for kinetic energy versus speed (holding mass constant). For grade 8 recognize from the data that the relationship is not proportional and that kinetic energy is a non-linear function of speed. Draw conclusions such as that doubling the speed more than doubles the kinetic energy. What are some possible implications for driving safety?

Statistics and Probability (6-8.SP). Science example: As part of carrying out a designed experiment, make a scatterplot showing the temperature change of a sample of water versus the mass of ice added. For grade 8 if the data suggest a linear association, form a straight line, and informally assess the model fit by judging the closeness of the data points to the line. Just for fun, compute the slope of the line. What are the units of the answer?

MS-PS4 WAVES AND THEIR APPLICATIONS IN TECHNOLOGIES FOR INFORMATION TRANSFER

As part of this work, teachers should give students opportunities to **use ratios and proportional relationships and functions**:

Ratios and Proportional Relationships (6-7.RP) and Functions (8.F). **Science examples: (1) Analyze an idealized set of bivariate measurement data for wave energy versus wave amplitude. Decide whether the two quantities are in a proportional relationship (e.g., by testing for equivalent ratios or graphing on a coordinate plane and observing whether the graph is a straight line through the origin). For grade 8 recognize that wave energy is a non-linear function of amplitude, and draw conclusions such as that doubling the amplitude more than doubles the energy. Discuss possible implications for the safety of wading in the ocean during a storm. (2) Interpret an idealized set of bivariate measurement data for wave energy versus wave speed.**

MS-LS1 FROM MOLECULES TO ORGANISMS: STRUCTURES AND PROCESSES

As part of this work, teachers should give students opportunities to **use order-of-magnitude thinking, write and solve equations, analyze data, and use concepts of probability**:

Expressions and Equations (6-8.EE). **Science examples: (1) Quantify the sizes of cells and parts of cells, using convenient units such as microns as well as (in grade 8) scientific notation. (2) Appreciate the orders of magnitude that span the difference in size between cells, molecules, and atoms. (3) Write a number sentence that expresses the conservation of mass as food moves through an organism. Assign values to the arrows in a diagram to show flows quantitatively. (4) Infer an unknown mass by using the concept of conservation to write and solve an equation with a variable.**

Statistics and Probability (6-8.SP). **Science examples: (1) For grade 8 use data in a two-way table as evidence to support an explanation of how environmental and genetic factors affect the growth of organisms. (2) For grade 8 use data in a two-way table as evidence to support an explanation that different local environmental conditions impact growth in organisms. (3) For grade 7 or 8 use probability concepts and language to describe and quantify the effects that characteristic animal behaviors have on the likelihood of successful reproduction.**

MS-LS2 ECOSYSTEMS: INTERACTIONS, ENERGY, AND DYNAMICS

As part of this work, teachers should give students opportunities to **work with ratios and proportional relationships, write and solve equations, and use basic statistics**:

Ratios and Proportional Relationships (6-7.RP). **Science example: Use ratios and unit rates as inputs for evaluating plans for maintaining biodiversity and ecosystem services (e.g., consider the net cost or net value of developing a wetland, using inputs such as the value of various wetland services in dollars per acre per year; and in analyzing urban biodiversity, rank world cities by the amount of green space as a fraction of total land area; in analyzing social factors, determine the amount of green space per capita [square meters per person]).**

Expressions and Equations (6-8.EE). **Science examples: (1) Write a number sentence that expresses the conservation of total matter or energy in a system as matter or energy flows into, out of, and within it. Assign values to the arrows in a diagram to show flows quantitatively. (2) Infer an unknown matter or** energy flow in a system by using the concept of conservation to write and solve an equation with a variable.

Statistics and Probability (6-8.SP). **Science example: For grade 8 use data in a two-way table as evidence to support an explanation of how social behaviors and group interactions benefit organisms' abilities to survive and reproduce.**

MS-LS3 HEREDITY: INHERITANCE AND VARIATION OF TRAITS

As part of this work, teachers should give students opportunities to **use concepts of probability:**

Statistics and Probability (6-8.SP). **Science examples: (1) Recognize a Punnett square as a component of a probability model, and compute simple probabilities from the model. (2) Use a computer to simulate the variation that comes from sexual reproduction, and determine probabilities of traits from the simulation.**

MS-LS4 BIOLOGICAL EVOLUTION: UNITY AND DIVERSITY

As part of this work, teachers should give students opportunities to **work with ratios and proportional relationships, use concepts of probability, and use order-of-magnitude thinking:**

Ratios and Proportional Relationships (6-7.RP) and Statistics and Probability (6-8.SP). **Science examples: (1) Apply several ratios in combination to determine a net survival rate. For example, if 50 animals in a population have trait A and 50 have trait B, and each winter the survival rates are 80% for trait A and 60% for trait B, how many animals with each trait will be alive after one winter? After two winters? Six winters? (2) Use scaled histograms to summarize the results of a simulation of natural selection over many generations. (3) For grade 7 or 8 use probability language and concepts when explaining how variation in traits among a population leads to an increase in some traits in the population and a decrease in others.**

Expressions and Equations (6-8.EE). **Science examples: (1) Quantify durations of time in interpreting the fossil record. (2) For grade 8 use scientific notation for long intervals of time or for dates in the distant past; also use convenient units (e.g.,**

Myr, Gyr, Ma, Ga). **(3) Appreciate the spans of time involved in natural selection.**

Alignment notes: (1) Exponential functions are not expected until high school. (2) Laws of probability such as $p(AB) = p(A)p(B|A)$ are not expected until high school.

MS-ESS1 EARTH'S PLACE IN THE UNIVERSE

As part of this work, teachers should give students opportunities to **use ratios and proportional relationships** and **use order-of-magnitude thinking:**

Ratios and Proportional Relationships (6-7.RP). **Science examples: For grade 7: (1) Create a scale model or scale drawing of the solar system or Milky Way galaxy. (2) Create scale-preserving descriptions, such as "If the solar system were shrunk down to the size of Earth, then Earth would shrink to the size of _____"; compute relevant scale factors and use them to determine a suitable object.**

Expressions and Equations (6-8.EE). **Science examples: For grade 8: (1) Use scientific notation for long intervals of time or for dates in the distant past; also use convenient units (e.g., Myr, Gyr, Ma, Ga). Appreciate the spans of time involved in Earth's history. (2) Are there more molecules of gas in a toy balloon or more stars in the Milky Way galaxy?**

MS-ESS2 EARTH'S SYSTEMS

As part of this work, teachers should give students opportunities to **work with positive and negative numbers and to use order-of-magnitude thinking:**

The Number System (6-8.NS). **Science examples: (1) Use positive and negative quantities to quantify changes in physical quantities such as atmospheric pressure and temperature. For example, if the temperature drops from 24°C to 11°C, the temperature change is –13°C. (2) Solve word problems relating to changes in signed physical quantities. For example, a shift in the jet stream caused a 10°C temperature increase in a single day; if the temperature before the shift was –32°C, what was the temperature after?**

Expressions and Equations (6-8.EE). **Science examples: For grade 8: (1) Use scientific notation for long intervals of time or for dates in the distant past; also use convenient units (e.g., Myr, Gyr, Ma, Ga). (2) Use order-of-magnitude data on the rate of seafloor spreading to estimate how long it has taken for two continents to separate. (3) Appreciate the spans of time involved in Earth's history. Recognize that a period of time is neither "long" nor "short" in itself, but only relatively long or relatively short compared to some other period of time. For example, the Hawaiian islands have been forming for several million years, and this time period is neither long nor short. It is a long time in comparison to the duration of the last glacial period, but a short time in comparison to Earth's entire history.**

MS-ESS3 EARTH AND HUMAN ACTIVITY

As part of this work, teachers should give students opportunities to **use ratios and proportional relationships** and **use order-of-magnitude thinking:**

Ratios and Proportional Relationships (6-7.RP). **Science example: Work with measurement quantities that are formed through division, such as atmospheric concentration of carbon dioxide, extraction cost per barrel of oil in different forms, per-capita consumption of given resources, and flow rates in freshwater rivers.**

Expressions and Equations (6-8.EE). **Science example: For grade 8 use orders of magnitude and order-of-magnitude estimates as part of oral and written arguments, evaluations of data from technical texts, design solutions, and explanations of the impact on Earth's systems of increasing population and per-capita consumption.**

MS-ETS1 ENGINEERING DESIGN

As part of this work, teachers should give students opportunities to **solve quantitative problems and use basic statistics:**

7.EE.3. Solve multi-step real-life and mathematical problems posed with positive and negative rational numbers in any form (whole numbers, fractions, and decimals), using tools strategically. Apply properties of operations to calculate with numbers in any form, convert between forms as appropriate, and assess the reasonableness of answers using mental computation and estimation strategies. *For example: If a woman making $25 an hour gets a 10% raise, she will make an additional 1/10 of her old hourly wage, or $2.50, for a new hourly wage of $27.50. If you want to place a towel bar 9¾ inches long in the center of a door that is 27½ inches wide, you will need to place the bar about 9 inches from each edge; this estimate can be used as a check on the exact computation.* **Science example: Work with tolerances, cost constraints, and other quantitative factors in evaluating competing design solutions.**

Statistics and Probability (6-8.SP). Develop a probability model and use it to find probabilities of events. Compare probabilities from a model to observed frequencies; if the agreement is not good, explain possible sources of the discrepancy. **Science example: For grade 7 use simulations to generate data that can be used to modify a proposed object, tool, or process.**

HS-PS1 MATTER AND ITS INTERACTIONS

As part of this work, teachers should give students opportunities to **reason quantitatively and use units to solve problems and to apply key takeaways from grades 6–8 mathematics:**

Quantities (N-Q)/Reason quantitatively and use units to solve problems:

N-Q.1. Use units as a way to understand problems and to guide the solution of multi-step problems; choose and interpret units consistently in formulas; choose and interpret the scale and origin in graphs and data displays.

N-Q.2. Define appropriate quantities for the purpose of descriptive modeling.

N-Q.3. Choose a level of accuracy appropriate to limitations on measurement when reporting quantities.

Science examples: (1) Recognize the difference between intensive and extensive quantities (e.g., a quantity with units of joules per kilogram is insensitive to the overall size of the sample in question, unlike a quantity with units of joules). (2) Attend to units properly when using formulas such as density = mass/volume. (3) Carefully format data displays and graphs, attending to origin, scale, units, and other essential items.

Applying key takeaways from grades 6–8 mathematics. **Science examples: (1) Convert a reference value of a quantity to match the units being used in a classroom experiment. (2) Interpret, write, or solve an equation that represents the conservation of energy or mass in a chemical reaction.**

HS-PS2 MOTION AND INSTABILITY: FORCES AND INTERACTIONS

As part of this work, teachers should give students opportunities to **model with mathematics, use basic algebra, reason quantitatively, and use units to solve problems and to apply key takeaways from grades 6–8 mathematics:**

Quantities (N-Q)/Reason quantitatively and use units to solve problems:

N-Q.1. Use units as a way to understand problems and to guide the solution of multi-step problems; choose and interpret units consistently in formulas; choose and interpret the scale and origin in graphs and data displays.

N-Q.2. Define appropriate quantities for the purpose of descriptive modeling.

N-Q.3. Choose a level of accuracy appropriate to limitations on measurement when reporting quantities.

Science examples: (1) Relate the units of acceleration (m/s²) to the fact that acceleration refers to a change in velocity over time. (2) Reconstruct the units of the universal gravitational constant G by reference to the formula $F = Gm_1m_2/r^2$, instead of having to memorize the units. (2) Attend to units properly when using formulas such as momentum = mass times velocity. (3) Carefully format data displays and graphs, attending to origin, scale, units, and other essential items.

Seeing Structure in Expressions (A-SSE). **Science example: Draw conclusions about gravitational or other forces by interpreting the algebraic structure of formulas. For example, conclude that the force on an object in a gravitational field is proportional to its mass, by viewing the formula $F = Gm_{source}m_{object}/r^2$ as $F = (Gm_{source}/r^2)(m_{object})$ and recognizing the same algebraic structure as in $y = kx$.**

Creating Equations (A-CED). **Science examples: (1) Rearrange a formula (such as $F = ma$ or $p = mv$) in order to highlight a quan-**

tity of interest. **(2) Write and solve a linear equation to solve a problem involving motion at a constant speed.**

Interpreting Functions (F-IF) and Interpreting Categorical and Quantitative Data (S-ID). **Science examples: (1) Informally fit a quadratic function to the position-time data for a cart that rolls up an incline (slowing as it climbs, then reversing direction and speeding up as it descends). Use the algebraic expression for the fitted function to determine the magnitude of the cart's acceleration and initial speed. Over several trials, graph various quantities (such as acceleration versus angle or peak displacement versus initial speed squared) and interpret the results. (2) Calculate and interpret the average speed of a moving object by using data from a distance-time graph.**

Applying key takeaways from grades 6–8 mathematics. **Science examples: (1) Compute ratios of distances and times in order to distinguish accelerated motion from motion with constant speed. Reason qualitatively on that basis (e.g., a dropped stone falls farther between $t = 1$s and $t = 2$s than between $t = 0$s and $t = 1$s). (2) For an object moving at constant speed, compute the speed by choosing a point from its distance-time graph.**

HS-PS3 ENERGY

As part of this work, teachers should give students opportunities to **reason quantitatively and use units to solve problems and to apply key takeaways from grades 6–8 mathematics:**

Quantities (N-Q)/Reason quantitatively and use units to solve problems:

N-Q.1. Use units as a way to understand problems and to guide the solution of multi-step problems; choose and interpret units consistently in formulas; choose and interpret the scale and origin in graphs and data displays.

N-Q.2. Define appropriate quantities for the purpose of descriptive modeling.

N-Q.3. Choose a level of accuracy appropriate to limitations on measurement when reporting quantities.

Science examples: (1) Analyze units in expressions like mgh and $\frac{1}{2}mv^2$ to show that they both refer to forms of energy. (2) Observe in a range of situations within science that quantities being added to one another or subtracted from

one another are always quantities of the same general kind (energy, length, time, temperature); express such terms in the same units before adding or subtracting. (3) Carefully format data displays and graphs, attending to origin, scale, units, and other essential items.

Applying key takeaways from grades 6–8 mathematics. **Science examples: (1) Fit a linear function to a data set showing the relationship between the change in temperature of an insulated sample of water and the number of identical hot ball bearings dropped into it (all with the same initial temperature). Find the slope of the graph and use it to determine the specific heat of the metal. (2) Interpret, write, or solve an equation that represents the conservation of energy in a given process.**

HS-PS4 WAVES AND THEIR APPLICATIONS IN TECHNOLOGIES FOR INFORMATION TRANSFER

As part of this work, teachers should give students opportunities to **work with basic algebra and to apply key takeaways from grades 6–8 mathematics:**

Seeing Structure in Expressions (A-SSE). **Science example: (1) Write expressions in equivalent forms to solve problems. For example, relate the formulas $c = \lambda f$ and $c = \lambda/T$ by seeing that $\lambda/T = \lambda(1/T) = \lambda f$, instead of remembering both forms separately. (2) See the conceptual and structural similarities between formulas such as $c = \lambda/T$ and $v = d/t$. How do these formulas relate to the formula (running speed) = (stride length) × (stride frequency), which is sometimes found in track-and-field coaching manuals?**

Creating Equations (A-CED). **Science examples: (1) Rearrange a formula in order to highlight a quantity of interest. (2) Write and solve an equation in a problem involving wave motion. For example, as part of an activity to use seismographic data to locate the epicenter of an earthquake.**

Applying key takeaways from grades 6–8 mathematics. **Apply several proportional relationships in combination. Science examples: (1) Estimate how long it would take a solar cell installation to pay for itself by combining such factors as per-square-meter cost of solar cells, collection efficiency, per-square-meter solar energy flux, and per-kilowatt-hour cost of conventional electricity. (2) Will 4 lbs of food in a microwave oven take approximately four times**

as long to reach the desired temperature as 1 lb of food? Why or why not? How is this situation similar to or different from cooking in a conventional oven?

HS-LS1 FROM MOLECULES TO ORGANISMS: STRUCTURES AND PROCESSES

As part of this work, teachers should give students opportunities to **model with mathematics:**

Interpreting Functions (F-IF) and Building Functions (F-BF).[17] **Science example: Use a spreadsheet or other technology to simulate the doubling in a process of cell division; graph the results; write an expression to represent the number of cells after a division in terms of the number of cells beforehand; express this in closed form as a population size in terms of time. Discuss real-world factors in the situation that lead to deviation from the exponential model over time.**

HS-LS2 ECOSYSTEMS: INTERACTIONS, ENERGY, AND DYNAMICS

As part of this work, teachers should give students opportunities to **reason quantitatively and use units to solve problems, represent quantitative data, and apply key takeaways from grades 6–8 mathematics:**

Quantities (N-Q)/Reason quantitatively and use units to solve problems:

N-Q.1. Use units as a way to understand problems and to guide the solution of multi-step problems; choose and interpret units consistently in formulas; choose and interpret the scale and origin in graphs and data displays.

N-Q.2. Define appropriate quantities for the purpose of descriptive modeling.

N-Q.3. Choose a level of accuracy appropriate to limitations on measurement when reporting quantities.

Science examples: (1) Recognize the difference between intensive and extensive quantities (e.g., a quantity with units of tons/acre is insensitive to the overall size of the area in question, unlike a quantity with units of tons). (2) Carefully format data

---

[17] See also Linear, Quadratic, and Exponential Models (F-LE).

displays and graphs, attending to origin, scale, units, and other essential items.

Interpreting Categorical and Quantitative Data (S-ID) and Making Inferences and Justifying Conclusions (S-IC). **Science example: Use a spreadsheet or other technology to analyze and display a historical or simulated data set as part of an investigation of ecosystem changes.**

Applying key takeaways from grades 6–8 mathematics. **Science examples: (1) Compute a percent change in a variable over the period of a historical data set, as part of an explanation of ecosystem changes (e.g., pesticide application, disease incidence, water temperature, invasive species population counts). (2) Merge two data sets by converting values in one data set as necessary to match the units used in the other. (3) Interpret, write, or solve an equation that represents the conservation of energy as it is transferred from one trophic level to another.**

HS-LS3 HEREDITY: INHERITANCE AND VARIATION OF TRAITS

As part of this work, teachers should give students opportunities to **apply key takeaways from grades 6–8:**

Applying key takeaways from grades 6–8 mathematics (see especially 7.SP.B, 7.SP.C, and 8.SP.4). **Science examples: (1) Use a probability model to estimate the probability that a child will inherit a disease or other trait, given knowledge or hypotheses about the parents' traits. (2) Use observed or simulated frequencies to identify cases of non-Mendelian inheritance.**

HS-LS4 BIOLOGICAL EVOLUTION: UNITY AND DIVERSITY

As part of this work, teachers should give students opportunities to **apply key takeaways from grades 6–8:**

Applying key takeaways from grades 6–8 mathematics (see especially 6.SP). **Science example: Assess differences between two populations using measures of center and variation for each. Analyze a shift in the numerical distribution of traits and use these shifts as evidence to support an explanation.**

HS-ESS1 EARTH'S PLACE IN THE UNIVERSE

As part of this work, teachers should give students opportunities to **model with mathematics, use basic algebra, reason quantitatively, and use units to solve problems and to apply key takeaways from grades 6–8 mathematics:**

Interpreting Functions (F-IF) and Interpreting Categorical and Quantitative Data (S-ID).[18] **Science example: Work with exponential models in connection with radiometric dating concepts and data.**

Creating Equations (A-CED). **Science examples: (1) Rearrange a formula (such as $E = mc^2$) in order to highlight a quantity of interest. (2) Use Kepler's Third Law to write and solve an equation in order to solve a problem involving orbital motion.**

Seeing Structure in Expressions (A-SSE). **Science example: Draw conclusions about astronomical phenomena by interpreting the algebraic structure of formulas. For example, conclude from $\lambda_{max} T = b$ that cooler stars are redder and hotter stars are bluer; conclude from Kepler's Third Law that Earth and the moon take the same amount of time to revolve around the sun, even though they have different masses (because only the mass of the sun appears in the law, not the mass of the orbiting body).**

Quantities (N-Q)/Reason quantitatively and use units to solve problems:

N-Q.1. Use units as a way to understand problems and to guide the solution of multi-step problems; choose and interpret units consistently in formulas; choose and interpret the scale and origin in graphs and data displays.

N-Q.2. Define appropriate quantities for the purpose of descriptive modeling.

N-Q.3. Choose a level of accuracy appropriate to limitations on measurement when reporting quantities.

Science examples: (1) Verify that mc^2 has units of energy (e.g., has the same units as mgh and mv^2). (2) Use SI units as well as convenient units (e.g., mm/yr for sea floor spreading, Gya for dates in the early history of Earth). (3) Attend to units properly when using formulas such as energy = mass times speed of light squared. (4) Carefully format data displays and graphs, attending to origin, scale, units, and other essential items.

---

[18] See also Linear, Quadratic, and Exponential Models (F-LE).

Applying key takeaways from grades 6–8 mathematics. **Science examples: (1) Pinnacles National Monument is believed to have been created when the San Andreas Fault moved part of a volcano 195 miles northward over a period of 23 million years. On average, how fast did this part of the volcano move, in centimeters per year? (2) Also express the answer in meters per second using scientific notation. (3) Use a spreadsheet to scatterplot the planets' orbital periods against their orbital semimajor axes, and explain how these data show non-linearity. Then scatterplot the squares of the orbital periods against the cubes of their orbital semimajor axes, and show that the relationship is linear.**

HS-ESS2 EARTH'S SYSTEMS

As part of this work, teachers should give students opportunities to **reason quantitatively and use units to solve problems and to apply key takeaways from grades 6–8 mathematics:**

Quantities (N-Q)/Reason quantitatively and use units to solve problems:

N-Q.1. Use units as a way to understand problems and to guide the solution of multi-step problems; choose and interpret units consistently in formulas; choose and interpret the scale and origin in graphs and data displays.

N-Q.2. Define appropriate quantities for the purpose of descriptive modeling.

N-Q.3. Choose a level of accuracy appropriate to limitations on measurement when reporting quantities.

Science examples: (1) When coastal erosion is measured, what are its units? What does this say about what quantity is being measured? (2) Use SI units as well as convenient units (e.g., My for durations of time or Gya for dates in the early history of Earth). (3) Carefully format data displays and graphs, attending to origin, scale, units, and other essential items.

Applying key takeaways from grades 6–8 mathematics. **Science example: Use order-of-magnitude thinking to appreciate relative timescales in the co-evolution of Earth's systems and life on Earth. For example, when did photosynthetic life alter the atmosphere? How long was it then until the appearance of land plants?**

HS-ESS3 EARTH AND HUMAN ACTIVITY

As part of this work, teachers should give students opportunities to **reason quantitatively and use units to solve problems and to apply key takeaways from grades 6–8 mathematics:**

Quantities (N-Q)/Reason quantitatively and use units to solve problems:

N-Q.1. Use units as a way to understand problems and to guide the solution of multi-step problems; choose and interpret units consistently in formulas; choose and interpret the scale and origin in graphs and data displays.

N-Q.2. Define appropriate quantities for the purpose of descriptive modeling.

N-Q.3. Choose a level of accuracy appropriate to limitations on measurement when reporting quantities.

Science examples: (1) Quantify the impacts of human activities on natural systems. For example, if a certain activity creates pollution that in turn damages forests, go beyond a qualitative statement by quantifying both the amount of pollution and the level of damage. (2) Carefully format data displays and graphs, attending to origin, scale, units, and other essential items.

Applying key takeaways from grades 6–8 mathematics. **Science examples: (1) Use concepts of probability to describe risks of natural hazards (e.g., volcanic eruptions, earthquakes, tsunamis, hurricanes, droughts) that impact human activity. (2) Use cost–benefit ratios to evaluate competing design solutions. (3) Use per-capita measures such as consumption, cost, and resource needs.**

HS-ETS1 ENGINEERING DESIGN

As part of this work, teachers should give students opportunities to **model with mathematics and to apply key takeaways from grades 6–8 mathematics:**

Modeling. **Science examples: (1) Identify variables and select those that represent essential factors to understand, control, or optimize. (2) Use technology to vary assumptions, explore consequences, and compare predictions with data.**

Applying key takeaways from grades 6–8 mathematics. **Science example: Work with tolerances, cost constraints, quantitative impacts, and other quantitative factors in evaluating competing design solutions.**

REFERENCES

Boyer, C. B., and Merzbach, U. C. (1991). *A history of mathematics*, Second Edition. New York: Wiley and Sons. Pp. vii–viii.

National Governors Association Center for Best Practices, Council of Chief State School Officers. (2010). *Common Core State Standards Mathematics*. Washington, DC: National Governors Association Center for Best Practices, Council of Chief State School Officers. Pp. 72–73.

SOURCES CONSULTED

Woodward, R. T., and Wui, Y.-S. (2001). The economic value of wetland services: A meta-analysis. *Ecological Economics* 37:257–270.

http://en.wikipedia.org/wiki/Atomic_mass_unit

http://en.wikipedia.org/wiki/Topsoil

http://learn.genetics.utah.edu/content/begin/cells/scale

http://learningcenter.nsta.org

http://libinfo.uark.edu/aas/issues/1964v18/v18a5.pdf

http://serc.carleton.edu/NAGTWorkshops/time/activities/61171.html

http://soils.usda.gov/technical/manual

http://www.agiweb.org/nacsn/40890_articles_article_file_1641.pdf

http://www.amazon.com/Complete-Guide-Running-How-Champion/dp/1841261629

http://www.clemson.edu/extension/natural_resources/wildlife/publications/fs8_cottontail%20rabbit.html

http://www.ewg.org/losingground/report/erosion-adds-up.html

http://www.fws.gov/economics/Discussion%20Papers/USFWS_Ecosystem%20Services_Phase%20I%20Report_04-25-2012.pdf

http://www.geo.mtu.edu/UPSeis/locating.html

http://www.nps.gov/pinn/naturescience/index.htm

http://www.nrcs.usda.gov/wps/portal/nrcs/detail/national/technical/nra/nri/?cid=stelprdb1041887

http://www.nyc.gov/html/dot/html/about/knowthespeedlimit.shtml

http://www.rssweather.com/climate/California/Sacramento

http://www.rssweather.com/climate/California/San%20Francisco%20County

http://www.teebweb.org/local-and-regional-policy-makers-report

http://www.thaiscience.info/Article%20for%20ThaiScience/Article/5/Ts-5%20coastal%20erosion%20and%20mangrove%20progradation%20of%20southern%20thailand.pdf

http://www.uky.edu/Ag/CritterFiles/casefile/spiders/wolf/wolf.htm

CONNECTIONS TO THE COMMON CORE STATE STANDARDS FOR LITERACY IN SCIENCE AND TECHNICAL SUBJECTS

Connections to the English/language arts (ELA) CCSS are included across all disciplines and grade bands in the final version of the NGSS. However, Appendix M focuses on connections to the Standards for Literacy in Science and Technical Subjects, which only cover grades 6–12. Therefore this appendix likewise only lists connections for grades 6–12. See the Common Core State Standards website for more information about the Literacy Standards, available at: http://www.corestandards.org/ELA-Literacy.

Literacy skills are critical to building knowledge in science. To ensure the Common Core State Standards (CCSS) for literacy work in tandem with the specific content demands outlined in the Next Generation Science Standards (NGSS), the NGSS development team worked with the CCSS writing team to identify key literacy connections to the specific content demands outlined in the NGGS. As the CCSS affirms, reading in science requires an appreciation of the norms and conventions of the discipline of science, including understanding the nature of evidence used, an attention to precision and detail, and the capacity to make and assess intricate arguments, synthesize complex information, and follow detailed procedures and accounts of events and concepts. Students also need to be able to gain knowledge from elaborate diagrams and data that convey information and illustrate scientific concepts. Likewise, writing and presenting information orally are key means for students to assert and defend claims in science, demonstrate what they know about a concept, and convey what they have experienced, imagined, thought, and learned.

Every effort has been made to ensure consistency between the CCSS and the NGSS. As is the case with the mathematics standards, the NGSS should always be interpreted and implemented in such a way that they do not outpace or misalign to the grade-by-grade standards in the CCSS for literacy (this includes the development of NGSS-aligned instructional materials and assessments). Below are the NGSS science and engineering practices and the corresponding CCSS Literacy Anchor Standards and portions of the Standards for Science and Technical Subjects.

Science and Engineering Practice: Asking Questions and Defining Problems

Students at any grade level should be able to ask questions of each other about the texts they read, the features of the phenomena they observe, and the conclusions they draw from their models or scientific investigations. For engineering, they should ask questions to define the problem to be solved and to elicit ideas that lead to the constraints and specifications for its solution (NRC, 2012, p. 56).

Supporting CCSS Literacy Anchor Standards and Relevant Portions of the Corresponding Standards for Science and Technical Subjects	Connection to Science and Engineering Practice
CCR Reading Anchor #1: Read closely to determine what the text says explicitly and to make logical inferences from it; cite specific textual evidence when writing or speaking to support conclusions drawn from the text. • **RST.6-8.1:** "support analysis of science and technical texts." • **RST.9-10.1:** "support analysis of science and technical texts, attending to the precise details of explanations or descriptions." • **RST.11-12.1:** "support analysis of science and technical texts, attending to important distinctions the author makes and to any gaps or inconsistencies in the account."	Evidence plays a critical role in the kinds of questions asked, information gathered, and findings reported in science and technical texts. The notion of close reading in Reading Standard 1 emphasizes the use of asking and refining questions in order to answer them with evidence that is either explicitly stated or implied.
CCR Reading Anchor #7: Integrate and evaluate content presented in diverse formats and media, including visually and quantitatively, as well as in words. • **RST.6-8.7:** "Integrate quantitative or technical information expressed in words in a text with a version of that information expressed visually (e.g., in a flowchart, diagram, model, graph, or table)." • **RST.9-10.7:** "Translate quantitative or technical information expressed in words in a text into visual form (e.g., a table or chart) and translate information expressed visually or mathematically (e.g., in an equation) into words." • **RST.11-12.7:** "evaluate multiple sources of information presented in diverse formats and media (e.g., quantitative data, video, multimedia) in order to address a question or solve a problem."	Scientists and engineers present data in a myriad of visual formats in order to reveal meaningful patterns and trends. Reading Standard 7 speaks directly to the importance of asking questions about and evaluating data presented in different formats.
CCR Reading Anchor #8: Delineate and evaluate the argument and specific claims in a text, including the validity of the reasoning as well as the relevance and sufficiency of the evidence. • **RST.6-8.8:** "Distinguish among facts, reasoned judgment based on research findings, and speculation." • **RST.9-10.8:** "Assess the extent to which the reasoning and evidence in a text support the author's claim or a recommendation for solving a scientific or technical problem." • **RST.11-12.8:** "Evaluate the hypotheses, data, analysis, and conclusions in a science or technical text, verifying the data when possible and corroborating or challenging conclusions with other sources of information."	Challenging or clarifying scientific hypotheses, arguments, experiments, or conclusions—and the evidence and premises that support them—are key to this practice. Reading Standard 8 emphasizes evaluating the validity of arguments and whether the evidence offered backs up the claims logically.

CCR Writing Anchor #7: Conduct short as well as more sustained research projects based on focused questions, demonstrating understanding of the subject under investigation. • **RST.6-8.7:** "answer a question (including a self-generated question) … generating additional related, focused questions that allow for multiple avenues of exploration." • **RST.9-12.7:** "narrow or broaden inquiry when appropriate."	Generating focused questions and well-honed scientific inquiries is key to conducting investigations and defining problems. The research practices reflected in Writing Standard 7 reflect the skills needed for successful completion of such research-based inquiries.
CCR Speaking and Listening Anchor #1: Prepare for and participate effectively in a range of conversations and collaborations with diverse partners, building on others' ideas and expressing their own clearly and persuasively. • **SL.8.1:** "Pose … specific questions by making comments that contribute to the discussion." • **SL.9-10.1:** "posing and responding to questions that relate the current discussion to broader themes or larger ideas." • **SL.11-12.1:** "posing and responding to questions that probe reasoning and evidence."	The ability to pose relevant questions, clarify or elaborate on the ideas of others, or request information from others is crucial to learning and conducting investigations in science class. Speaking and Listening Standard 1 speaks directly to the importance of asking and refining questions to clarify ideas that generate solutions and explanations.
CCR Speaking and Listening Anchor #3: Evaluate a speaker's point of view, reasoning, and use of evidence and rhetoric. • **SL.8.3:** "evaluating the soundness of the reasoning and sufficiency of the evidence, and identifying when irrelevant evidence is introduced." • **SL.9-10.3:** "identifying fallacious reasoning or exaggerated or distorted evidence." • **SL.11-12.3:** "assessing the stance, premises, links among ideas, word choice, points of emphasis."	Evaluating the soundness of a speaker's reasoning and evidence concerning scientific theories and concepts through a series of inquiries teaches students to be discriminating thinkers. Speaking and Listening Standard 3 directly asserts that students must be able to critique a point of view from the perspective of the evidence provided and reasoning advanced.

Science and Engineering Practice: Planning and Carrying Out Investigations

Students should have opportunities to plan and carry out several different kinds of investigations during their K–12 years. At all levels, they should engage in investigations that range from those structured by the teacher—in order to expose an issue or question that they would be unlikely to explore on their own (e.g., measuring specific properties of materials)—to those that emerge from students' own questions (NRC, 2012, p. 61).

Supporting CCSS Literacy Anchor Standards and Relevant Portions of the Corresponding Standards for Science and Technical Subjects	Connection to Science and Engineering Practice
CCR Reading Anchor #3: Analyze how and why individuals, events, or ideas develop and interact over the course of a text. • **RST.6-8.3:** "Follow precisely a multistep procedure when carrying out experiments, taking measurements, or performing technical tasks." • **RST.9-10.3:** "Follow precisely a complex multistep procedure when carrying out experiments, taking measurements, or performing technical tasks, attending to special cases or exceptions defined in the text." • **RST.11-12.3:** "Follow precisely a complex multistep procedure when carrying out experiments, taking measurements, or performing technical tasks; analyze the specific results based on explanations in the text."	Systematic investigations in the field or laboratory lie at the heart of scientific inquiry. Reading Standard 8 emphasizes the importance of accuracy in carrying out such complex experiments and procedures, in following a course of action that will provide the best evidence to support conclusions.
CCR Writing Anchor #7: Conduct short as well as more sustained research projects based on focused questions, demonstrating understanding of the subject under investigation.	Planning and carrying out investigations to test hypotheses or designs is central to scientific and engineering activity. The research practices reflected in Writing Standard 7 reflect the skills needed for successful completion of such research-based inquiries.
CCR Writing Anchor #8: Gather relevant information from multiple print and digital sources, assess the credibility and accuracy of each source, and integrate the information while avoiding plagiarism. • **WHST.6-8.8:** "quote or paraphrase the data and conclusions of others." • **WHST.9-10.8:** "assess the usefulness of each source in answering the research question." • **WHST.11-12.8:** "assess the strengths and limitations of each source in terms of the specific task, purpose, and audience."	Collecting relevant data across a broad spectrum of sources in a systematic fashion is a key element of this scientific practice. Writing Standard 8 spells out the importance of gathering applicable information from multiple reliable sources to support claims.
CCR Speaking and Listening Anchor #1: Prepare for and participate effectively in a range of conversations and collaborations with diverse partners, building on others' ideas and expressing their own clearly and persuasively. • **SL.8.1:** "Come … having read or researched material under study; explicitly draw on that preparation by referring to evidence on the topic, text, or issue to probe and reflect on ideas under discussion … define individual roles as needed." • **SL.9-10.1:** "Come … having read and researched material under study; explicitly draw on that preparation by referring to evidence from texts and other research on the topic or issue to stimulate a thoughtful, well-reasoned exchange of ideas … make new connections in light of the evidence and reasoning presented." • **SL.11-12.1:** "Determine what additional information or research is required to deepen the investigation or complete the task."	Carrying out investigations in collaborative settings is crucial to learning in science class and engineering settings. Speaking and Listening Standard 1 speaks directly to the importance of exchanging theories and evidence cooperatively and collaboratively to carrying out investigations.

Science and Engineering Practice: Analyzing and Interpreting Data

Once collected, data must be presented in a form that can reveal any patterns and relationships and that allows results to be communicated to others. Because raw data as such have little meaning, a major practice of scientists is to organize and interpret data through tabulating, graphing, or statistical analysis. Such analysis can bring out the meaning of data—and their relevance—so that they may be used as evidence.

Engineers, too, make decisions based on evidence that a given design will work; they rarely rely on trial and error. Engineers often analyze a design by creating a model or prototype and collecting extensive data on how it performs, including under extreme conditions. Analysis of this kind of data not only informs design decisions and enables the prediction or assessment of performance but also helps define or clarify problems, determine economic feasibility, evaluate alternatives, and investigate failures (NRC, 2012, pp. 61–62).

Supporting CCSS Literacy Anchor Standards and Relevant Portions of the Corresponding Standards for Science and Technical Subjects	Connection to Science and Engineering Practice
CCR Reading Anchor #7: Integrate and evaluate content presented in diverse formats and media, including visually and quantitatively, as well as in words. • **RST.6-8.7:** "Integrate quantitative or technical information expressed in words in a text with a version of that information expressed visually (e.g., in a flowchart, diagram, model, graph, or table)." • **RST.9-10.7:** "Translate quantitative or technical information expressed in words in a text into visual form (e.g., a table or chart) and translate information expressed visually or mathematically (e.g., in an equation) into words." • **RST.11-12.7:** "Evaluate multiple sources of information presented in diverse formats and media (e.g., quantitative data, video, multimedia) in order to address a question or solve a problem."	Scientists and engineers present data in a myriad of visual formats in order to reveal meaningful patterns and trends. Reading Standard 7 speaks directly to the importance of understanding and presenting information that has been gathered in various formats to reveal patterns and relationships and allow for deeper explanations and analyses.
CCR Reading Anchor #9: Analyze how two or more texts address similar themes or topics in order to build knowledge or to compare the approaches the authors take. • **RST.6-8.9:** "Compare and contrast the information gained from experiments, simulations, video, or multimedia sources with that gained from reading a text on the same topic." • **RST.9-10.9:** "Compare and contrast findings presented in a text to those from other sources (including their own experiments), noting when the findings support or contradict previous explanations or accounts." • **RST.11-12.9:** "Synthesize information from a range of sources (e.g., texts, experiments, simulations) into a coherent understanding of a process, phenomenon, or concept, resolving conflicting information when possible."	Scientists and engineers use technology to allow them to draw on multiple sources of information in order to create data sets. Reading Standard 9 identifies the importance of analyzing multiple sources in order to inform design decisions and create a coherent understanding of a process or concept.
CCR Speaking and Listening Anchor #2: Integrate and evaluate information presented in diverse media and formats, including visually, quantitatively, and orally. • **SL.8.2:** "Analyze the purpose of information presented in diverse media and formats (e.g., visually, quantitatively, orally)." • **SL.9-10.2:** "Integrate multiple sources of information presented in diverse media or formats (e.g., visually, quantitatively, orally), evaluating the credibility and accuracy of each source." • **SL.11-12.2:** "Evaluating the credibility and accuracy of each source and noting any discrepancies among the data."	Central to the practice of scientists and engineers is integrating data drawn from multiple sources in order to create a cohesive vision of what the data mean. Speaking and Listening Standard 2 addresses the importance of such synthesizing activities to building knowledge and defining and clarifying problems. This includes evaluating the credibility and accuracy of data and identifying possible sources of error.
CCR Speaking and Listening Anchor #5: Make strategic use of digital media and visual displays of data to express information and enhance understanding of presentations. • **SL.8.5:** "Integrate multimedia and visual displays into presentations to clarify information, strengthen claims and evidence." • **SL.9-12.5:** "Make strategic use of digital media (e.g., textual, graphical, audio, visual, and interactive elements) in presentations to enhance understanding of findings, reasoning, and evidence."	Presenting data for the purposes of cross-comparison is essential for identifying the best design solution or scientific explanation. Speaking and Listening Standard 5 stresses the importance of visual displays of data within presentations in order to enhance understanding of the relevance of the evidence. That way others can make critical decisions regarding what is being claimed based on the data.

Science and Engineering Practice: Constructing Explanations and Designing Solutions

Asking students to demonstrate their own understanding of the implications of a scientific idea by developing their own explanations of phenomena, whether based on observations they have made or models they have developed, engages them in an essential part of the process by which conceptual change can occur.

In engineering, the goal is a design rather than an explanation. The process of developing a design is iterative and systematic, as is the process of developing an explanation or a theory in science. Engineers' activities, however, have elements that are distinct from those of scientists. These elements include specifying constraints and criteria for desired qualities of the solution, developing a design plan, producing and testing models or prototypes, selecting among alternative design features to optimize the achievement of design criteria, and refining design ideas based on the performance of a prototype or simulation (NRC, 2012, pp. 68–69).

Supporting CCSS Literacy Anchor Standards and Relevant Portions of the Corresponding Standards for Science and Technical Subjects	Connection to Science and Engineering Practice
CCR Reading Anchor #1: Read closely to determine what the text says explicitly and to make logical inferences from it; cite specific textual evidence when writing or speaking to support conclusions drawn from the text. • **RST.6-8.1:** "support analysis of science and technical texts." • **RST.9-10.1:** "support analysis of science and technical texts, attending to the precise details of explanations or descriptions." • **RST.11-12.1:** "support analysis of science and technical texts, attending to important distinctions the author makes and to any gaps or inconsistencies in the account."	Evidence plays a critical role in determining a theory in science and a design solution in engineering. The notion of close reading in Reading Standard 1 emphasizes pursuing investigations into well-supported theories and design solutions on the basis of evidence that is either explicitly stated or implied.
CCR Reading Anchor #2: Determine central ideas or themes of a text and analyze their development; summarize the key supporting details and ideas. • **RST.6-8.2:** "provide an accurate summary of the text distinct from prior knowledge or opinions." • **RST.9-10.2:** "trace the text's explanation or depiction of a complex process, phenomenon, or concept." • **RST.11-12.2:** "summarize complex concepts, processes, or information presented in a text by paraphrasing them in simpler but still accurate terms."	Part of the power of a scientific theory or engineering design is its ability to be cogently explained. That ability to determine and clearly state an idea lies at the heart of Reading Standard 2.
CCR Reading Anchor #8: Delineate and evaluate the argument and specific claims in a text, including the validity of the reasoning as well as the relevance and sufficiency of the evidence. • **RST.6-8.8:** "Distinguish among facts, reasoned judgment based on research findings, and speculation." • **RST.9-10.8:** "Assess the extent to which the reasoning and evidence in a text support the author's claim or a recommendation for solving a scientific or technical problem." • **RST.11-12.8:** "Evaluate the hypotheses, data, analyses, and conclusions in a science or technical text, verifying the data when possible and corroborating or challenging conclusions with other sources of information."	Constructing theories and designing solutions both require analysis that is rooted in rational argument and in evidence stemming from an understanding of the world. Reading Standard 8 emphasizes evaluating the validity of arguments and whether the evidence offered backs up the claim logically.

CCR Writing Anchor #2: Write informative/explanatory texts to examine and convey complex ideas and information clearly and accurately through the effective selection, organization, and analysis of content. • **WHST.6-8.2:** "Develop the topic with relevant, well-chosen facts, definitions, concrete details, quotations, or other information and examples." • **WHST.9-10.2:** "Develop the topic with well-chosen, relevant, and sufficient facts, extended definitions, concrete details, quotations, or other information and examples appropriate to the audience's knowledge of the topic." • **WHST.11-12.2:** "Develop the topic thoroughly by selecting the most significant and relevant facts, extended definitions, concrete details, quotations, or other information and examples appropriate to the audience's knowledge of the topic."	Building a theory or model that explains the natural world requires close attention to how to weave together evidence from multiple sources. With a focus on clearly communicating complex ideas and information by critically choosing, arranging, and analyzing information, Writing Standard 2 requires students to develop theories with the end goal of explanation in mind.
CCR Writing Anchor #8: Gather relevant information from multiple print and digital sources, assess the credibility and accuracy of each source, and integrate the information while avoiding plagiarism. • **WHST.6-8.8:** "quote or paraphrase the data and conclusions of others." • **WHST.9-10.8:** "assess the usefulness of each source in answering the research question; integrate information into the text selectively to maintain the flow of ideas." • **WHST.11-12.8:** "assess the strengths and limitations of each source in terms of the specific task, purpose, and audience; integrate information into the text selectively to maintain the flow of ideas."	Collecting relevant data across a broad spectrum of sources in a systematic fashion is a key element of constructing a theory with explanatory power or a design that meets multiple constraints. Writing Standard 8 spells out the importance of gathering applicable information from multiple reliable sources in order to construct well-honed explanations.
CCR Writing Anchor #9: Draw evidence from literary or informational texts to support analysis, reflection, and research. • **WHST.6-12.9:** "Draw evidence from informational texts to support analysis, reflection, and research."	The route toward constructing a rigorous explanatory account centers on garnering the necessary empirical evidence to support a theory or design. That same focus on generating evidence that can be analyzed is at the heart of Writing Standard 9.
CCR Speaking and Listening Anchor #4: Present information, findings, and supporting evidence such that listeners can follow the line of reasoning and the organization, development, and style appropriate to the task, purpose, and audience. • **SL.8.4:** "Present claims and findings, emphasizing salient points in a focused, coherent manner with relevant evidence, sound and valid reasoning." • **SL.9-10.4:** "Present information, findings, and supporting evidence clearly, concisely, and logically." • **SL.11-12.4:** "Present information, findings, and supporting evidence, conveying a clear and distinct perspective … alternative or opposing perspectives are addressed."	A theory in science and a design in engineering are a rational explanatory account of how the world works in light of the evidence. Speaking and Listening Standard 4 stresses how the presentation of findings crucially relies on how the evidence is used to illuminate the line of reasoning embedded in the explanation offered.

Science and Engineering Practice: Engaging in Argument from Evidence

The study of science and engineering should produce a sense of the process of argument necessary for advancing and defending a new idea or an explanation of a phenomenon and the norms for conducting such arguments. In that spirit, students should argue for the explanations they construct, defend their interpretations of the associated data, and advocate for the designs they propose (NRC, 2012, p. 73).

Supporting CCSS Literacy Anchor Standards and Relevant Portions of the Corresponding Standards for Science and Technical Subjects	Connection to Science and Engineering Practice
CCR Reading Anchor #6: Assess how point of view or purpose shapes the content and style of a text. • **RST.6-8.6:** "Analyze the author's purpose in providing an explanation, describing a procedure, or discussing an experiment in a text." • **RST.9-10.6:** "Analyze the author's purpose in providing an explanation, describing a procedure, or discussing an experiment in a text, defining the question the author seeks to address." • **RST.11-12.6:** "Analyze the author's purpose in providing an explanation, describing a procedure, or discussing an experiment in a text, identifying important issues that remain unresolved."	The central motivation of scientists and engineers is to put forth what they believe is the best explanation for a natural phenomenon or design solution and to verify that representation through well-wrought arguments. Understanding the point of view of scientists and engineers and how that point of view shapes the content of the explanation is what Reading Standard 6 asks students to attune to.
CCR Reading Anchor #8: Delineate and evaluate the argument and specific claims in a text, including the validity of the reasoning as well as the relevance and sufficiency of the evidence. • **RST.6-8.8:** "Distinguish among facts, reasoned judgment based on research findings, and speculation...." • **RST.9-10.8:** "Assess the extent to which the reasoning and evidence in a text support the author's claim or a recommendation for solving a scientific or technical problem." • **RST.11-12.8:** "Evaluate the hypotheses, data, analyses, and conclusions in a science or technical text, verifying the data when possible and corroborating or challenging conclusions with other sources of information."	Formulating the best explanation or solution to a problem or phenomenon stems from advancing an argument whose premises are rational and supported with evidence. Reading Standard 8 emphasizes evaluating the validity of arguments and whether the evidence offered backs up the claim logically.
CCR Reading Anchor #9: Analyze how two or more texts address similar themes or topics in order to build knowledge or to compare the approaches the authors take. • **RST.6-8.9:** "Compare and contrast the information gained from experiments, simulations, video, or multimedia sources with that gained from reading a text on the same topic." • **RST.9-10.9:** "Compare and contrast findings presented in a text to those from other sources (including their own experiments), noting when the findings support or contradict previous explanations or accounts." • **RST.11-12.9:** "Synthesize information from a range of sources (e.g., texts, experiments, simulations) into a coherent understanding of a process, phenomenon, or concept, resolving conflicting information when possible."	Implicit in the practice of identifying the best explanation or design solution is comparing and contrasting competing proposals. Reading Standard 9 identifies the importance of comparing different sources in the process of creating a coherent understanding of a phenomenon, concept, or design solution.

CCR Writing Anchor #1: Write arguments to support claims in an analysis of substantive topics or texts using valid reasoning and relevant and sufficient evidence. • **WHST.6-8.1:** "Support claim(s) with logical reasoning and relevant, accurate data and evidence that demonstrate an understanding of the topic or text, using credible sources." • **WHST.9-10.1:** "Develop claim(s) and counterclaims fairly, supplying data and evidence for each while pointing out the strengths and limitations of both claim(s) and counterclaims in a discipline-appropriate form and in a manner that anticipates the audience's knowledge level and concerns." • **WHST.11-12.1:** "Develop claim(s) and counterclaims fairly and thoroughly, supplying the most relevant data and evidence for each while pointing out the strengths and limitations of both claim(s) and counterclaims in a discipline-appropriate form that anticipates the audience's knowledge level, concerns, values, and possible biases."	Central to the process of engaging in scientific thought or engineering practices is the notion that what will emerge is backed up by rigorous argument. Writing Standard 1 places argumentation at the heart of the CCSS for science and technology subjects, stressing the importance of logical reasoning, relevant evidence, and credible sources.
CCR Speaking and Listening Anchor #1: Prepare for and participate effectively in a range of conversations and collaborations with diverse partners, building on others' ideas and expressing their own clearly and persuasively. • **SL.8.1:** "Pose questions that connect the ideas of several speakers and respond to others' questions and comments with relevant evidence, observations, and ideas. Acknowledge new information expressed by others, and, when warranted, qualify or justify their own views in light of the evidence presented." • **SL.9-10.1:** "Actively incorporate others into the discussion and clarify, verify, or challenge ideas and conclusions. Respond thoughtfully to diverse perspectives, summarize points of agreement and disagreement, and, when warranted, qualify or justify their own views and understanding and make new connections in light of the evidence and reasoning presented." • **SL.11-12.1:** "Respond thoughtfully to diverse perspectives; synthesize comments, claims, and evidence made on all sides of an issue; resolve contradictions when possible; and determine what additional information or research is required to deepen the investigation or complete the task."	Reasoning and argument require critical listening and collaboration skills in order to identify the best explanation for a natural phenomenon or the best solution to a design problem. Speaking and Listening Standard 1 speaks directly to the importance of comparing and evaluating competing ideas through argument to cooperatively and collaboratively identify the best explanation or solution.
CCR Speaking and Listening Anchor #3: Evaluate a speaker's point of view, reasoning, and use of evidence and rhetoric. • **SL.8.3:** "evaluating the soundness of the reasoning and sufficiency of the evidence, and identifying when irrelevant evidence is introduced." • **SL.9-10.3:** "identifying fallacious reasoning or exaggerated or distorted evidence." • **SL.11-12.3:** "assessing the stance, premises, links among ideas, word choice, points of emphasis."	Evaluating the reasoning in an argument based on the evidence present is crucial for identifying the best design or scientific explanation. Speaking and Listening Standard 3 directly asserts that students must be able to critique the point of view within an argument presented orally from the perspective of the evidence provided and reasoning advanced by others.
CCR Speaking and Listening Anchor #4: Present information, findings, and supporting evidence such that listeners can follow the line of reasoning and the organization, development, and style appropriate to the task, purpose, and audience. • **SL.8.4:** "Present claims and findings, emphasizing salient points in a focused, coherent manner with relevant evidence, sound and valid reasoning." • **SL.9-10.4:** "Present information, findings, and supporting evidence clearly, concisely, and logically." • **SL.11-12.4:** "Present information, findings, and supporting evidence, conveying a clear and distinct perspective … alternative or opposing perspectives are addressed."	The practice of engaging in argument from evidence is a key ingredient in determining the best explanation for a natural phenomenon or the best solution to a design problem. Speaking and Listening Standard 4 stresses how the presentation of findings crucially relies on how the evidence is used to illuminate the line of reasoning embedded in the explanation offered.

Science and Engineering Practice: Obtaining, Evaluating, and Communicating Information

Any education in science and engineering needs to develop students' ability to read and produce domain-specific text. As such, every science or engineering lesson is in part a language lesson, particularly reading and producing the genres of texts that are intrinsic to science and engineering (NRC, 2012, p. 76).

Supporting CCSS Literacy Anchor Standards and Relevant Portions of the Corresponding Standards for Science and Technical Subjects	Connection to Science and Engineering Practice
CCR Reading Anchor #2: Determine central ideas or themes of a text and analyze their development; summarize the key supporting details and ideas. • **RST.6-8.2:** "provide an accurate summary of the text distinct from prior knowledge or opinions." • **RST.9-10.2:** "trace the text's explanation or depiction of a complex process, phenomenon, or concept." • **RST.11-12.2:** "summarize complex concepts, processes, or information presented in a text by paraphrasing them in simpler but still accurate terms."	Part of the power of a scientific theory or engineering design is its ability to be cogently explained. That ability to determine and clearly state or summarize a salient scientific concept or phenomenon lies at the heart of Reading Standard 2.
CCR Reading Anchor #7: Integrate and evaluate content presented in diverse formats and media, including visually and quantitatively, as well as in words. • **RST.6-8.7:** "Integrate quantitative or technical information expressed in words in a text with a version of that information expressed visually (e.g., in a flowchart, diagram, model, graph, or table)." • **RST.9-10.7:** "Translate quantitative or technical information expressed in words in a text into visual form (e.g., a table or chart) and translate information expressed visually or mathematically (e.g., in an equation) into words." • **RST.11-12.7:** "Evaluate multiple sources of information presented in diverse formats and media (e.g., quantitative data, video, multimedia) in order to address a question or solve a problem."	A key practice within scientific and engineering communities is communicating about data through the use of tables, diagrams, graphs, and models. Reading Standard 7 speaks directly to the importance of understanding information that has been gathered by investigators in visual formats that reveal deeper explanations and analyses.
CCR Reading Anchor #9: Analyze how two or more texts address similar themes or topics in order to build knowledge or to compare the approaches the authors take. • **RST.6-8.9:** "Compare and contrast the information gained from experiments, simulations, video, or multimedia sources with that gained from reading a text on the same topic." • **RST.9-10.9:** "Compare and contrast findings presented in a text to those from other sources (including their own experiments), noting when the findings support or contradict previous explanations or accounts." • **RST.11-12.9:** "Synthesize information from a range of sources (e.g., texts, experiments, simulations) into a coherent understanding of a process, phenomenon, or concept, resolving conflicting information when possible."	The end goal of these science and engineering practices is to position scientists and engineers to be able to evaluate the merit and validity of claims, methods, and designs. Reading Standard 9 identifies the importance of synthesizing information from a range of sources to the process of creating a coherent understanding of a phenomenon or concept.
CCR Reading Anchor #10: Read and comprehend complex literary and informational texts independently and proficiently. • **RST.6-8.10:** "By the end of grade 8, read and comprehend science/technical texts in the grades 6–8 text complexity band independently and proficiently." • **RST.9-10.10:** "By the end of grade 10, read and comprehend science/technical texts in the grades 9–10 text complexity band independently and proficiently." • **RST.11-12.10:** "By the end of grade 12, read and comprehend science/technical texts in the grade 11 CCR text complexity band independently and proficiently."	When reading scientific and technical texts, students need to be able to gain knowledge from challenging texts that often make extensive use of elaborate diagrams and data to convey information and illustrate concepts. Reading standard 10 asks students to read complex informational texts in these fields with independence and confidence.

CCR Writing Anchor #2: Write informative/explanatory texts to examine and convey complex ideas and information clearly and accurately through the effective selection, organization, and analysis of content. • **WHST.6-8.2:** "include formatting (e.g., headings), graphics (e.g., charts, tables), and multimedia when useful to aiding comprehension…. Develop the topic with relevant, well-chosen facts, definitions, concrete details, quotations, or other information and examples." • **WHST.9-10.2:** "include formatting (e.g., headings), graphics (e.g., figures, tables), and multimedia when useful to aiding comprehension…. Develop the topic with well-chosen, relevant, and sufficient facts, extended definitions, concrete details, quotations, or other information and examples appropriate to the audience's knowledge of the topic." • **WHST.11-12.2:** "include formatting (e.g., headings), graphics (e.g., figures, tables), and multimedia when useful to aiding comprehension…. Develop the topic thoroughly by selecting the most significant and relevant facts, extended definitions, concrete details, quotations, or other information and examples appropriate to the audience's knowledge of the topic."	The demand for precision in expression is an essential requirement of scientists and engineers, and using the multiple means available to them is a crucial part of that expectation. With a focus on clearly communicating complex ideas and information by critically choosing, arranging, and analyzing information—particularly through the use of visual means—Writing Standard 2 requires students to develop their claims with the end goal of explanation in mind.
CCR Writing Anchor #8: Gather relevant information from multiple print and digital sources, assess the credibility and accuracy of each source, and integrate the information while avoiding plagiarism. • **WHST.6-8.8:** "using search terms effectively … quote or paraphrase the data and conclusions of others." • **WHST.9-10.8:** "using advanced searches effectively; assess the usefulness of each source in answering the research question; integrate information into the text selectively to maintain the flow of ideas." • **WHST.11-12.8:** "using advanced searches effectively; assess the strengths and limitations of each source in terms of the specific task, purpose, and audience; integrate information into the text selectively to maintain the flow of ideas."	Collecting relevant data across a broad spectrum of sources in a systematic fashion is a key element of assessing the validity of claims, methods, and designs. Writing Standard 8 spells out the importance of gathering applicable information from multiple reliable sources so that information can be communicated accurately.
CCR Speaking and Listening Anchor #1: Prepare for and participate effectively in a range of conversations and collaborations with diverse partners, building on others' ideas and expressing their own clearly and persuasively. • **SL.8.1:** "Pose questions that connect the ideas of several speakers and respond to others' questions and comments with relevant evidence, observations, and ideas. Acknowledge new information expressed by others, and, when warranted, qualify or justify their own views in light of the evidence presented." • **SL.9-10.1:** "Actively incorporate others into the discussion and clarify, verify, or challenge ideas and conclusions. Respond thoughtfully to diverse perspectives, summarize points of agreement and disagreement, and, when warranted, qualify or justify their own views and understanding and make new connections in light of the evidence and reasoning presented." • **SL.11-12.1:** "Respond thoughtfully to diverse perspectives; synthesize comments, claims, and evidence made on all sides of an issue; resolve contradictions when possible; and determine what additional information or research is required to deepen the investigation or complete the task."	Reasoning and argument require critical listening and collaboration skills in order to evaluate the merit and validity of claims, methods, and designs. Speaking and Listening Standard 1 speaks directly to the importance of comparing and assessing competing ideas through extended discussions grounded in evidence.
CCR Speaking and Listening Anchor #4: Present information, findings, and supporting evidence such that listeners can follow the line of reasoning and the organization, development, and style appropriate to the task, purpose, and audience. • **SL.8.4:** "Present claims and findings, emphasizing salient points in a focused, coherent manner with relevant evidence, sound and valid reasoning." • **SL.9-10.4:** "Present information, findings, and supporting evidence clearly, concisely, and logically." • **SL.11-12.4:** "Present information, findings, and supporting evidence, conveying a clear and distinct perspective … alternative or opposing perspectives are addressed."	Central to the professional activity of scientists and engineers alike is communicating their findings clearly and persuasively. Speaking and Listening Standard 4 stresses how the presentation of findings crucially relies on how the evidence is used to illuminate the line of reasoning embedded in the explanation offered.
CCR Speaking and Listening Anchor #5: Make strategic use of digital media and visual displays of data to express information and enhance understanding of presentations. • **SL.8.5:** "Integrate multimedia and visual displays into presentations to clarify information, strengthen claims and evidence." • **SL.9-12.5:** "Make strategic use of digital media (e.g., textual, graphical, audio, visual, and interactive elements) in presentations to enhance understanding of findings, reasoning, and evidence."	Presenting data for the purposes of communication is essential for evaluating the merit and validity of claims, methods, and designs. Speaking and Listening Standard 5 stresses the importance of visual or digital displays of data within presentations in order to enhance understanding of the evidence. That way others can make critical decisions regarding what is being claimed based on the data.

REFERENCE

NRC (National Research Council). (2012). *A framework for K–12 science education: Practices, crosscutting concepts, and core ideas.* Washington, DC: The National Academies Press.